Concurrent Programming

INTERNATIONAL COMPUTER SCIENCE SERIES

Consulting Editor   **A D McGettrick**   University of Strathclyde

SELECTED TITLES IN THE SERIES

Concurrent Programming

Alan Burns

University of York

Geoff Davies

University of Bradford

ADDISON-WESLEY
PUBLISHING
COMPANY

Wokingham, England · Reading, Massachusetts · Menlo Park, California · New York
Don Mills, Ontario · Amsterdam · Bonn · Sydney · Singapore
Tokyo · Madrid · San Juan · Milan · Paris · Mexico City · Seoul · Taipei

Cover designed by Chris Eley incorporating photograph
© Bernard Van Berg/The Image Bank
and printed by The Riverside Printing Co. (Reading) Ltd.
Typeset by Columns Design and Production Services Ltd, Reading.
Printed in Great Britain by Mackays of Chatham plc, Chatham, Kent.

First printed 1993.

British Library Cataloguing in Publication Data
A catalogue record for this book is available from the British Library.

Library of Congress Cataloging in Publication Data is available.

Preface

Concurrency is one of the key abstractions in Computer Science. It has relevance to hardware design and operation, operating systems, multiprocessor and distributed computation, real-time systems, programming languages and system design methods. It is also true that the environment of most computer systems is inherently parallel in nature. Although the standard von Neumann computer (and computer languages such as FORTRAN, COBOL and Pascal) make use of a sequential view of action and progress, computer scientists and software engineers must see this as the exception rather than the rule. Parallel and pseudo-parallel behaviour is the norm and must be fully understood by those aiming to become (or remain!) professionals in computer-based engineering.

General approach of the book

This is an *introductory* book on concurrency and concurrent programming. The author of an introductory book on programming, whether sequential or concurrent, is faced with a variety of possible approaches. One possibility is to adopt a rigorously mathematical approach from the beginning: methods of proving correctness can be introduced and used in the systematic development of programs. This approach has been very effectively used by Andrews (1991) in his recent book on concurrent programming.

It can be argued that this rigorous approach is particularly important when constructing concurrent (as distinct from sequential) software because of the greater complexity in the reasoning involved in establishing the correctness of such software. The present authors would not disagree with this. However, taking such a route necessitates either the exposition of the necessary mathematical background, or assuming that students have already taken a course providing the relevant discrete mathematics. We have not wanted to impose such prerequisites, however. Nor do we provide the necessary mathematical background for such an approach. What we have favoured is providing readers with an intuitive grasp of concurrency and the classic problems found in concurrent programming, and of the synchronization and communication primitives introduced into languages for their solution, together with practical experience with a variety of such primitives.

Whereas there is general agreement as to the primitives to support in a sequential programming language, there is less uniformity in the design of concurrency features. We therefore survey and describe many common language primitives, including various forms of process representation, shared-variable interaction, asynchronous and synchronous message passing, rendezvous structures, semaphores, monitors (with conduction variables) and protected resources. Specific consideration is given to the language features found in occam, Ada and Ada 9X.

Practical work

The authors have found that the concept of concurrency, although eventually surmountable, does cause many students considerable initial difficulty. A practical approach is therefore advocated. Students are encouraged to undertake programming exercises with all the language features. Once the concepts are fully grasped, the student is able to take on more advanced and theoretical material. Indeed, the book does lay the foundation to these more theoretical courses by introducing, where appropriate, formal notation and some of the more important laws concerning the concurrency operations. However, a fully rigorous approach is left to more advanced courses.

One of the major difficulties in running a practical course in concurrency is the need for a variety of languages (and hence compilers) to be available. Without these the student is merely undertaking a course about the concurrency features of a specific language. However, expecting students to learn and effectively use, say, occam 2, Ada, Concurrent Pascal and Concurrent C is clearly undesirable. Most students put all their energies into learning the different language syntaxes rather than the underlying concurrency features. Because of this the authors have developed a teaching language – Pascal-FC (Functionally Concurrent) – that supports all the major primitives described and used in this book. Virtually all examples are given in Pascal-FC. Moreover, the compiler is available to support this book. It is written in Pascal and hence is portable. Information on how to obtain a copy is given at the end of this preface.

As Pascal-FC supports various synchronization primitives, it is possible to use the language in a number of distinct modes; in particular it is possible to program process communications via:

- shared variables
- semaphores
- monitors with condition variables

- synchronous message passing – the occam model
- remote invocation – the Ada rendezvous model
- protected resources with requeue – the new Ada 9X model.

The last mode is particularly important and useful. It allows practical experience to be gained in the new Ada features (the protected type with requeue).

Intended readership

Although there are many books on concurrency, the material presented here is distinctive because of its practical emphasis, the use of a single language but a variety of primitives, the availability of the language to support the material and the inclusion of modern topics such as the Ada 9X model. The book is primarily aimed at supporting courses in concurrent programming and operating systems. It is, however, equally feasible for professional software engineers to use the book for self-directed study, particularly if the Pascal-FC system is available – it runs on all PCs. Readers should be familiar with a sequential programming language prior to reading this book. A knowledge of Pascal is ideal, but Ada C or FORTRAN is sufficient.

This book has grown out of courses taught by the authors at the Universities of Bradford and York, and elsewhere. The courses have been provided to a variety of students, including undergraduates in computer science and electrical engineering, graduate students undertaking conversion courses in computing, and graduate students taking courses in real-time systems. The material is suitable for courses involving approximately 100 hours of student time, of which approximately one-third consists of lectures, one-third of practical work and resulting discussions, and one-third in reading (including some recommended further reading).

The aim of the authors is to make concurrent programming a widely understood skill. Concurrency should not remain a topic of study for the universities alone. Colleges and even high schools can begin to address the issues if a practical approach is taken. Although the design of a large safety-critical distributed real-time embedded system is a complex activity, one of the enabling skills is a detailed and knowledgeable understanding of concurrency (in general) and its realization in the chosen implementation language. This book attempts at least to start the process of obtaining these enabling skills.

Structure and content

The material is presented in nine main chapters and two appendices. As one might expect from a book on concurrency, a purely sequential reading of the chapters is not absolutely necessary (the chapters are *partially ordered*).

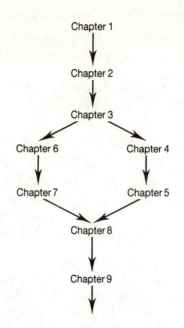

Figure 1 Valid reading paths.

Figure 1 illustrates the book's form. After the first three chapters, Chapters 4 and 5 (on message-passing models) may be read before or after Chapters 6 and 7 (on shared-variable models). Both activities should, however, be completed before starting Chapter 8.

In the first chapter the basic nature of concurrency is introduced and examples of its use are given. Although for much of this book the implementation of concurrency is not a major issue, some consideration of this topic is given. The chapter concludes by introducing the sequential features of Pascal-FC: these represent a slightly extended subset of standard Pascal.

Chapter 2 introduces the concept of process and addresses the issues of representation, structure, granularity and basic behaviour – how processes are created, how they start their execution and how they terminate. A simple state diagram for the life-cycle of a process is given. In addition, some of the simple laws that apply to the concurrency operator are described.

The third chapter introduces the important topic of inter-process synchronization and communication. In general, process interaction falls into three classes: independence, competition and cooperation. Many of the difficulties of competition and cooperation are illustrated by the classic problems of multiple update, Readers and Writers, and the Dining Philosophers. Attempts to solve some of these problems with only shared variables amply demonstrate the need for further primitives in concurrent programming languages.

Chapters 4 and 5 discuss one set of such primitives, the message-passing models. Both asynchronous and synchronous models are considered, although most attention is given to the latter. The standard rendezvous model of occam (and CSP) is discussed in Chapter 4. Issues of process naming and symmetry of interaction are discussed. In order to increase the expressive power of message-passing models, it is necessary to allow a process to choose between alternative communications. This non-deterministic language feature (called selective waiting) is discussed in detail in this chapter. Also introduced are some of the more theoretical issues surrounding non-determinism.

Consideration of message passing is continued into Chapter 5, where the remote invocation or extended rendezvous model of Ada is discussed. Whereas the occam model is characterized by point-to-point communication, one-directional data flow and the use of an intermediary for naming purposes (the channel), remote invocation uses direct naming, bidirectional data flow and many-to-one communication. It more directly supports the client–server paradigm of process interaction. Selective waiting is, of course, still required, and is extended to incorporate remote invocation. In doing this, the adequacy of the asymmetric select construct becomes apparent.

The alternative to message passing is to stay with shared variables for inter-process communication but to add synchronization primitives to ease the programming effort. Chapter 6 discusses the historically significant primitive, the semaphore. Examples of its use are given, as is a discussion of its implementation. Semaphores are powerful low-level constructs that allow many concurrency problems to be solved, but they fail to provide an adequate high-level abstraction that genuinely supports concurrent programming. The nature of this criticism is discussed in the chapter.

The most important and necessary synchronization for shared variables is mutual exclusion. Rather than program this with semaphores, languages based on conditional critical regions or monitors give direct support to mutual exclusion. Though Pascal-FC does not support conditional critical regions, some consideration is given to them in Chapter 7 as, like monitors, they represent a structured version of the shared-variable approach. Chapter 7 concentrates on the use of monitors and the necessary internal synchronization primitive, the condition variable. This allows a process to be suspended if the conditions are not appropriate for it to continue.

One of the advantages of experimenting with the primitives supported by Pascal-FC is that it is possible to combine different primitives. Many language designers take the understandable view that a language should support only the minimum of abstractions. The programmer should not be faced with alternative ways of achieving the same end result. This has resulted in concurrent programming languages being either message based or monitor based. However, Pascal-FC does allow programs to be written that combine, say, monitors for mutual exclusion, and synchronous message passing for direct inter-process communication. This theme of a unified, though extensive, set of language features is discussed in Chapter 8. First an assessment of the primitives described in the preceding four chapters is given. A number of observations are made: in particular that avoidance synchronization (the use of guarded communication) is a more appropriate synchronization abstraction than the use of semaphores or condition variables. Another often-debated issue concerns the correct abstraction for a passive entity that needs to protect itself against inappropriate access (for example, a buffer that cannot allow concurrent reads or writes, and must suspend a reader if the buffer is empty). Should the entity be a 'passive' process or a 'protected' module such as a monitor? Whilst not conclusively coming down on one side of this debate or the other, the second part of Chapter 8 introduces a unified language model that closely follows the language proposals for Ada 9X. This language model incorporates remote invocation for direct inter-process communication and a passive entity, called a resource, that gives mutual exclusion. Unlike monitors, resources enforce other synchronizations by using guards on the allowed operations. A requeue facility is also supported which aids the programming of certain algorithms.

The unified model is used in a series of examples in Chapter 9. These have been chosen to exemplify the main forms of process architecture used in concurrent programs. Consideration is given to embedded systems, simulation, data flow models, LINDA-type structures and process farms. It is not possible to give a detailed description of all of these architectures. Rather, a brief description followed by a programmed example (using the unified model) is given.

A short conclusion completes the book, although there are also two useful appendices. The first constitutes a Language Reference Manual for the Pascal-FC features used in the book. The second appendix discusses the implementation of Pascal-FC.

Braille copies

Braille copies of this book, on paper or Versabraille cassette, can be made available. Enquiries should be addressed to Dr G.L. Davies, Department of Computing, University of Bradford, West Yorkshire BD7 1DP, United Kingdom.

Acknowledgements

The material presented in this book has been developed over a number of years and we would like to thank all the students who have experienced these courses and provided feedback.

This book would not have been so easily constructed without the extensive use of electronic mail over JANET. We would like to thank the Computer Board of the UK Universities' Funding Council and the UK Science and Engineering Research Council for providing this invaluable service.

Earlier versions of Pascal-PC have been used in a number of institutions in the UK, mainland Europe and the USA. We thank all those who have provided feedback on their experiences. In particular, we are grateful to Dr Andrzej Buller of the Politechnika Gdanska, Poland: his visit to Bradford during the summer of 1991, which was generously supported by the British Council, provided the opportunity for many stimulating discussions. Nor can we underestimate the debt we owe to Ben Ari's (1982) work: Pascal-FC has grown out of his 'implementation kit' for concurrent Pascal-S.

A number of colleagues have made valuable comments on drafts of the book. In particular, we must thank Jane Peers, Phil Davies and Julia Jackson.

Availability of Pascal-FC

Copies of the Pascal-FC system and User Manuals can be made available on payment of a small handling charge. Unlimited permission to copy the software and manuals is granted. Please send enquiries to Dr G.L. Davies at the Department of Computing, University of Bradford, Bradford, West Yorkshire BD7 1DP, UK. Email: gld@computing.bradford.ac.uk

Alan Burns
Geoff Davies
January 1993

Contents

1 The Nature and Uses of Concurrent Programming

In this chapter, we shall attempt to define our field. We prefer to approach this by first considering what is more familiar to the reader: sequential programming. Concurrent programming is then introduced by way of contrast.

The concurrent programming paradigm is in part an attempt to free the software developer from what Booch (1987) has called the 'von Neumann mind-set'. Programming languages not only furnish us with a means of expression, but they also constrain our thinking in certain ways by imposing on us a particular model of computation. Sequential languages such as FORTRAN and Pascal embody an abstraction of the uniprocessor von Neumann architecture which totally dominated the early decades of computer science. One of the consequences is that the user of such languages is constantly tempted to think in a way that may have more to do with such machines than with what would really be appropriate for the problem at hand. It will be seen that one of the principal differences between sequential and concurrent programs is that, whilst the former define a total ordering of events, the latter only require a partial ordering. Concurrent programs do not necessarily execute their operations in the same order when run repeatedly, even if the same input data is used. We shall see that this provides a more powerful means of expression, which can be used to advantage in a variety of applications.

More powerful tools almost always allow us to make more spectacular mistakes, and concurrent programming opens up a new set of potential difficulties that do not afflict the sequential programmer. The tools for solving such problems are the focus of the bulk of this book, but we provide an example of the problems in this chapter to motivate the solutions that are presented later.

This is a book about software rather than computer architecture. As such, it does not concern itself much with the implementation of concurrency. In this first chapter, however, we make a minor exception to this by briefly considering the kinds of architecture on which concurrent software may be run.

Finally, we shall introduce some of the basic features of the language that we shall be using for our examples throughout the book: Pascal-FC (Functionally Concurrent Pascal). This was specially developed to provide students with a range of practical experiences in the programming of concurrent systems.

1.1 Introduction

A dominant theme in the evolution of computer programming languages has been the trend towards increased **abstraction**. Abstraction is simply ignoring what is irrelevant in order to focus on the essence of a problem. Programming languages have fostered abstraction by providing programmers with ways of expressing themselves in terms appropriate to their application domains, rather than being constrained by the peculiarities of the hardware running their programs. Not only does this make the application programmer's task easier but, by eliminating hardware dependencies from the source code, it makes a program **portable**: it does not have to be rewritten in order to run it on different hardware.

For example, FORTRAN introduced **expression abstraction**, which meant that programmers could use familiar mathematical notation for arithmetic expressions. This was a major improvement on the assembly languages which were used before FORTRAN was introduced. The assembly language programmer would have to set out the exact sequence of additions, subtractions, and so on required to carry out a computation. Care would have to be taken to make sure that the order of the operations was correct, and places would have to be found to store the partial results produced during the evaluation of a complicated expression. Finally, it might not be at all clear to a reader of the program *what* expression the resulting code was actually evaluating. In all these respects, FORTRAN made life easier both for writers and for readers of programs.

Another benefit of expression abstraction was that the FORTRAN programmer was able, for example, to specify multiplication without needing to be aware that the machine which ran the program might not even have a multiplication operation in its instruction set: it was the compiler writer's job to implement the multiplication abstraction (for example. by repeated addition). Applications programmers want to solve application problems, not to fight primitive hardware!

Later, Pascal incorporated improvements in the area of **data abstraction**. For example, enumeration types eliminated the need explicitly to code application-relevant attributes (such as colour) as integers. Structured data types, such as records, and the ability to nest structures within structures, allowed programmers to build data models of arbitrary complexity. This meant that real-world data objects could be modelled without the need to understand that the main memory of the machine was, for example, a linear array of 8-bit storage locations.

Though FORTRAN and Pascal provide some degree of abstraction, they are still strongly influenced by the underlying machine architecture which was prevalent when they were designed, and which still characterizes the majority of systems that run programs written in these languages. These are *uniprocessor* systems using the von Neumann architecture. The essence of this architecture can be summarized as follows:

- there is a single processing element (CPU), which is connected to Random Access Memory (RAM) and to input/output devices by means of a **bus**;
- both program instructions and data are stored in RAM;
- the processor executes a repeating cycle in which the next instruction is fetched from RAM and then executed;
- as there is only one CPU, the system can at most be executing one instruction at any moment.[†]

At the assembly language level, the natural way to program such a machine is to write a *sequence* of instructions which, when executed one after another, implement the required algorithm. Of course, slavishly executing

---

[†] It is true that, in the interests of performance, such techniques as execute/fetch overlap and pipelining are now often used: in such cases, there is a sense in which the processing of instructions is overlapped. However, the **semantics** of the instructions are not affected by this: the assembly language programmer writes the same program whether or not such techniques are used.

instructions in the order in which they are stored in RAM is not very flexible, so we shall immediately want to incorporate facilities for branching and looping into our instruction set, but these do not violate the principle that the system proceeds by executing instructions one after another. This is also the model that underlies higher-level sequential programming languages such as FORTRAN and Pascal: they proceed by executing one higher-level language **statement** (for example, assignment statement, procedure call, **case** statement) after another.

Concurrent programming is an abstraction away from the von Neumann hardware architecture. The step-by-step view is not always the most useful model. As Booch (1987) says: 'concurrent programming frees the programmer from the von Neumann mind-set'.

1.2 Sequential programming as a total ordering

This section will not introduce anything that is new to the student. Instead, it will make explicit what the experienced user of sequential programming languages already must assume in order to use them successfully. We shall see later that a partial relaxation of these assumptions is a fundamental feature of concurrent programming.

Below is an abstract fragment from a sequential program:

```
P;
Q;
R
```

The fragment consists of three statements: it does not matter for our purposes what they are. What is important is that in a sequential programming language we are giving the system (hardware and software) which runs our program very strict instructions about the order in which it may carry out these statements. What we are saying is that P *must* precede Q and that, in turn, Q *must* precede R. (For now, we shall pretend that our programming language does not contain branching and looping structures, but we shall see later that the argument is the same even if it does.) Any implementation of our sequential language must ensure that this is true *for every possible execution* of the program. Any assertion that is true of every possible execution of a program is said to be a **property** of that program.

We shall state the required property slightly more formally as:

$$\forall e \bullet P \rightarrow Q \rightarrow R$$

where the '$\rightarrow$' operator means 'precedes' or 'happens before'. The symbol '$\forall e$' means 'for all legitimate executions of the program'. The period in this case may be read as 'it is true that'.

In case this should seem too abstract, suppose that our three statements are:

```
x := 1;        (* P *)
y := x + 1;    (* Q *)
x := y + 2     (* R *)
```

It is clear that the final values of the variables depend on the order in which the statements are executed. Indeed, the algorithms which we write in such languages rely on the assumption that the textual order of the statements is the order in which they are executed. The implementor and the user of a sequential language have, in effect, a contract that the language implementation will behave in that way.

Consider further what it means when we write:

$$P \rightarrow Q$$

Clearly, it implies that P must begin before Q begins, but it also means that P must finish before Q begins. Another way to say this is that there should be no overlap in the execution of the component operations of P and Q.

Suppose, for example, that P and Q are assignment statements in a high-level language. It is very likely that each statement would be compiled into several machine-code instructions: $p1 \ldots pm$ and $q1 \ldots qn$. Execution of the assignment statements would consist of the execution of these component instructions in sequence, so that:

$$\forall e \bullet p1 \rightarrow p2 \ldots \rightarrow pm \rightarrow q1 \rightarrow q2 \ldots \rightarrow qn$$

What we have here is a **total ordering** of the components of P and Q: given *any* pair of different machine instructions, x and y, we can always say which must precede the other, for either:

$$\forall e \bullet x \rightarrow y$$

or

$$\forall e \bullet y \rightarrow x$$

One of these alternatives *must* be true. This is so whether x and y are drawn both from the same assignment, or one is from P and the other is from Q.

In reality, the program probably will include control structures for looping and branching. These may at first sight appear to undermine the assertion that the statements of a sequential program are totally ordered. The decision structures (**if** and **case**, for example) in particular mean that the path through a program may vary from one run to another, so that different orderings of program statements may be observed on different runs. This is so because the path traced during a particular execution will depend on the input data. However, if we repeatedly run a sequential program with the *same* input data, then it will *always* trace the same path. Hence, decision structures do not provide any special problems: for any given set of input data, we could write down the order of execution of the program statements. Similarly, loops can be easily accommodated. If P and Q are enclosed in a loop, then it is clearly not sufficient to say that P precedes Q, because (for example) the first execution of Q precedes the second execution of P. However, the *i*th execution of P precedes the *i*th execution of Q, for all values of *i*. In fact, we may write:

$$\forall e \bullet P^i \to Q^i$$

and

$$\forall e \bullet Q^i \to P^{i+1}$$

for all *i*.

We can say, then, that a sequential program is **deterministic**: given the same input data, it will always execute the same sequence of instructions and it will always produce the same results.[†] We should be very surprised if it did otherwise.

In summary, the sequential paradigm has the following two characteristics:

- the textual order of statements specifies their order of execution;
- successive statements must be executed without any overlap (in time) with one another.

We shall see that neither of these properties applies to concurrent programs.

1.3   Breaking away from the sequential paradigm

1.3.1   Multiple processors

The sequential paradigm described in the previous section is clearly rooted in the traditional uniprocessor architecture. Sometimes, however, the total ordering of the sequential paradigm is not the most appropriate model. Suppose, for example, that we have the following three statements:

[†] This is an over-simplification if the program involves floating-point arithmetic and is run on two different systems. In such a case, real values may differ somewhat because of differences in the precision of representation of floating-point numbers in the two systems.

```
x := 0;      (* P *)
y := 0;      (* Q *)
z := 0       (* R *)
```

It is not necessary here to insist that P → Q → R. That ordering is no more the *correct* one than R → Q → P, because both will have exactly the same results as far as the final values of the variables are concerned. Writing the statements in any particular sequence could be considered misleading, as it implies an ordering that is not essential to the algorithm. Another way to say this is that writing the statements as a sequence is over-specifying the execution of the program: it is constraining the execution in a way that is not required by the logic of the algorithm.

This line of thought is no idle exercise: it could have important practical consequences. Suppose that, whenever we wish to execute a program, we can use as many central processors as we like, without economic penalty. For example, we could use three processors in the above case. This would allow each of P, Q and R to have its own private processor, so that they could all be executed in parallel. We would expect three processors to allow us to execute up to three instructions at any one time. Hence, the section of code ought to execute more quickly than when run on a single CPU; this is certainly of practical significance. However, we should bear in mind that this parallelism might not be applicable to *all* sections of the program because, in some cases, the logic of the algorithm *does* demand sequential execution.

We should introduce some programming notation to indicate when parallel execution is sensible and when it is not. We can then have a mixture, within a single program, of sequential and parallel execution. We shall use a **cobegin/coend** structure to indicate where parallel execution is permitted, as follows:

```
J;
K;
cobegin
  P;
  Q;
  R
coend;
L;
M
```

This notation means that:

$$\forall e \bullet J \rightarrow K \rightarrow (\textbf{cobegin} \ldots \textbf{coend}) \rightarrow L \rightarrow M$$

Within the **cobegin/coend**, however, we expect parallel execution of P, Q and R on three separate processors. This will be symbolized by:

P || Q || R

In English, we shall say that P, Q and R are to be executed concurrently with one another. Remember, though, that we have made the (unrealistic) assumption that we can always have as many processors as we like: we may *expect* separate processors, but our expectation might not always be realized.

Note that the || and **cobegin/coend** notations are simply two different ways of expressing the same idea. The former is an algebraic notation which is useful in reasoning about the behaviour of programs, while the latter is a programming language notation used in writing programs.

1.3.2 Return to reality

In reality, central processors *do* have to be paid for. Real processors also sometimes break down. We may not, therefore, always have three processors when executing P, Q and R. However, we want our source code to be portable: we do not want to have to rewrite the **cobegin/coend** structure (or perhaps even eliminate it altogether) each time the program is to be run on a different hardware configuration. In other words, we want to work at a higher level of abstraction where we can ignore the hardware configuration.

What we should do is to generalize the **cobegin/coend** structure so that it has some meaning regardless of the number of processors available. For true portability, it should even have a meaning for a uniprocessor. A reasonable approach is to say that statements in the **cobegin/coend** *may* overlap when the program is executed, but we cannot say that they *must* do so. If P, Q and R are each a single assembly language statement and the system is a uniprocessor, they *could not* be overlapped because a uniprocessor can only execute one instruction at a time.

We can now give the following definition of the meaning of the concurrency operator ||:

$$P \parallel Q \leftrightarrow \exists e \bullet \text{not}(P \to Q) \text{ and not } (Q \to P)$$

In English, this means: 'P and Q are concurrent if and only if there exists at least one legal execution of the program in which P and Q overlap'.

1.3.3 Logical processors

In keeping with our aim of using abstractions that are independent of hardware, we can say that P || Q means that P and Q are each given a **logical processor**. Each logical processor is itself a sequential machine which executes instructions one at a time. These instructions are taken from the *processes* that are allocated to it, that is, P and Q are now considered to be processes that embody the statements that were previously associated with P and Q. How the logical processors are mapped onto *physical* ones is an implementation detail in just the same way that the implementation of multiplication (by a multiply instruction or by repeated addition) was. It is the **properties** of the logical processors that we shall concentrate on, not their implementations.

In the interests of portability, we shall make very weak assumptions about the temporal properties of logical processors: they may, after all, be implemented on various types and numbers of physical processors. The first temporal property is that:

> No assumptions must be made about the speeds of operation of logical processors relative to one another.

Certainly, we should not assume that any two logical processors operate at comparable speeds: they could, for example, be mapped onto physical processors of significantly different performance.

The second temporal property of logical processors may appear peculiar at first. It is that:

> No relationship exists between the speeds of operation of logical processors and our normal clocks for measuring time ('real' time). Logical processors do not necessarily proceed at a constant rate when measured in real time units.

One reason for this is that more than one logical processor might be mapped onto a single physical processor. What happens in such a case is that the logical processors must share the instruction-cycles of the shared CPU. Typically, a few instructions are executed from one process and then the CPU is switched to another (this is called **interleaving**). In this way, each logical processor appears to progress in a series of bursts of activity interspersed with periods of dormancy. Each logical processor may be regarded as having its own logical clock, the rate of which is in no way tied to real time or to the logical clocks of other processors.

1.4   Concurrent programming as a partial ordering

What can we now say about the ordering of events in a concurrent program, bearing in mind the temporal properties of logical processors? Suppose that we write:

```
cobegin
   P;
   Q;
   R
coend
```

What can we say about the legitimate orderings of P, Q and R?

By definition, P, Q and R may overlap. However, we saw earlier that we cannot say that they must do so: we are unwilling to make any stipulation about the speeds of the processors, either relative to one another or to real time. Hence, the following are all legitimate executions:

- $Q \rightarrow R \rightarrow P$
- $R \rightarrow Q \rightarrow P$
- $P \rightarrow Q \rightarrow R$

In fact, if we just consider executions in which there is no overlap of the three operations, there are six legal orderings.

However, P, Q and R *are* allowed to overlap, so the number of legal executions of the program may be larger than six. Again, consider P and Q (for example) to be assignment statements consisting of machine-code components $p1 \ldots pm$ and $q1 \ldots qn$. Because each 'assignment process' is running on a sequential logical processor, we can say, for example, that:

$$\forall e \bullet p2 \rightarrow p3$$

and that

$$\forall e \bullet q4 \rightarrow q5$$

More generally, we can write that:

$$\forall e, i < j \bullet pi \rightarrow pj$$

An analogous assertion can be made for the components of Q.

To put this another way, we can take any pair of operations from within P and state the order in which they will be executed on all runs of the program (with a particular data set). Considered on its own, therefore, P is sequential. Hence it is misleading to speak of *a* concurrent process: processes are only concurrent *with respect to one another*. A more abstract way of saying this is that the concurrency operator $\parallel$ is not a unary operator.[†]

[†] We shall, however, follow common usage sometimes and refer to P and Q, for example, as 'concurrent processes'. The reader should understand that this is a short way of saying that P and Q are concurrent with respect to one another.

Suppose now that we take two operations, x and y, and that one of them comes from P and the other from Q. What can we now say about the order of execution? In fact, we can say very little. They may overlap (if we have more than one physical processor) or either one may precede the other. The best that we can say at this stage is that:

$$\text{not}(\forall e \bullet x \rightarrow y) \text{ and not } (\forall e \bullet y \rightarrow x)$$

This allows a considerable degree of flexibility in the ordering of these two operations. When we consider that each of P and Q consists potentially of a large number of such operations, it is clear that the number of legal orderings for a concurrent program (even a fairly small one) can be very large indeed.

Because of the temporal variability of logical processors, we may observe different orderings on different runs of a concurrent program, even with the same input data. This can lead to a variation in output results, which is not at all what we would expect to find in sequential programming! Experienced practitioners of sequential programming can be disturbed by this when they first begin to study concurrent programming. Leach (1987), for example, notes that his students were often surprised when their own concurrent programs exhibited this variability. Indeed:

> 'Two of the students were so shocked by the different behaviour of the sample runs that they turned in their projects with signatures of witnesses that their program ran successfully, at least once.' (p. 41)

In summary, if two operations are concurrent with one another:

- the operations are permitted (but not obliged) to overlap in time;
- the textual order does not define the order of execution.

Another way to express the second point is that the operations of a concurrent program are **partially ordered**. Concurrent programs can behave **non-deterministically**, in the sense that they can deliver differing results when repeatedly run on the same input data.

The fact that concurrent programs are non-deterministic should always be borne in mind: an algorithm may appear to work on one implementation of the language, but fail when run on another. This can happen because the algorithm depends for its success on a particular subset of the legal orderings that just happen to be favoured by the first implementation. Another implementation may exercise different orderings, legality of which was overlooked when the program was written and tested. Lack of dependence on order is the contract which the user of a concurrent language makes with the implementor of the language. Writing an algorithm which breaks this contract is likely to lead to a program that ' . . . works, but only sometimes'. We usually try to do better than this!

1.5   The motivation for concurrent programming

So far we have concentrated on the characteristics of concurrent systems: we have said very little about *why* we might want to allow the system to execute some parts of a program concurrently. Three possible reasons are given below: it is not an exhaustive list, but it will serve our purpose.

- Using multiprocessor hardware, we can achieve gains in execution speed by assigning different physical processors to different processes.
- It is generally the case that a program is unable to keep a physical processor fully occupied throughout its execution. We can eliminate potential processor idle time by sharing the processor between a number of programs that are run as concurrent processes. Individual processes may take longer to execute, but CPU utilization and the system's throughput of work will be improved.
- The total ordering of the sequential paradigm may be an inappropriate model for a given application. The order in which program operations should occur may be determined at run time by events external to the computer system. Moreover, it may not be possible to say in what order these external events may occur. (For example, if we are producing software to control traffic lights at a crossroads, we cannot predict in what order the various sensors will be triggered by vehicles approaching the junction, because that will depend on who decides to drive where, and at what time.) In short, the problem domain may be inherently non-deterministic and concurrent.

In the following subsections we shall explore the first two reasons for concurrency in a little more detail. The third will be considered later.

1.5.1   Parallelism for faster execution

Suppose that we have an array of real numbers, and that, in order to calculate statistics, we want to know the sum of elements of the array and the sum of the squares of these elements. Each of these values could be computed by a function. Suitable code is given below in a Pascal-like syntax:

```
function SUM(DATA:  REALARRAY): real;
var
   INDEX: integer;
```

```
      TOTAL: real;
  begin
    TOTAL := 0.0;
    for INDEX := 1 to ARRAYSIZE do
      TOTAL := TOTAL + DATA[INDEX];
    SUM := TOTAL
  end;

  function SUMOFSQUARES(DATA: REALARRAY): real;
  var
    INDEX: integer;
    TOTAL: real;
  begin
    TOTAL := 0.0;
    for INDEX := 1 to ARRAYSIZE do
      TOTAL := TOTAL + sqr(DATA[INDEX]);
    SUMOFSQUARES := TOTAL
  end;
```

If we assume that two processes can read simultaneously from an array without interfering with one another, then we can execute the functions concurrently, as follows:

```
  cobegin
    TOTAL := SUM(DATA);
    TOTALSQ := SUMOFSQUARES(DATA)
  coend
```

The two assignment statements are concurrent processes, and may be run on two different physical processors, if available. As we have seen, they are not, however, required to do so, and the same program could also be run on a uniprocessor.

1.5.2 Improving processor utilization

Until recently, processors were expensive and their owners wanted to get as much work out of them as possible. Yet a single program is unlikely to keep a processor working flat out throughout its execution. One reason for this is that most programs need to perform input and output operations. For example, the program may need to input some data before it can carry out any calculations. Yet the Input/Output (I/O) devices that are connected to computers are often very slow in comparison with the rate at which a processor can execute instructions. Hence there is likely to be a significant delay between making a request for input and actually receiving the data. If the requesting program has nothing to do in the meantime, it makes sense to switch the processor to one that *can* make use of the available processor-cycles. Multiple programs are then run as concurrent processes (a practice known as **multi-programming**). The exploitation of this possibility in operating systems was one of the earliest applications of concurrency and is still one of the most important.

This kind of behaviour is one of the reasons why we do not assume that logical processors function at a constant rate as measured in real-time units. Typically, logical processors progress in a series of bursts of activity interspersed with periods when they are dormant.

1.6 An inherently concurrent problem domain

Here, we shall consider a more extended example, which highlights the shortcomings of sequential programming in the field of **embedded computer systems**. An embedded system is a computer which forms a component of a larger engineering system, such as an aircraft or process control system, the primary purpose of which is not computation. The role of the computer is to monitor variables such as temperature, pressure and flow-rate, both in subcomponents of the system and in the external environment, and to set controls to ensure the system's correct operation.

The use of embedded computers in the control of aircraft and spacecraft has now reached the stage at which such vehicles are often designed for fly-by-wire operation. This means that the various controls that the pilot uses are not connected directly (e.g. by hydraulics or cables) to the control surfaces and other effectors of the aircraft, but rather that the pilot's control signals are fed to a computer, which then computes an appropriate output signal to send to the effectors. Similarly, status signals from the various components of the aircraft are routed via the computer, which then controls suitable display devices.

We are not going to consider a specific embedded system in detail. Instead we shall abstract the important characteristics of a typical application. We consider a system for monitoring four facets of the environment, A, B, C and D, which must carry out some task in respect of each of these. For the present, task D will be ignored. As the sequential paradigm is based on the uniprocessor hardware model, we shall assume a single CPU.

1.6.1 Periodic tasks

What are the tasks that must be carried out? In the case of A, B and C, we shall suppose that we have periodically to make a measurement and take some appropriate action. For example, this may involve taking a temperature and then turning a heater on or off, as appropriate. As a first attempt at writing the software for the system, we might use a traditional sequential approach to provide a **control loop**, as follows:

```
repeat
    DEAL_WITH_A;
    DEAL_WITH_B;
    DEAL_WITH_C
forever
```

Each DEAL_WITH procedure implements the required task.

This code is premature. We should have considered the timing requirements of the application before writing the control loop. It is typical in such systems that different periods are appropriate for different variables. Intuitively, it would seem that the required period would depend on how quickly the variable concerned might *change significantly*.

Suppose, for example, that this is a system for a 'drive-by-wire' car and that one of its tasks is to display the amount of fuel remaining in the tank. How often should the level be measured and the driver's display updated? Under normal operating conditions, the level would be expected to change quite slowly, so that checking once every few minutes would probably suffice: fuel gauges in cars are not, after all, read to the nearest millilitre! To measure the level more frequently would be a waste of CPU time, which might be better employed elsewhere.

Suppose that another task is to monitor the position of the steering wheel and control the movements of the front wheels. How many readers would be prepared to travel in the car if the position of the steering wheel were measured once every few minutes? Once every few tens of milliseconds would be more appropriate here.

Forget about the car for a moment and think more generally about the three tasks. Each one is characterized by a periodic repetition of some action. Suppose that the periods are as shown in Table 1.1. The times are in some unspecified time units.

Table 1.1 Three periodic tasks.

Task	Period
A	20
B	40
C	80

The only way that we can meet these requirements with the control loop given above is to ensure that the loop is executed once every 20 units. However, that means that DEAL_WITH_B is being carried out twice as frequently, and DEAL_WITH_C four times as frequently, as required. At best this is a waste of processor resources, which might be required for other purposes. At worst it may be impossible to achieve the required performance with the processor at hand, as we can see if we now consider how much time is required by each execution of the various DEAL_WITH procedures.

How long each procedure requires obviously depends both on the speed of the processor and the operations required to carry out the procedure. Suppose that the required execution times are as set out in the third column of Table 1.2. The table shows that, for example, 40 units of CPU time are required every 80 units to meet the requirements of C. We shall suppose that this is the *total* time required per period. It is not necessary to have the processor for an unbroken period of 40 units: a series of **slices** of processor time is satisfactory.

Table 1.2 Periodic tasks and their execution times.

Task	Period	Time
A	20	4
B	40	10
C	80	40

The problem can now obviously not be solved by running the loop once every 20 units: DEAL_WITH_C alone will take 40 units per iteration, so that the loop simply will not execute quickly enough! Yet in a sense it appears that it should be possible to satisfy the requirements of all of the tasks if we consider the total CPU time required per period of 80 time units. The total is, in fact, 76 units, and is calculated as follows:

- A requires $4 \times 4 = 16$
- B requires $2 \times 10 = 20$
- C requires 40.

The fact that enough CPU time does appear to be available, and that the times are total times per period of 80 units, suggests a possible solution along the following lines:

- the loop is run at one iteration per 80 time units;
- DEAL_WITH_A is called four times per iteration;
- DEAL_WITH_B and DEAL_WITH_C are split into as many sub-procedures as necessary to fit the timing requirements.

Table 1.3 shows the way in which the new scheme could use the available CPU time. The first column indicates the time elapsed since the beginning of a single 80-unit period. Task C has been divided into four components, which have been chosen to fit the gaps not occupied by A and B. In this example it has not been necessary to subdivide DEAL_WITH_B, but a different set of timing requirements might have made that necessary.

Table 1.3 Meeting the timing requirements.

Elapsed	Task	Time
0	A	4
4	B	10
14	C_1	6
20	A	4
24	C_2	16
40	A	4
44	B	10
54	C_3	6
60	A	4
64	C_4	12
76	(spare)	4

A second version of the control loop, incorporating these ideas, is given below:

```
repeat
    DEAL_WITH_A;
    DEAL_WITH_B;
    DEAL_WITH_C_1;
    DEAL_WITH_A;
    DEAL_WITH_C_2;
    DEAL_WITH_A;
    DEAL_WITH_B;
    DEAL_WITH_C_3;
    DEAL_WITH_A;
    DEAL_WITH_C_4;
    (* sleep for 4 units *)
forever
```

This has clearly been a rather painful design process, even though the system is very simple. Moreover, the structure of the resulting code is poor and it is difficult to maintain. A change in the timing requirements or the use of alternative hardware with different performance could necessitate significant changes to the source code. There is worse to come: enter task D!

1.6.2 Introduction of an aperiodic task

Tasks A, B and C were periodic and typified one of the two main classes of tasks found in embedded systems. They are characterized by the need to repeat some action at regular and predictable intervals. The second major class are known as **aperiodic tasks**. These are not characterized by the repetition of a predictable cycle of activity, but instead may require action at unpredictable times, perhaps only on an occasional basis. Often they represent alarm conditions, which happen rarely (if at all). If the alarm is raised, however, prompt remedial action must be carried out.

Task D in our example is aperiodic. It is concerned with the control of the inertia-reel seat belts. Normally, the belt can be fed out from the reel so that the user has freedom of movement. However, the reel must lock whenever a sensor detects a rapid deceleration so that the user is held secure. The deceleration need not be the result of a collision: it may be caused by heavy braking. Hence, the car may need to continue normal operation after the event has occurred.

We suppose that a sensor sends a signal (ALARM) to the embedded computer when a rapid deceleration is detected. When the car is no longer decelerating rapidly, a second signal (CLEAR) is sent, but we shall not have so much to say about this. The computer must lock the seat belt reels when the ALARM signal is received and unlock them when CLEAR is received.

What are the timing requirements for task D? Suppose that two units of CPU time are required when either the ALARM or the CLEAR signal is received. There are two other important timing characteristics. First, we need some indication of how frequently these signals might occur. This could be difficult to determine. Perhaps the best we can do is to indicate the worst-case behaviour: what is the minimum possible time between any two signals? Suppose that the mechanical characteristics of the seat belt system are such that the minimum is 80 time units. Second, it should be obvious in this case that the **latency** of response of the system is crucial: if the belt locks too late, then the system is useless. Suppose that the execution of DEAL_WITH_D must complete within three time units of the occurrence of an ALARM signal.

The requirements imposed on the system by task D typify those presented by aperiodic tasks:

- it may be required to act at times that are not predictable (though in some cases we may be able, as here, to specify the minimum time between two successive required actions);
- when action is required, it must be completed within a specified time.

We shall not even attempt to modify our control loop to incorporate task D: it would involve including code which polled for the occurrence of D every time unit.[†] By now the reader will be convinced that the sequential approach has led us into a swamp. The concurrent approach to such a

---

[†] It might be observed by seasoned sequential programmers that the way to cope with D is to generate an interrupt on its occurrence. This is then serviced by a routine that does not have to be placed in the control loop at all. However, the interrupt service routine is executed *concurrently* with the DEAL_WITH procedures in our sense of 'concurrent'.

problem avoids that particular hazard. The essence of a concurrent solution is as follows:

- a separate process is assigned to each of the tasks A to D;
- the processes run concurrently with one another;
- each process contains a loop;
- periodic processes need some way of tying the rate of iteration of their loop to the required period for the task;
- aperiodic processes need some way of remaining dormant when they have no work to do and becoming active when required.

An outline of a concurrent program for the system will be presented in Section 2.6.3, after some foundation material has been presented.

This example highlights an important difference between the general field of concurrent programming, which is the main focus of this book, and real-time programming, which is a specific area of application of concurrency techniques. Whereas in concurrent programming we attempt to make no assumptions about the real-time behaviour of logical processors, in real-time programming we *must* do so because there are deadlines to be met. We shall not consider here how the logical clocks can be brought into synchrony with real-time clocks; we shall return to this question in Section 2.7. For the present, we shall simply assume that this can be done.

1.7 Problems in concurrent programming

The model presented so far is that a concurrent program consists of a set of processes, each with its own logical processor. Because each processor is sequential, *within* a process there is a total ordering of operations (with a given data set). However, we did not want to make any assumptions about the speeds of the logical processors relative to one another. Because of this, we were not prepared to say much about the order of execution of two operations from different processes (i.e. executed on different logical processors). In consequence, we said that concurrent programs could produce different output results on different runs, even with the same input data. This was because there may be a very large number of legal execution orders of the component operations of the program.

This is often not what we want. Some of the orderings may be compatible with the purpose of the program, while others may be detrimental to it. In such cases the concurrent language must provide us with a way of constraining the execution of the program so that only the acceptable orders can ever be used. Languages do this by providing facilities for **process synchronization**. Such facilities, and how we use them to eliminate all the unacceptable orderings, are a central theme of the study of concurrent programming.

Processes also sometimes need to communicate information among one another. Some concurrent languages use ordinary variables (such as are found in a sequential language) as a way of passing information from one process to another, and the programmer must use the language's synchronization facilities to allow processes to know when valid information is ready. In other cases, synchronization and communication are bundled together in a single, higher-level construct. Both of these approaches will be described later in this book.

To motivate the study of synchronization and communication presented in later chapters, we now consider a different problem where not all interleavings are desirable.

1.7.1   Outline of the seat reservation problem

A central computer connected to remote terminals via communication links is used to automate seat reservations for a concert hall. The remote terminals are located in booking offices which are geographically dispersed. When a client enters a booking office, the clerk displays the current state of reservations on a screen. The client chooses one of the free seats and the clerk enters the number of the chosen seat at the terminal. A ticket for that seat is then issued. Clearly, a fundamental requirement is to avoid multiple bookings for any seat, whilst allowing the client a free choice among the available seats.

1.7.2   A first attempt at a solution

Suppose that we decide to implement the software for this system as a single program. A reasonable approach is to write a **terminal handler** module which manages the input and display of information at a single terminal. Since there are n terminals in the system, we could then have n instances of this module running concurrently. We could express this as follows:

```
cobegin
    HANDLER1;
    HANDLER2;
    HANDLER3
        . . .
    HANDLERn
coend
```

In a pseudocode form, the outline of each handler might be as follows:

```
repeat
  display seat plan on screen;
  read(CLIENT_CHOICE);
  SEAT[CLIENT_CHOICE] := RESERVED;
  issue ticket
forever
```

We do not need any knowledge of concurrent programming to see one of the problems with this attempt: there is nothing to stop the booking of a seat which is already displayed as reserved. This could occur through human error; a properly designed system should trap such errors. Even if we assume perfect users (who make no errors and are never malicious), we still have a problem with this attempt, which *is* caused by the concurrency in our program.

The problem is not difficult to see. If two clients were shown the seating plan at approximately the same time (perhaps in different booking offices), they could both see that a particular seat is still free and tell the clerk to book it. We have a double booking and our system has failed.

1.7.3 A second attempt

Below is a second attempt at the terminal handler:

```
repeat
  if SOLD_OUT then
  begin
    present a suitable display;
    await further instructions
  end
  else
  begin
    SUCCESS := false;
    repeat
      display seat plan on screen;
      read(CLIENT_CHOICE);
      if SEAT[CLIENT_CHOICE] = FREE then
      begin
        SEAT[CLIENT_CHOICE] := RESERVED;
        SUCCESS := true;
        issue ticket
      end
      else
        give_error_message
    until SUCCESS
  end
forever
```

We have now inserted a check before committing a reservation to ensure that the position has not changed since the display was presented. Unfortunately this has not solved the problem, and multiple bookings are still possible. Consider, for simplicity, two terminal handler processes: HANDLER*x* and HANDLER*y*. There is nothing to prevent the following sequence from occurring:

(1)   HANDLER*x* tests SEAT[K] and finds it FREE,

(2)   HANDLER*y* tests SEAT[K] and finds it FREE,

(3)   HANDLER*x* marks SEAT[K] RESERVED,

(4)   HANDLER*y* marks SEAT[K] RESERVED.

This is simply the same problem we had in the first version: in the previous case, the clients were making the tests rather than the computer.

1.7.4   Atomic actions

The essence of this problem is that a compiler will not treat the testing and setting operations as a single action. The **if** statement in the above code would be translated into a sequence of several machine instructions. The following is a simplified pseudocode example of the machine code that might be produced (each line represents a single machine instruction):

```
load SEAT[CLIENT_CHOICE] to CPU register
test value of CPU register
jump to L1 if RESERVED
set SEAT[CLIENT_CHOICE] to RESERVED
set SUCCESS to TRUE
code to issue ticket
jump to L2
L1: code to output error message
L2: code following if statement
```

We can regard each of these machine instructions as an **atomic** action. An atomic action is one that appears to take place as a single indivisible operation. Hence no other process can observe the effects of an atomic action while it is actually in progress, nor can any other process interfere with the execution of an atomic action while it is being executed. Although we can be sure that there will be no interference from any other process while P (for example) is executing an atomic instruction, we cannot make any such assumption about what might happen *between* the execution of two successive atomic instructions from P. Thus, by writing our terminal handlers as concurrent processes, we have explicitly allowed the system to use the unfortunate ordering given above.

It is not *always* the case that we want the test and the subsequent actions of an **if** statement to be carried out as an atomic action. Hence, building a compiler that always did this would not be a solution to the problem, because we do not want to constrain execution ordering any more than is necessary (we do not want to overspecify the execution). What we need instead is a way of telling the compiler when to do this. In this particular case, we want to generate the following, where the instructions contained in angle brackets are to be carried out as an atomic action:

```
        <
        load SEAT[CLIENT_CHOICE] to CPU register
        test value of CPU register
        jump to L1 if RESERVED
        set SEAT[CLIENT_CHOICE] to RESERVED
        >
        set SUCCESS to TRUE
        code to issue ticket
        jump to L2
    L1: code to output error message
    L2: code following if statement
```

In more general terms, we need to be able to build arbitrary atomic actions by marking in some way a sequence of statements that needs to be carried out as an indivisible step in the computation. Ideally, what we want to do is to declare as illegal all execution orders that are not acceptable while allowing complete freedom of choice among the acceptable orderings. This is the role of the synchronization facilities of a concurrent language.

A piece of code that must appear (from the point of view of some other process) as an atomic action is called **a Critical Section** (CS). If processes P and Q both contain critical sections whose overlapped executions could interfere with one another, then we need to ensure that these sections are executed under **mutual exclusion**. Hence, each process's critical section appears as an atomic action from the other's point of view. The critical sections are still not totally ordered, as we do not want to specify the order in which different processes are allowed to start their critical sections. More formally, we want to insist that:

$$\forall e \bullet (CS_P^i \rightarrow CS_Q^j) \text{ or } (CS_Q^j \rightarrow CS_P^i)$$

for all pairs of processes P and Q and repetitions of their critical sections i and j. We say that two operations are **serialized** when they may be executed in either order but without overlap.

1.8 Hardware architectures for supporting concurrent programming

For most of this book, we shall not be concerned with the implementation of logical processors on hardware. However, a brief outline of alternative architectures does provide a useful background, because the features provided in concurrent languages have often been abstractions of hardware architectures. We can distinguish between two broad types of system on which we might run concurrent programs:

- uniprocessors
- multiprocessors.

We now briefly consider these in turn.

1.8.1 Uniprocessor systems

People are sometimes perplexed by the idea of executing concurrent programs on a uniprocessor: it can, after all, execute at most one machine instruction at any time. However, the reader should now understand that:

- high-level language statements can be overlapped because their associated machine instructions can be interleaved;
- writing P and Q as concurrent processes means that overlap is *legal*, not that it is *mandatory*.

What is the motivation for running a concurrent program on a uniprocessor? It is certainly not an increase in program execution speed, for a program such as the statistical one in Section 1.5.1 would not execute any more quickly on a uniprocessor than would a sequential version.[†] This is because both processes are capable of keeping the CPU working flat out: they are said to be **processor bound**, which means that their rate of progress is limited by the speed with which the CPU can execute instructions. The main reasons for running concurrent programs on a uniprocessor, therefore, are:

- the desire to improve CPU utilization when running **I/O bound** processes;
- to provide an interactive service to multiple users;
- to take advantage of the partial ordering of the concurrent paradigm when the problem domain is itself not totally ordered.

[†] Indeed, it may even be slower, because the action of interleaving involves some overhead, as we shall see in Section 2.5.

As, in principle, all processes running on a uniprocessor can access the same primary memory space, a natural way to implement inter-process synchronization and communication on such a system is by **shared variables**. One process can place information in an agreed place and the other can read it. The earliest language primitives for synchronization and communication were based on this model, and will be described in Chapters 6 and 7.

1.8.2 Multiprocessors

We can make a rough distinction between two types of multiprocessor.

- In a **tightly-coupled** system there is a bus to which memory and I/O devices are connected, but there is more than one CPU attached to the bus. There is, therefore, some memory which is common to the processors. In addition, some or all of the processors may have local memory, which is not accessible from any of the other processors.

- In a **loosely-coupled** (or **distributed**) system we have a collection of **nodes**, which may be geographically dispersed. Each node may itself be a uniprocessor or multiprocessor computer system. No two nodes share any memory, but nodes are connected by communication links (otherwise, we should simply have a collection of independent computers rather than a multiprocessor system).

In both types of multiprocessor, it is possible to execute instructions in parallel. Hence these architectures are chosen for applications where a gain in execution speed is a motive for the use of concurrency. We could assign a separate processor to each process running in such a system, but for economic reasons usually there are more processes than processors. It is, therefore, likely that each processor will be shared by a set of processes.

On a tightly-coupled multiprocessor, communication between processes can again be implemented by shared memory. This may, however, raise the following question:

> What happens if two processors simultaneously attempt to access the same memory location?

The reader should now have enough insight into the potential pitfalls of concurrency to know that simultaneous accesses could lead to incorrect system behaviour. In fact, the problem is avoided by some form of **bus arbitration**: if two different processors wish to use the system bus at the same time, then the hardware **serializes** these accesses (they are atomic actions).

In a loosely-coupled system there is no memory which is shared by all processors. This does not mean that a concurrent language could not be based on the **abstraction** of shared memory: the language implementor could present the illusion that synchronization and communication variables could be seen by processes running on different processors. However, this illusion might be difficult to implement efficiently, and some people do not consider it to be the most appropriate abstraction to use with distributed systems.

A distributed system does, however, have communication links between its processors, and we can easily think of communication between processes in terms of **messages** being sent from one to another. It can be argued that thinking of inter-process communication in this way is a more satisfactory abstraction than the shared memory model: it seems natural to think of processes sending messages to one another whether the underlying hardware has shared memory or not. The message-passing model appears intuitively to fit all three of the basic architectures we have considered. Since this is so, we lay more emphasis on message passing in this book, and it is considered in detail in Chapters 4 and 5.

1.9   Introducing Pascal-FC

Most of the programming examples in this book are written in Pascal-FC (Davies and Burns, 1990). This language was developed for use in the teaching of concurrent programming, and readers with access to it will be able to carry out practical work. However, those without access to a Pascal-FC system can treat it as a Pascal-like pseudocode. For both groups of readers, we introduce some of the features of the language here as a foundation for their understanding of the examples given later in the book. The features that support concurrency will be described at various points when required: only sequential features are considered now.

Pascal-FC is based on a subset of Pascal developed by Wirth and named Pascal-S. Pascal-S (and Pascal-FC) have been designed to be simple compact languages, so certain features present in standard Pascal are not included because they are not essential to a study of concurrent programming. We shall assume that the reader is familiar with standard Pascal in this section, so that what follows is largely a description of what is missing from Pascal-FC. (The remainder of the book will redeem the language by introducing its many features that are not in standard Pascal.) At least this should explain what might otherwise be regarded as eccentric programming style in some of our examples. A definition of the Pascal-FC features used in this book and an explanation of our syntax notation are given in Appendix A.

1.9.1   Standard Pascal features not supported by Pascal-FC

The following facilities are not supported by Pascal-FC.

(1)   **Files.** There are no files, apart from the standard input and output. Hence Pascal-FC does not allow file parameters in a program header: it is assumed, in effect, that all programs are likely to require the

standard input and output. The form of the program header is:

```
program_header ::=
    program identifier;
```

(2) The **with statement**. Record types (excluding variant records) may be declared as in standard Pascal, but there is no **with** statement.

(3) **Sets.** There are no set types, except for the added type bitset, which is intended for use in real-time implementations of Pascal-FC.

(4) **Subrange types.** Subrange types are not supported.

(5) **Dynamic storage.** There are no pointer types, and the standard procedures new and dispose are not provided.

(6) **Packed data**. The language does not support the **packed** qualifier, and consequently there is no facility for string variables (though string literals in the write and writeln procedures are supported).

1.9.2 Useful enhancements of standard Pascal features

A few features have been added which are not directly concerned with processes and their communication and synchronization:

(1) **Extension to the repeat ... until loop**. We shall find that a useful abstraction in concurrent programming is a cyclic process which executes indefinitely. Pascal-FC allows this idea to be represented in a **repeat ... forever** loop, which is semantically equivalent to **repeat ... until** false.

(2) The **null statement**. The **null** statement has been introduced as an alternative to Pascal's empty statement. Its execution has no effect.

(3) **The** random **function**. This function returns a pseudorandom integer. A call has the form:

```
i := random(n)
```

The integer returned will be in the range 0 ... abs(n).

1.9.3 Other characteristics

(1) **Case of alphabetic characters in the source program**. Case is not significant, except in string and char literals. The source code in this book, however, uses the following conventions: reserved words are in bold lower case; predefined identifiers are in lower case; user defined identifiers use a mixture of upper and lower case.

(2) **Order of declarations**. Originally, Pascal declarations had to be made in a specific order (**label**, **const**, **type**, **var**, followed by **procedure** and **function** declarations). In Pascal-FC, however, the order of declarations is not restricted.

SUMMARY

The sequential paradigm considered at the beginning of the chapter gives a total ordering of program operations. However, this often results in overspecification, and we next considered the concurrent paradigm. Each process considered by itself is sequential, but we presented a view in which pairs of operations from different processes are unordered. We saw that, though this model may be useful in cases such as the statistical program of Section 1.5.1, a problem such as the seat reservation application needs a compromise between this and the total ordering of sequential programming. It turns out that cases such as the statistical program are rather rare in concurrent programming. Concurrent languages, therefore, invariably provide facilities (in the form of synchronization primitives) to allow the programmer to specify exactly the degree of control over event-ordering that is required for an application, while allowing full advantage to be taken of the benefits of concurrency.

The various degrees of freedom in the ordering of two operations, P and Q, which we have considered are:

(1) The operations must be executed sequentially, so that:

$$\forall e \bullet P \to Q$$

(2) P and Q are unordered, but must be executed under mutual exclusion:

$$\forall e \bullet (P \to Q) \text{ or } (Q \to P)$$

This is serial execution: as long as the statements never overlap, we do not care in which order they are executed.

(3) P and Q may be overlapped (P and Q are concurrent processes):

$$\exists e \bullet \text{not } (P \to Q) \text{ and not } (Q \to P)$$

If P and Q are run on different physical processors, then we say that they are run in parallel. Even if they share a physical processor, it may still be possible to overlap them by interleaving. Hence, we see parallelism as a particular instance of the more general concept of concurrency.

Finally, the following implication expresses the indeterminacy of a concurrent program:

$$P \parallel Q \Rightarrow \text{not } (\forall e \bullet P \to Q) \text{ and not } (\forall e \bullet Q \to P)$$

EXERCISES

1.1 'The problem with the seat-reservation example is easily solved if we always make sure that the screen displays the latest information on bookings.' Discuss.

1.2 In languages such as Pascal and C, the order of evaluation of an expression such as:

A + B + C + D

is not defined. Should we consider this as a case of concurrency?

1.3 A binary operator *op* is said to be **commutative** if a *op* b => b *op* a. It is said to be **transitive** if ((a *op* b) and (b *op* c)) => a *op* c. Does the '→' operator introduced in this chapter have these properties?

1.4 Consider a concurrent program consisting of two processes. Each process consists of three atomic operations. How many legal orderings are there for the program, assuming that no synchronization primitives have been used?

1.5 Consider the activities involved in cooking a substantial meal. You, as cook, are the processor. What resources are you using? What are the concurrent processes involved? Would more cooks (multiprocessors) help? How would the cooks share resources?

1.6 Can a multiprocessor allow us to solve computational problems that *cannot* be solved with a uniprocessor, or does it merely permit us to solve the same problems more quickly?

2 Process Representation and Life-cycle

In the last chapter the notion of concurrency was introduced. Following the pioneering work of Dijkstra (1968), a concurrent program is conventionally viewed as consisting of a collection of sequential processes. Each process is considered to execute on its own logical processor and progresses by executing a sequence of statements. The designers of concurrent programming languages are concerned with the representation and behaviour of processes and the means by which sets of processes exchange information and synchronize their executions. In this chapter we review a number of process structures found in modern concurrent programming languages. We then describe the features supported in Pascal-FC and give some example programs. The necessary support for executing process systems is also discussed.

2.1 The concept of process

Consider a program that consists of three processes {P, Q, R}. To show that the processes can be executed concurrently we write:

P ∥ Q ∥ R

Each of the processes is said to have its own **thread of control** and it is useful to consider each as having its own logical processor (even though, in reality, the execution of all three processes may be interleaved onto the same physical processor). If P, Q and R have no interactions with each other, then they can progress at different rates; the behaviour of the complete program should not depend on any particular ordering of the statements of P with respect to Q or R.

A number of simple laws (Hoare, 1985) apply to the **concurrency operator**. The first law expresses symmetry (states that the concurrency operator is **commutative**):

P ∥ Q = Q ∥ P

If P is concurrent with Q then Q is concurrent with P. Next there is a law of associations:

P ∥ (Q ∥ R) = (P ∥ Q) ∥ R

It follows that the brackets can be done away with and that the ordering is irrelevant:

P ∥ Q ∥ R = Q ∥ P ∥ R = R ∥ P ∥ Q

Finally we can note that ∥ is **transitive**:

P ∥ Q and Q ∥ R => P ∥ R (=> P ∥ Q ∥ R)

If P is concurrent with Q and Q is concurrent with R, then P is also concurrent with R. Indeed, all three processes are concurrent (with respect to each other).

The behaviour of each process is defined by the sequence of statements it executes. The actual sequence may, of course, depend on input data but we can (as in Chapter 1) ignore this refinement for the moment. Let the first event of process P be represented by the action a. We can write:

P = (a → P')

Process P is said to engage in event a and then behave like process P'. This can be extended as follows:

$$P' = (b \rightarrow P'')$$

It follows that:

$$P = (a \rightarrow b \rightarrow P'')$$

Eventually either the sequence of events must terminate or repeat itself (and, therefore, conceptually, run for ever). If it terminates then we distinguish between correct termination (SUCCESS) and error termination (FAILURE):

$$P = (a \rightarrow b \rightarrow \ldots \rightarrow SUCCESS)$$
$$P = (a \rightarrow b \rightarrow \ldots \rightarrow FAILURE)$$

Whereas it is usually considered an error for a sequential program not to terminate, this is not the case with concurrent programs. Many embedded control programs involve the repeated execution of a number of control loops. (The concurrent solution to the drive-by-wire car, which is shown in Section 2.6.3, will illustrate this). In our concurrent program each loop will be represented by a cyclic process:

$$P = (a \rightarrow P')$$
$$P' = (b \rightarrow P')$$

Process P engages in action a (which may, for example, be some form of data initialization) and then repeatedly engages in action b. We shall see in later chapters that process interactions can be modelled by actions that are undertaken by more than one process.

It is often convenient to introduce a process that engages in no significant events, always terminates and terminates successfully. This process is usually called the SKIP process. It is a genuine process but does no work and is always ready to terminate; it should not be confused with the **null** statement (or event) that a process may engage in. Indeed, the SKIP process could be defined as follows:

$$SKIP = (null \rightarrow SUCCESS)$$

Finally, we should note, for completeness, that the set of actions that any process can engage in is called the **alphabet** of that process. The alphabet of P is written αP, so we write:

$$\alpha P = \{a, b\}$$
$$P = (a \rightarrow P')$$
$$P' = (b \rightarrow P')$$

A clock can be modelled as a process that, once initialized, repeatedly engages in the tick event:

$$\alpha \text{ clock} = \{\text{init, tick}\}$$
$$\text{clock} = \text{init} \rightarrow \text{repeat}$$
$$\text{repeat} = \text{tick} \rightarrow \text{repeat}$$

As a final example, consider the first attempt, in the previous chapter, at solving the seat reservation problem. The program consists of a collection of terminal handlers:

$$H_1 \parallel H_2 \parallel H_3 \parallel \ldots \parallel H_n$$

Each H_i is defined by:

$$\alpha H_i = \{\text{display, read, reserve, issue}\}$$
$$H_i = (\text{display} \rightarrow \text{read} \rightarrow \text{reserve} \rightarrow \text{issue} \rightarrow H_i)$$

2.2 Process structures

The model presented above forms the basis for analysing the behaviour of a concurrent program. In terms of designing a concurrent programming language there are, however, many factors still to be considered. A number of these will be addressed in this section; they give rise to a wide variety of possible language designs. The factors that will be considered are:

- structure
- level
- initialization
- termination
- representation.

2.2.1 Structure

Process structure is classified as follows:

Static: the number of processes in a program is fixed and known prior to execution.

Dynamic: processes may be created dynamically; the number of processes created can only be determined at execution time.

(This is the same distinction that applies to passive data structures in languages such as Pascal: dynamic data structures are built by using pointers.) Some languages provide a dynamic process structure but define a fixed upper limit to the maximum number of extant processes.

2.2.2 Level

The process level refers to the possibility of using process hierarchies. Such hierarchies may be constructed by nesting process declarations within process declarations. Some languages allow such nesting, but those with a flat process structure do not. For example, Ada allows nested dynamic processes (called tasks), while Concurrent Pascal (Brinch Hansen, 1975) supports only static flat processes.

When there are nested levels a parent/child relationship exists between processes: a process is the child of the process in which it is declared. Even with a flat level, the main program can be considered to be the parent of all the processes. The important property of the parent/child relationship is that the parent cannot terminate until all children have terminated. This (unnatural) role is required to prevent a parent from removing any resources that the child may be using. Only when all children have terminated is it safe for the parent to terminate. With block-structured languages it is possible for an inner block or procedure (or even a function) to be the parent of a process. If this is the case, then that block cannot terminate until internal processes have done so.

2.2.3 Initialization

Initialization refers simply to the ability, within the language, to pass initialization data to a process when it is being created. This is useful when, for example, an array of processes is being used: initialization data can be utilized to indicate to each process which member of the array it is. The lack of an initialization facility means that such information can only be supplied to a process by explicit communication with it (for example, from its parent) after it has started its execution.

2.2.4 Termination

Process termination can be accomplished (or not) in a variety of ways. These can be summarized as follows:

(1) completion of execution (occurrence of a SUCCESS action);

(2) occurrence of an untrapped error condition (occurrence of FAILURE action);

(3) suicide by execution of a 'self terminate' statement (internally forced FAILURE action);

(4) forced abortion by another process (externally forced FAILURE);

(5) when no longer needed;

(6) never, as a result of an error condition (occurrence of an unintended recursive set of actions);

(7)   never, as a result of executing a non-terminating loop (occurrence of an intended recursive set of actions).

The fifth condition for termination perhaps needs some further clarification; it can informally be defined as follows:

> If a process wishes to terminate and its parent process wishes to terminate, and all other child processes of the parent are either terminated or similarly wish to terminate, then all child processes and the parent will terminate.

We shall see in Chapter 4 how this rule can be incorporated into a language syntax.†

Whether an abort facility or an explicit suicide action is supported is very much a question of style and intended application area. If it is possible for a process to run amok then it may be advisable to have the ability for another process to abort it. Although this seems reasonable, it could, as Hoare pointed out, be a guardian process that goes astray and starts aborting processes that are behaving correctly.

2.2.5 Process representation

We have left the main language issue until last: how are processes represented and, related to this, what rules govern process creation? Although the concept of process is central to concurrent programming, some concurrent programming languages have no explicitly-named process construct. Instead, they define a way of denoting concurrent execution of ordinary statements by introducing a **cobegin/coend** structure (also called a **PAR** construct or a **parbegin**). 'Cobegin' indicates a concurrent begin; it was used in Chapter 1, as follows:

```
cobegin
  S1;
  S2;
  S3;
  S4;
  . . .
  Sn
coend
```

In the above the S1 . . . Sn are arbitrary language statements. If they are procedure calls then a significant sequence of code is defined to be executing

---

† In the above description a single parent/child relationship has been used to define the creation and termination relationship between processes. For some languages, such as Ada, this is too simplistic; the parent of a process (that process which caused creation) may not be the process that is responsible for termination.

concurrently (with the other statements). A statement could even be another **cobegin/coend**, thereby supporting nesting.

The alternative to this use of **cobegin/coend** to indicate concurrent execution of ordinary language statements is to support the explicit definition of processes. Processes can be first class, in that process types can be defined and process objects (of the types) declared. In this way, more than one process can be generated from the same type. When explicit process structures are used there are two ways in which the initial execution can be controlled. First, the **cobegin/coend** structure can be employed (but with process objects instead of arbitrary statements). The second method involves using the scope rules of the language to control execution. A process declared in a procedure declarative part (for example) will start its execution when the procedure is ready to proceed through its first **begin**. The process will then run concurrently with the procedure's body. This is the model used in Ada. The following example illustrates it using a Pascal-like syntax:

```
procedure PROC;
  process P;
  begin
    . . .
  end;

  process Q;
  begin
    . . .
  end;

begin
  (* PROC, P and Q execute concurrently as three *)
  (* separate threads. No explicit code is required  *)
  (* here to initiate the execution of P and Q.      *)
end;    (* PROC *)
```

2.2.6 Summary

This section has reviewed a wide variety of language features. All are aimed at supporting concurrent programming but present very different models. There is, as yet, no consensus as to what makes a good concurrent programming language. Some languages support very flexible structures but pay the price of poor run-time performance. In this book we use a single language, Pascal-FC, for most of our examples. Its process model is described below. Although it does not support the most flexible language model possible, it does allow a wide range of styles to be experimented with. Later in this book we shall see that Pascal-FC supports different, competing, synchronization primitives. It is not possible, however, for more than one process model to be supported in a single language.

2.3   The process model in Pascal-FC

Given the earlier discussion, it is possible to provide a succinct description of the process model in Pascal-FC. It supports explicit process (type) definitions with **cobegin/coend** execution control (and initialization). The process level is flat with a semi-static structure†. All termination conditions are allowed other than explicit suicide and abort.

Consider the following schema outline of a concurrent Pascal-FC program:

```
program SCHEMA;
  (* definition of process types: *)
  process type EXAMPLE(I : integer);
  begin
    . . .
  end;
var
  (* definition of process objects: *)
  P : EXAMPLE;
  . . .
begin
  (* sequential execution prior to      *)
  (* execution of concurrent processes *)
  cobegin
    (* process activation: *)
    P(42)
  coend;
  (* sequential execution after concurrent *)
  (* processes have all terminated         *)
end.
```

All processes identified in the **cobegin/coend** structure must have been previously declared. Moreover, concurrent execution *only* applies to explicitly declared processes (not arbitrary language statements). The **cobegin/coend** statement is the parent of all the processes: it cannot terminate until all child processes have terminated. The example above had only one process, but the following has three instances of type PTYPE:

```
program SIMPLE;
  process type PTYPE(I : integer);
  begin
    . . .
  end;
```

---

† We say *semi*-static because it is possible to declare an array of processes and then decide at run-time (for example, by input from the keyboard) how many elements of the array will be activated. However, the *maximum* number is constrained by the size of the array, which must be known at compile time.

```
var
   P1,P2,P3 : PTYPE;
begin
  cobegin
     P1(1);
     P2(2);
     P3(3)
  coend
end.
```

This will cause three processes to start their execution. Each will be defined by the same sequence of statements, but will have a different initialization parameter (which may subsequently cause the processes to diverge in their activities). When all these processes have terminated the parent program will proceed beyond the **coend**. As the **cobegin/coend** structure is a syntactical representation of the || operator, the law of symmetry applies, that is, there is no significance to the order in which processes are placed within the **cobegin/coend**. They all execute concurrently in the sense introduced in Chapter 1.

Within the **cobegin/coend**, constructor statements (loops) are allowed in order to make the program notation more concise. The three processes could therefore have been represented by an array and a **for**† statement used as follows:

```
program SIMPLE;
   process type PTYPE(I : integer);
   begin
     . . .
   end;
var
   COUNT : integer;
   P : array[1..3] of PTYPE;
begin
  cobegin
     for COUNT := 1 to 3 do
     P[COUNT](COUNT)
  coend
end.
```

It is important to understand that this is not an ordinary **for** loop, which carries out sequential iteration. The processes are still executed concurrently with one another. Note also that the Pascal-FC notation places the array subscript before the actual parameter(s).

If a program has a process type from which only a single process is declared, then an anonymous process type can be used (in an analogous way to anonymous array types). For example, the following code fragment:

---

† The **while** and **repeat** loops can be used for the same purpose in Pascal-FC.

```
process type PT;
var ...
begin
    ...
end;

P : PT;
```

is equivalent to:

```
process P;
var ...
begin
    ...     (* as before *)
end;
```

As the above examples show, a process can be passed initialization data via value parameters to the process itself. Indeed, Pascal-FC allows data to be returned to the main program, after process termination, via **var** parameters. This is useful with processes designed to compute a result and then terminate. An example of the use of this feature is given in Section 4.6.2.

2.4   Process states and transitions

2.4.1   The life-cycle of a process

Although Pascal-FC has a relatively simple process structure, it is still possible to distinguish a number of unique states through which a process proceeds during its lifetime. Figure 2.1 illustrates the states that have been implicitly considered so far. A process is created by the declaration of some object of a process type. It starts its execution when designated within a

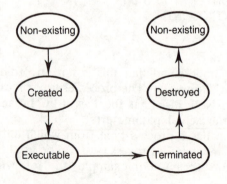

Figure 2.1   Simple state diagram for a process.

cobegin/coend structure. At some point a process may terminate as a result of normal completion or because of an error condition. When all processes have terminated, the **cobegin/coend** structure will also terminate – all processes are then considered to have been destroyed. On completion of the program the processes return to the state of non-existing. It should be noted that in a language that supports process nesting, the state behaviour of a process becomes considerably more complicated.

2.4.2 The executable state

An **executable** process is one that is currently running on a logical processor. For the most part, as we have said before, we should not be concerned with the way in which logical processors are implemented. We make an exception to this in the next few sections and work at a lower level of abstraction, where implementation issues are relevant.

The most productive, and therefore important, condition for a process is clearly when a physical processor is executing instructions on its behalf. However, we usually want to run more processes than we have physical processors, so that not all processes can be in this condition at once. This is why the term *executable*, rather than *executing*, has been used in Figure 2.1: a process may be currently running on a logical processor, but that does not necessarily imply that the logical processor's clock is currently ticking. For a uniprocessor system, for example, only one of the logical clocks is ticking at any one time; the process concerned is called the **running process**. More generally, there can never be more than N running processes at any time, where N is the number of physical processors in the system.

A process that is executable, but for which no processor is currently available, is said to be **ready**. There may be several ready processes at any time: when a processor becomes available, one of them can become a running process. Which one of them makes the transition from ready to running is the decision of a system component called the **CPU scheduler**. The ready processes may be kept in a **First In First Out** (FIFO) queue, although this is only one of a wide range of possible scheduling policies. The ready condition can be defined as follows:

> A ready process is one that could immediately make use of processor instruction cycles if they were offered to it.

The executable state of Figure 2.1 can now be seen to consist of two different conditions (ready and running) whenever there are more processes than processors. Figure 2.2 shows this in more detail. Note that a newly created process first enters the ready condition, and that it is only from the running condition that a process can make the transition to terminated. The

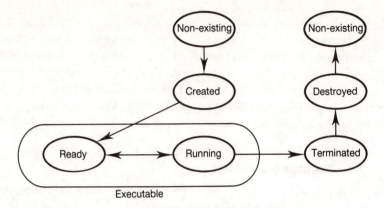

Figure 2.2   The *executable* state when processors are shared.

bidirectional transition between ready and running indicates that a process may alternate between these conditions many times during its execution.

It is easy to imagine that a process makes the transition from ready to running when a physical processor becomes available. This can happen, for example, because a running process terminates, so having no further use for the processor. Why would a process make the transition from running to ready? The answer depends on the type of system we are dealing with.

First, in a general purpose multi-user computer system, it is typical to employ **time sharing**: there are not enough physical processors to assign a different one to each user, so they must share the processors. Each user's process has a regular **time slice** in a CPU: if the process is still executable when the time slice expires, the processor is **pre-empted** from that user, and another user's process is given a time slice. In this way, the users are all given the illusion of exclusive use of a processor because they all receive regular bursts of CPU time. Of course, their process proceeds less rapidly than it would if it really did have exclusive use of one of these processors.

The second kind of reason for a process changing from the running to the ready condition is typical of embedded systems, which must respond to externally generated stimuli by specified deadlines. Consider the seat belt process in the drive-by-wire car introduced in Section 1.6. Most of the time it has no work to do. During this time it can be considered to be in a **non-executable state** (see Section 2.4.3). On rapid deceleration, this process must not only become ready, but must actually execute in a processor. Suppose that the fuel gauge process is in the processor when this occurs. The seat belt process cannot afford to be delayed for such a trivial reason, so the CPU must be pre-empted from the less urgent task and assigned instead to the time critical one. The fuel gauge task is making the transition from running to ready: it could still use processor cycles if it were permitted to continue.

Finally, some readers may have noticed that we have used the word 'condition', rather than 'state', in association with ready and running. That is because we want to reserve 'state' for more abstract descriptions where we are not concerned with the details of implementation of logical processors. Perhaps we should have used the term 'logically executing', rather than 'executable', if we wanted to be thorough in this respect, but we have retained the more orthodox terminology.

2.4.3   The non-executable or blocked state

For brevity, we shall use the term **blocked** from now on to refer in general to the **non-executable** state. (We also adopt the common practice of referring to processes as 'sleeping' and 'waking' when they enter and leave this state, respectively.) We can work with the following definition:

> A blocked process is an extant process that is waiting for an event to occur, and cannot in the meantime make use of processor cycles.

By *extant*, we mean a process that has been created but has not yet terminated.

Later in this book we shall see that this state is the key to the inter-process synchronization and communication that is essential in almost all concurrent programs. We shall find that there are many different ways in which a process may become blocked, so this term can be considered a generic description for a variety of discriminable states. In the previous section we saw one use of blocking: a process that has no work to do for now is blocked so that it does not compete for a CPU. Another common reason for blocking is that a process has made a request for input that cannot be satisfied immediately. In Section 2.7 we shall introduce a specific example of blocking from Pascal-FC: the sleep procedure. This is used to block a process for a specified period of time.

Note that there is a clear distinction between being blocked (unable to execute) and being pre-empted (able to execute but no processor available). The addition of more processors may help a pre-empted process, but it will have no direct effect on a blocked one.

Figure 2.3 is a modification of Figure 2.1 to include the blocked state. In practice, a process can only become blocked from the running condition, and a process which is unblocked enters the ready condition: there is no direct transition from blocked to running.

2.5   Process management and the run-time support system

From the above discussion on process states it should be clear that the execution of a concurrent program is not as straightforward as that of a sequential program. Processes must be created and terminated, and

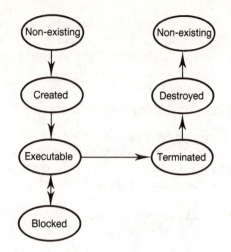

Figure 2.3 Addition of the *blocked* state.

despatched to the available processors. These activities are undertaken by software that is usually generated by the compiler with the object code representing the program. It is called the **Run-Time Support System** (RTSS) or the **Run-Time Kernel** (RTK). The RTSS has many of the properties of the scheduler of a multi-user operating system and sits logically between the hardware and the application software. We now briefly consider the way in which it carries out its work.

2.5.1 Process descriptors

The RTSS must keep track of all the processes as a concurrent program runs. A process may visit a CPU and be removed from it many times during its life-cycle and, each time it is despatched to a processor, it must be able to continue from where it left off the last time. This means that process switching can only occur after the completion of one machine instruction but before the start of the next. When a process leaves a CPU, copies must be made of the contents of all CPU registers. The copies must be stored somewhere that is private to the process, so that they can be restored into the registers when the process makes its next visit. Although other processes will probably have used that CPU in the meantime, this sharing must be transparent to all processes because they would otherwise interfere with one another.

The register copies are stored in a per-process data structure called a **process descriptor** or **process control block**. In programming language terms, the process descriptor can be thought of as a record. Figure 2.4 shows a typical example. The fields of the process descriptor are:

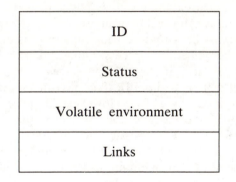

ID
Status
Volatile environment
Links

Figure 2.4 A typical process descriptor.

- The **ID** field gives a unique identifier to every process. It could, for example, be interpreted as an integer.
- **Status** will be one of the possible process states (or conditions) described earlier.
- **Volatile environment** is the private copy of CPU registers, including the program counter and the stack pointer.
- **Links** will be one or more pointers which link this descriptor to others. These are used by the RTSS to facilitate the handling of process descriptors, to assemble them into queues and so on.

There may be other fields in a process descriptor, depending on the specific requirements of the system, but this set will suffice for our purposes.

2.5.2 Where is the RTSS?

When running a concurrent program under a standard operating system (such as Unix), two implementation strategies are possible:

(1) The compiler can generate an RTSS which contains all the process management and scheduling facilities. The RTSS, together with the code generated from the user's program, are linked to form a single program, which is then executed as a single operating system thread.

(2) Process management and scheduling are done by the underlying operating system, while the compiler generates calls to this system, as required. Each process in the user program can then be mapped onto an individual operating system thread.

The second method is the most effective if the concurrency model of the language and that of the operating system are compatible. The first model is, by comparison, much easier to implement, and is the method of choice when there is no underlying concurrent operating system. Its only major drawback (apart from a performance penalty) concerns the behaviour of the program if one of the embedded processes undertakes an I/O request. From the program's point of view, if one of its processes is blocked attempting I/O (for example, input from a keyboard), then the other executable concurrent processes should continue executing. However, from the operating system's perspective, the 'program' has executed an I/O request and therefore the 'program' is blocked. The RTSS is itself not scheduled and so none of the other processes can continue. Most current implementations of Pascal-FC use this easier method of implementation; the following illustrative program does not therefore print a series of 'hello' messages while the LISTENER process is waiting for user input:

```
program HELLO;
  process SPEAKER;
  begin
    repeat
      writeln('hello')
    forever
  end;
  process LISTENER;
  var DATA: integer;
  begin
    repeat
      read(DATA)
    forever
  end;
begin
  cobegin
    LISTENER; SPEAKER
  coend
end.
```

This type of problem is not limited to Pascal-FC: there are, for example, commercial implementations of Ada and other concurrent languages that exhibit the same characteristics.

2.6 Process scheduling

During the execution of a concurrent program there will usually be more processes wishing to execute (i.e. in the executable state) than there are processors available. The RTSS usually supports a queue of ready processes. As the order of execution of these processes is undefined, the RTSS can implement whatever scheduling scheme it wishes. We can assert that:

> The functional behaviour of a concurrent program should not depend on the scheduling policy of the RTSS.

Only the functional behaviour is constrained by this rule, as the temporal behaviour clearly will be affected by scheduling decisions. If two processes both output data, then the order in which the processes execute will determine the order in which the data is produced. If in some application the order is significant, then the program must be designed to constrain the processes (using process synchronization).

We noted in Chapter 1 that one of the major differences between general concurrent programming and real-time programming (a specific application of concurrency) is that, in the latter, the scheduler must be designed so as to ensure that real-time (temporal) requirements are met. Another way to say this is that in real-time programming the clocks of logical processors *must* be brought into some relation with real-time clocks. As the emphasis of this book is largely on general concurrent programming, the influence of different scheduling decisions on temporal behaviour will not be a focus of attention. However, the influence of the scheduler will be considered in the remainder of this section. Some general influences of scheduling policy are considered first, then scheduling in real-time systems is illustrated when we return to the drive-by-wire car in Section 2.6.3.

Consider two extreme scheduling policies:

(1) execute one process to completion, then choose another process and execute it to completion, and so on;

(2) share out the processor time by giving regular time slices to the processes.

The first approach is extremely unfair but has the advantage that it incorporates the smallest number of **context switches**. A context switch is the action of switching from executing one process to executing another. It can be a time-consuming activity, because it involves copying the CPU registers to the process descriptor of the outgoing process and loading the CPU registers from the descriptor of the incoming process. Therefore the cost (in time) of a context switch is important (particularly in real-time systems). Only switching when really necessary is often the approach adopted in a real-time scheduler.

By comparison, the second approach is very fair. More context switches are performed but all processes proceed at roughly the same rate. This type of approach is favoured in multi-user operating systems where (independent) user programs should be given equal usage of the processor.

Because the functional behaviour of the program should not be affected by the RTSS, program debugging is particularly problematic. A program may work perfectly on one implementation but fail when moved (ported) to another environment because it contains a dormant fault that only produces an error (and failure)† when a different scheduling policy is applied. In order to help debugging and to emphasize the need for functional behaviour to be independent of scheduling policy, the Pascal-FC system includes two different policies:

- the *fair* scheduler
- the *unfair* scheduler.

2.6.1 Pascal-FC's fair scheduler

This does not use time slicing, but instead is driven by random numbers.‡ This approach was first used by Ben Ari (1982) in his concurrent Pascal-S (another teaching language) and involves the RTSS in:

- choosing at random which executable process to run next;
- running the chosen process for a random number of statements (machine instructions) before pre-empting the processor from it.

Using this policy, different executions of a program will tend to follow different paths. Running a Pascal-FC program many times with this scheduler allows some of the legal executions to be exercised. Even a simple program has so many legal executions, however, that exhaustive testing is not feasible, and so this practice must not be regarded as any kind of proof of the program's correctness.

Execution of the following simple program will illustrate this random behaviour. Note that each process has a local variable defined. This variable is hidden inside the process and is not accessible from outside. In the full program three Is are defined – one in each process. Three ch value parameters are also defined. This ability of the process abstraction to support data encapsulation is an important feature as it allows a program to be structured as a set of process modules:

```
program CharOutput;
   process type printer(ch : char);
   var I : integer;
   begin
     for I := 1 to 10 do
        write(ch)
   end;
```

† A fault is a problem in a piece of software that may be the cause of an error. An error is an internal state of a system not provided for in the system specification: it is the effect of a fault. A failure is an unwanted piece of external system behaviour resulting from an error (Burns and Wellings, 1990).
‡ Strictly speaking, this does not guarantee fair allocation of CPU time to each process, because the probability of repeatedly choosing the same process is not zero. In practice, the number generator used in existing implementations is reasonably fair.

```
      var print1, print2, print3 : printer;

begin
  cobegin
    print1('A');
    print2('B');
    print3('C')
  coend
end.
```

Each of the three process instances loops round and outputs its designated character. A long series of executions will typically not produce the same pattern. The following are example output streams:

```
CCCACCCCABCAACCAABBBBABBABBAAB
ABAAACCCCCAAAAABBABBBBBBBCCCCC
BBBBCCCAAABBCCCCCCAABBBCAAABAA
BCCABABAAACAAABCCAABBBBBBCCCCC
CBBBAAABBAACCCAAAAABBCBBBCCCCC
BBCCCAAACAACCAABBCCACCABBBBABB
```

2.6.2   Pascal-FC's unfair scheduler

Experience with Pascal-FC indicates that many common programming errors are illuminated by a small number of test runs using the fair scheduler. However, some errors are more easily found if the completely unfair policy is used (Davies, 1990). Hence the system also contains an unfair scheduler, which operates according to the following policy:

- the ready processes are initially ordered according to their textual order in the **cobegin/coend** structure;

- when a process is to make the transition from ready to running, the one at the front of the queue is chosen;

- once a process is running, it is allowed to execute as many instructions as it likes, including running to completion or entering an infinite loop.

With this policy the above program always produces ten As followed by ten Bs followed by ten Cs. When debugging programs, it is sometimes useful to combine the use of the unfair scheduler with rearranging the order in which the processes are listed inside the **cobegin/coend**.

To illustrate further the effect of different scheduling policies, consider the following pathological program:

```
            program CharOutput;
              process type printer(ch : char);
              var I : integer;
              begin
                for I := 1 to 10 do
                  writeln(ch)
              end;

              process PIG;
              begin
                repeat
                  null
                forever      (* Pascal-FC syntax for an infinite loop *)
              end;

              var print1, print2 : printer;

        begin
          cobegin
            PIG;
            print1('A');
            print2('B')
          coend
        end.
```

Note that writeln is used here to flush the output buffer as each character is produced. As the program never terminates, there is otherwise no guarantee that the characters produced by the printer processes would be sent to the terminal screen.

The program consists of three processes, one of which incorporates an infinite (null) loop. As a consequence, the **cobegin/coend** statement, and hence the program itself, will never terminate. If this program is run with the fair scheduler, eventually all the 20 character outputs will be produced and the program will hang. With the unfair policy, no output will ever be produced! Process PIG will be scheduled first (it is textually the first), but it never terminates and is never blocked (it hogs the processor): the unfair scheduler will therefore continue to execute it indefinitely. If process PIG is moved to be the last process before **coend**, then the unfair policy will result in the immediate output of the ten As and the ten Bs and then the program will hang as PIG is scheduled.

2.6.3 Scheduling in a real-time system

We now have enough background to return to the drive-by-wire car of Chapter 1. An outline of a concurrent program to solve the problem is as follows:

```
program EMBEDDED;
  (* Simple concurrent embedded system control *)
process A;
begin
  repeat
    ACTION_A;
    (* sleep until next iteration due *)
  forever
end;

process B
begin
  repeat
    ACTION_B;
    (* sleep until next iteration due *)
  forever
end;

process C;
begin
  repeat
    ACTION_C;
    (* sleep until next iteration due *)
  forever
end;

process D;
begin
  repeat
    (* sleep until alarm received;        *)
    (* then carry out the requirements    *)
    (* imposed on the system by Task D *)
  forever
end;

begin
  cobegin
    A; B; C; D
  coend
end.
```

Suppose that the concurrent processes are to be run on a uniprocessor system. There may be a large number of executions that are acceptable in the sense that all timing requirements are met. However, there may also be many interleavings that are unsuitable because they cause deadlines to be missed. We need some way of giving the computer system some hints, so that it can choose a suitable interleaving. One way of providing such hints is to introduce a notion of **process priority**.

In the above example, we can assist the system to restrict itself to acceptable orderings by attaching a unique priority to each process, such that:

priority(D) > priority(A) > priority(B) > priority(C)

The CPU scheduler behaves according to the following scheduling policy:

> Always make sure that any process running in the CPU has the highest priority among the executable processes.

This is a pre-emptive policy: if a process awakes which has a higher priority than the one currently using the CPU, then the CPU is switched from the lower to the higher-priority process (pre-empted from the lower-priority process when it has completed its current machine instruction).

Using this scheduling policy, and in the absence of an alarm from the seat belts, the above program would operate as shown in Table 2.1.† The first column gives the time elapsed since the beginning of an 80-unit period. Note that this is the same pattern of CPU usage as in Table 1.3. This time, however, the scheduler is deciding on the order of work – not the programmer, whose job has been significantly simplified because it has not been necessary manually to chop the code into pieces to meet timing requirements. The reader may like to verify that all deadlines would still be met even in the event of an alarm from the seat belts, whenever it occurred.

Table 2.1 Use of the processor by the processes.

Elapsed	Running	Time
0	A	4
4	B	10
14	C	6
20	A	4
24	C	16
40	A	4
44	B	10
54	C	6
60	A	4
64	C	12
76	(spare)	4

† We have assumed that it takes no time to switch from one process to another. In practice, time is required, but we have assumed that it is negligible in this example. In reality, process switching time can be a serious problem when the limits of processor performance are being approached.

2.6.4 Schedulability and scheduling theory

We have deliberately chosen an example that is conveniently simple. In practice, there are at least two important questions which need to be answered:

- For a given set of timing requirements, how do we determine whether it is *possible* to schedule all the work in accordance with the required deadlines? In short, how do we know that there are *any* acceptable executions of the program on the given hardware?
- How do we arrive at the process priorities?

This is not the place to consider either of these questions. The interested reader is referred to the Further Reading section at the end of the chapter for an introduction to this active field of research.

2.6.5 Priority in Pascal-FC

Pascal-FC provides a priority procedure for indicating the relative priorities of processes (Davies and Burns, 1990). This feature was included for the benefit of implementations intended for real-time programming: other implementations are free to ignore calls to priority. As the focus of this book is not on real-time programming, we shall always assume that processes have equal priority and the priority procedure will not be used.

2.7 Timing in Pascal-FC

We have now seen that in real-time programming it is sometimes necessary for a process to be able to delay its execution for a time. A useful abstraction, of which we have seen an example in the drive-by-wire car, is that of the periodic process that executes regularly and is blocked for the time between the completion of one periodic action and the start of the next. In this section, we shall see in detail how Pascal-FC facilities can be used to tailor the period of the loop to fit the timing requirements.

Various forms of timing facility have been provided in existing languages for real-time work (Burns and Wellings, 1990). Though there is a considerable variety, those provided in Pascal-FC are representative. Here, we shall discuss two facilities:

- a standard function, clock
- a standard procedure, sleep

The Pascal-FC RTSS maintains a system clock, which ticks at a rate that is implementation dependent. However, in most cases the clock rate is one tick per second, and that is what will be assumed in this book. The function, clock, returns the current value of the system clock; the sleep procedure causes the calling process to be blocked for the number of seconds specified as a parameter. These can then be used to give some degree of control over the period of a loop, as in the example below.

```
process X;
  const PERIOD = ...;
  var START, NOW: integer;
begin
  repeat
    START := clock;
    ACTION_X;
    NOW := clock;
    sleep(PERIOD - (NOW - START))
  forever
end;    (* X *)
```

Similar facilities exist in Ada. It is important to understand, however, that such techniques only provide approximate control over a process's temporal behaviour. There is no guarantee that the process will be dormant for exactly the time specified. This is because a process which sleeps enters the blocked state and, as we have seen, there is no direct transition from blocked to running. Hence the expiry of the time does not *force* the scheduler to run the process: it merely makes the processes executable again. Resumption will only occur when the process is next chosen for execution by the scheduler.

When writing general concurrent algorithms, in which the meshing of program actions with real time is not a consideration, a sleep statement is not necessary. It can, however, be useful in overcoming the unfairness of a scheduler by forcing the RTSS to switch between processes. In this way a collection of independent processes can cooperate in 'passing the processor around' without having to rely on the vagaries of the scheduler.

The Pascal-FC sleep procedure takes a single integer parameter. If a negative or zero value is given as the argument, the calling process will be switched out and placed back in the ready queue. The scheduler will then choose one of the executable processes to execute. (It could be the same one that was just removed from the processor.) For example, the PIG process could have been written in a less hoggish way as follows:

```
process PIG;
  begin
    repeat
      sleep(0)
    forever
  end;
```

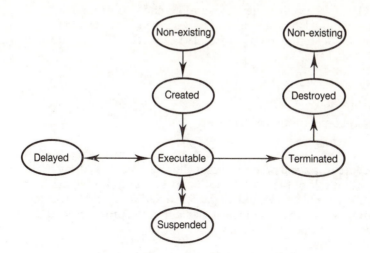

Figure 2.5 Introduction of a delayed state.

The sleep procedure (or, as it is called in Ada, the **delay** statement) provides one form of process blocking. The *blocked* state can be considered to consist of a variety of substates because, as we shall show later in the book, there are many different ways of becoming blocked. Figure 2.5 illustrates the introduction of the new state of **delayed**. A process moves from executable to delayed and then back to executable. When, in the earlier discussions, the unfair scheduler of Pascal-FC was said to run a process to termination this should now be described as run to termination or blocking.

The significance of the **suspended** state of Figure 2.5 will become clear in later chapters. Delayed and suspended processes are all blocked: the distinction reflects the way in which they became blocked (and the way in which they may eventually become unblocked). Delayed processes have become blocked by use of a timing primitive, such as Pascal-FC's sleep procedure: they will eventually become unblocked when the specified interval expires. 'Suspended' processes have become blocked by one of the process synchronization and communication primitives which we shall begin to survey in Chapter 4: action by another process is required to unblock them.

SUMMARY

In this chapter we have considered concurrent programs that have been built from independent processes. This has not enabled interesting programs to be developed as all meaningful concurrent programs use process interactions in order to meet requirements. Nevertheless, the notion of process has been introduced together with some of the laws that govern concurrency. The factors that give rise to the wide variety of notations and styles found in concurrent programming languages have been described and a detailed description of the model found in Pascal-FC has been given. The key features of this language model are:

- process types
- process initialization
- use of **cobegin/coend** for process start-up
- flat semi-static structure.

Pascal-FC also contains a sleep procedure that allows a process to delay itself.

The important role of the Run-Time Support System (RTSS) has been noted, in particular the policy adopted by the scheduler. The golden rule for a concurrent program is that the functional behaviour of the program should not depend upon the RTSS scheduling policy.

FURTHER READING

Allworth S.T. and Zobel R.N. (1987). *Introduction to Real-time System Design*. Macmillan

Ben-Ari M. (1982). *Principles of Concurrent Programming*. Prentice-Hall

Ben-Ari, M. (1990). *Principles of Concurrent and Distributed Programming*. Prentice-Hall

Bennett S. (1987). *Real-Time Computer Control: An Introduction*. Prentice-Hall

Burns A. and Wellings A.J. (1990). *Real-Time Systems and Their Programming Languages*. Addison-Wesley

Hoare C.A.R. (1985). *Communicating Sequential Processes*. Prentice-Hall

Lawrence P.D. and Mauch, K. (1988). *Real-Time Microcomputer System Design: An Introduction*. McGraw-Hill

Lister A.M. and Eager R.D. (1988). *Fundamentals of Operating Systems*. Macmillan

Milner R. (1989). *Communication and Concurrency*. Prentice-Hall

Peterson J. and Silberschatz A. (1985). *Operating System Concepts*. Addison-Wesley

EXERCISES

2.1 A process controlling a drinks machine accepts coins followed by a user's beverage request; it then dispenses the drink and any change before waiting a short time and then repeating the behaviour. Write out the alphabet for this process and its sequence of actions.

2.2 In order to speed up the service of the drinks machine in the previous exercise, the process is split into two concurrent processes: one dealing with the user's inputs, the other controlling the dispensing of drink and change. Write out the alphabets and behaviours of the two new processes; you may assume that the processes can pass data between them.

2.3 The following code uses nested **cobegin/coend** structures to initialize two important variables:

```
cobegin
  begin
    A := some initial value
    cobegin
        (* actions using A *)
    coend
  end;
  begin
    B := some initial value
    cobegin
        (* actions using B *)
    coend
  end
coend
```

Transform this program so that it uses only one (flat) **cobegin/coend** but behaves identically.

2.4 Some concurrent programming languages allow one process to abort another. Consider the state diagram in Figure 2.5 and show how this would change if abort were allowed in Pascal-FC.

2.5 Consider the following Pascal-FC program:

```
program sleeper;
  const period = 4;
  var start : integer;

  process A;
    var time : integer;
  begin
    repeat
      time := clock;
      if (time – start) mod 4 < 2 then
        writeln('Uninterrupted write by A');
      sleep(1)
    forever
  end;

  process B;
    var time : integer;
```

```
      begin
        repeat
          time := clock;
          if (time – start) mod 4 >= 2 then
            writeln('Uninterrupted write by B');
          sleep(1)
        forever
      end;

    begin
      start := clock;
      cobegin
        A;B
      coend
    end.
```

Are the writeln statements uninterruptible as the program claims?

2.6   With the program in Exercise 2.5, is the fair scheduler actually fair? What is the output of the program likely to look like with the unfair scheduler? If the two sleep statements are removed, what will the behaviour of the program be with the fair and unfair schedulers?

2.7   Assume that the clock and sleep statements work on a one-second time constant. Write a program that consists of five processes. Each process is periodic, but the periods differ. One process should run every 2 seconds, one every 3, one every 5, one every 7 and the last every 9 seconds. Use the unfair scheduler. Each process should simulate an intensive computational load by executing:

```
for I := 1 to MAX do
  temp := 1673*10 mod 975
```

where temp is a local variable (to each process) and MAX is a global constant. Experiment with different values of MAX. When is the computational load too excessive for each process to complete its executions before its next period should start?

2.8   In Exercise 2.7, what will be the effect of using the fair scheduler? Can a statement such as:

```
sleep(PERIOD – (NOW – START))
```

(as used in Section 2.7) be executed reliably with the fair scheduler?

3 Process Interaction

Although constructs for concurrent programming vary from one language to another, three fundamental facilities must be present in one form or another in any concurrent programming language. These facilities allow:

(1)   the expression of concurrent execution

(2)   inter-process synchronization

(3)   inter-process communication.

The previous chapter introduced the notion of process and much of the remainder of this book is concerned with inter-process synchronization and communication. In considering such interactions it is useful to distinguish between three types of process behaviour:

- independent
- competing
- cooperating.

As was indicated in the summary of the previous chapter, concurrent programs that consist of totally independent processes are rare and are essentially uninteresting. Processes compete when the available system resources are in short supply (as is usually the case); in a typical multi-user operating system, for example, the objectives of one executing program (operating system process) are independent of other programs. Nevertheless they must compete with these programs for memory buffers, disk usage and so on. One of the main requirements of an operating system is the management of competing processes.

By comparison, the processes contained within a concurrent program have a common goal (that of meeting the program's requirements). Such processes therefore regularly communicate and synchronize activities in order to perform some common operations. The basic nature of process interaction is thus one of cooperation. This does not, however, imply that there are not situations in which competition seems more significant. For example a number of processes may be competing to pass on data to a single process that has a coordination role. Nevertheless, in general the competition is not absolute as the indefinite postponement of a subset of the processes would be detrimental to the complete system.

We introduce a number of typical problems in concurrent programming in this chapter, namely: the Ornamental Gardens, the Producer–Consumer, the Readers and Writers and the Dining Philosophers problems. They will become familiar, as they are used in later chapters as test cases for language features provided for inter-process synchronization and communication.

3.1 Active and passive entities

The object-oriented programming paradigm encourages system (and program) builders to consider the artifact under construction as a collection of cooperating objects (or, to use a more neutral term, **entities**). Within this paradigm it is constructive to consider two kinds of object – active and passive. Active objects undertake spontaneous actions (with the help of a processor): they enable the computation to proceed. Passive objects, by comparison, only perform actions when 'invoked' by an active object. Any worthwhile program needs active entities. Passive objects are also important as they can be used to encapsulate resources needed by their active peers. More significantly, they can *control access* to resources that cannot be used in an arbitrary manner by groups of active objects. Some resources can only be used by one object at a time; in other cases the operations that can be carried out at a given time depend on the object's current state. A common example of the latter is a data buffer that cannot have an element extracted if it is empty. In general we shall use the term *passive* to indicate an entity that must control, in some way, the manner in which it is used. Non-active entities that can allow open access are called *neutral*. We shall see that there are few neutral entities in a concurrent program.

In a concurrent programming language, active objects are represented by processes. Neutral objects can be represented either directly as data variables or be encapsulated by some module construct that provides a procedural interface. The key question of what is the appropriate representation for passive objects is more open (and problematic). Two approaches can be identified:

(1) also use processes to represent passive entities;
(2) introduce a new primitive to represent passive entities explicitly.

The advantage of the first approach is that the language is simple: a single abstraction (the process) is sufficient. All protections necessary for the passive entity can be directly programmed. It is therefore an eminently flexible model. The drawback is that it can lead to proliferation of processes, with the resulting high number of context switches during execution.

The simple primitives usually provided for constructing passive objects are more efficient (at least on single processor systems) but are less flexible. They complicate the language by introducing different levels of abstraction.

With a model based entirely on processes, interactions are modelled as direct message passing between the processes; this approach is considered in Section 3.6 and Chapters 4 and 5. The more traditional data-oriented language features are discussed in Section 3.5 and Chapters 6 and 7. Once all this material has been considered the reader will have a good understanding of all the major synchronization and communication primitives found in modern concurrent programming languages.

3.2   The Ornamental Gardens problem

The simplest way for two (or more) processes to communicate is via a shared variable that is in scope for all processes. Let us first explore the possibility of implementing such communication using the ordinary data types (integer, boolean, etc.) that are provided in a modern programming language. Unfortunately, we shall find that achieving reliable communication with these simple raw materials is non-trivial.

As an introduction, consider the following allegory, which we have called the problem of the Ornamental Gardens. A large ornamental garden, probably formerly the grounds of a British stately residence, is open to members of the public, who must pay an admission fee to view the beautiful collection of roses, shrubs and aquatic plants. Entry is gained by two turnstiles. The management of the gardens want to be able to determine, at any time, the total number of members of the public currently in the grounds. They propose that a computer system should be installed which has connections to each turnstile and a terminal from which the management can ascertain the current total. We shall attempt to construct some prototype software for the proposed system.

Clearly, there needs to be a way of counting the visitors as they enter and leave the gardens. We shall suppose that the turnstiles are able to send a signal to the computer to indicate each arrival and each departure. However, the hardware details will not be considered: we shall construct a simplified simulation of what would be required.

This appears to be a case ripe for the application of concurrency. The two turnstiles are objects that exist and behave in parallel with one another, and the events they monitor do not have a predictable order: we do not know, when we write the software, at what time individual visitors will arrive and leave, nor which turnstile they will choose to use. Let us, then, propose the following:

- each turnstile will be handled by a separate process in the program;
- the turnstile processes will run concurrently with one another;
- a global integer variable will represent the current number of visitors in the garden;
- a terminal-handler process (which we shall not consider further) will provide the management information.

A full simulation of the required system would lead us too far afield at this stage. Instead, we shall concentrate on reliably counting visitors as they enter the grounds. We shall simulate an experiment in which 20 people enter the gardens through each turnstile: no-one is allowed to leave until the experiment has been completed. The global counter should show that there are 40 people in the grounds at this point. The following program simulates the experiment.

```
program gardens1;
var count : integer;

process turnstile1;
var
   loop : integer;
begin
   for loop := 1 to 20 do
   count := count + 1
end;     (* turnstile1 *)
```

```
process turnstile2;
var loop : integer;
begin
  for loop := 1 to 20 do
  count := count + 1
end;     (* turnstile2 *)

begin
  count := 0;
  cobegin
    turnstile1;
    turnstile2
  coend;
  writeln('Total admitted: ',count)
end.
```

If this program is run with Pascal-FC's unfair scheduler, it always produces the 'correct' result. However, the fair scheduler almost always gives faulty output. For example, the following string of values was produced from ten successive runs of the program:

25 29 31 20 21 26 27 18 31 35

Note that one of the values is actually below 20!

As the two processes have a similar structure they could have been generated from a single type:

```
   . . .
process type turnstile(num : integer);
var loop: integer;
begin
  for loop := 1 to num do
  count := count + 1
end;     (* turnstile *)

var turnstile1, turnstile2 : turnstile;
   . . .
  cobegin
    turnstile1(20);
    turnstile2(20)
  coend;
   . . .
```

This has no influence on the output results, however.

If the program is modified so that there is only one turnstile, then the expected result of 20 is always observed, but two such processes running concurrently may interfere with one another. Evidently, the turnstile processes in this case cannot be allowed to operate independently of one another: some form of synchronization must be introduced.

3.3 Mutual exclusion and other synchronizations

The Ornamental Gardens case illustrates what is usually known as the *multiple update problem*. It can be understood by considering the addition of a simple value to a shared variable:

    x : = x + 1

Let two processes, P and Q, concurrently undertake this assignment. If the hardware could perform this update as a single instruction, then the result would always be correct. This is so because:

(1) on a uniprocessor, only one instruction can be carried out at once;
(2) on a multiprocessor there is arbitration on simultaneous attempts by different processors to access the same location.

The result, either on a uniprocessor or on a multiprocessor, is that accesses to memory are serialized (in some undefined order).

However, on almost all current hardware platforms, the update action is broken down into three instructions:

(1) load value of x into some processor register,
(2) increment the value in the register,
(3) store the value in the register at the address for x.

It is now possible for the actions of P and Q to interfere with each other. For illustration, let x have an initial value of 2, and consider the following ordering of operations:

(1) P loads the value of x into a CPU register,
(2) Q loads the value of x into a CPU register,
(3) Q increments the value in its register,
(4) P increments the value in its register,
(5) Q stores the value in its register at the address of x,
(6) P stores the value in its register at the address of x.

Remember that, as each process has exclusive use of a logical processor, P and Q are in effect using different processor registers, no matter how many physical processors are being used to execute them. However, they both use the same main memory location for x.

On completion of step (2) in the above scenario, P and Q each have a processor register with a value of 2. Each then proceeds to add 1 to this value, so that each then has a register with a value of 3. It is this value that each process then stores at the address of *x*. Hence the value of *x* on completion of step (6) will be 3, even though two processes have attempted to increment the same variable, whose initial value was 2. We appear to have 'lost' an increment, and this is what was happening in the Ornamental Gardens simulation. In the terms introduced at the beginning of the chapter, our error is that we are treating *x* as a *neutral* object: a *passive* object is what we really need in this case.

It is important to note that it is only when the scheduler interleaves the two assignments that the error occurs. Pascal-FC's fair scheduler finds these situations frequently. The unfair scheduler, on the other hand, will run the first turnstile process to completion before beginning the second, so that no interleaving takes place.† A scheduler between these extremes might only rarely generate an 'unfortunate' interleaving. Testing may never find the fault: it will remain dormant, perhaps until the implementation is changed during software maintenance. Movement from a single processor to a multiprocessor system will usually activate such faults!

What the above example illustrates is that, even with a single resource such as a shared variable, there is a need to prohibit a certain form of interaction. Fundamentally, the problem is the same one that afflicted the seat-reservation program of Chapter 1, and the solution is the same. What we need to do is to code the updates to the shared variable in a critical section. As we saw in Chapter 1, a critical section, by definition, must be accessed under mutual exclusion.

A solution to the mutual exclusion problem was first described by Dijkstra (1965): it is a problem which lies at the heart of most concurrent programming primitives and is of great theoretical interest as well as practical importance. There are, however, other important synchronizations. Consider, for example, the following program, which attempts to show how the process sender can pass a data item to the process receiver via a shared variable. It is a primitive version of the Producer–Consumer problem: an outline of the requirements for a more sophisticated version follows:

```
program passing;
var value : integer;

  process sender;
  var message : integer;
  begin
     . . .
```

---

† This is so because turnstile1 remains executable throughout its run: it never becomes blocked (for example, by calling sleep).

```
      message := 42;
      value := message;
      . . .
   end;

   process receiver;
   var data : integer;
   begin
      . . .
      data := value;
      write(data);
      . . .
   end;

begin
   cobegin
      sender; receiver
   coend
end.
```

As only one process is updating the variable, there is no multiple update problem. There is, however, a potential error: if receiver reads value before sender has written into it, then it will get an undefined value rather than the 42 that is intended. Using the notation introduced in Chapter 1, we must stipulate that:

$$\forall e \bullet \text{produce} \rightarrow \text{consume} \qquad\qquad (3.1a)$$

This means that, for all legal executions of the program, produce must precede consume.

Condition synchronization is the name given to the required property that one process should not perform an event until some other process has undertaken a designated action. Section 3.4.1 presents a program that fulfills Requirement 3.1a.

As the Producer–Consumer problem will be encountered at various points in this book, it is worthwhile here to consider a more complex (and realistic) version. In the above program, a single item is intended to be produced and consumed. Following this, both processes terminate. More typically, each process is cyclic, so that the producer repeatedly produces items, which are then consumed. Requirement 3.1a needs to be modified to:

$$\forall e \bullet \text{produce}^i \rightarrow \text{consume}^i \qquad\qquad (3.1b)$$

This is not yet sufficient: it is usually stipulated that all items produced must eventually be consumed (that is, there must be no losses). Using the approach of the above program, where a single variable (value) is used to store each new item produced, a second condition synchronization must be added to the requirements to avoid overwriting an item before it has had the chance to be consumed:

$$\forall e \bullet \text{consume}^i \rightarrow \text{produce}^{i+1} \tag{3.2a}$$

One of the exercises at the end of this chapter invites the reader to write a program incorporating Requirements 3.1b and 3.2a.

Even if both of these condition synchronizations are included, we still do not have a realistic solution for most applications. It is common for the instantaneous rates of production and consumption to vary. For example, the rate of production may be 'bursty': there are periods when several items are produced in quick succession, and other periods when the producer is comparatively quiet. Not uncommonly, the consumer is able to keep pace with the *average* rate of production, but is unable to match the *peak* rate. It is common in these circumstances to *decouple* the producer and the consumer by interposing a *buffer* between them. A buffer is simply an area of storage capable of holding a suitable number of items. The example program could be said to have a one-item buffer, but this constrains the two processes always to operate at the same rate. In practice, larger buffers are used. Then, when the producer is being particularly active, it is able to proceed without blocking (up to a point) by building up an accumulation of items in the buffer. During periods of low production, the consumer can steadily work on this accumulation. The aim of this scheme is to keep both the producer and the consumer executable: only when the buffer is full must the producer block, and only when it is empty must the consumer block.

Requirement 3.2a must now be generalized, as follows:

$$\forall e \bullet \text{consume}^i \rightarrow \text{produce}^{i+\text{buffsize}} \tag{3.2b}$$

Here, buffsize is the capacity of the buffer. Programs that correctly implement a buffered producer–consumer relationship will be presented in later chapters.

Finally, we leave the Producer–Consumer problem and consider a generalization of mutual exclusion, which is required in another typical application, known as the Readers and Writers problem. Here, the 'read' and 'write' actions are considered to be non-trivial events; they are not atomic operations. To increase the concurrency of the system it should be possible for readers to be concurrently active in the file. However, a writer process must exclude all reader processes and competing writer processes. To make *all* accesses to the file mutually exclusive would be too restrictive in this case: what we need is rather to make all *write* accesses mutually exclusive of all other accesses. Again, solutions to this problem will be studied in later chapters.

The Readers and Writers problem can itself be generalized by considering a typical commercial database. Here a large number of competing concurrent requests must be dealt with efficiently but correctly. To make the whole database a single area of mutual exclusion would be too restrictive. Indeed, concurrent reads but exclusive writes are not sufficient to gain the necessary performance. The internal structure of the database must be used to limit the area over which a write **lock** is imposed. This area then behaves as if it were supporting a readers and writers protocol. To cater for more extensive access to the database, a request may obtain locks on different areas.

Many different **concurrency control** protocols are used in database design. They are specific to this application area and are not of general interest to the topic of concurrent programming. Interested readers (or writers) should refer to the Further Reading section.

3.4   Synchronization using simple shared variables

The discussions above have concluded that the naive use of shared variables for inter-process communication is insufficient; we need some way of providing mutual exclusion and condition synchronization. But does that imply that new language features are needed? The question must be asked: is it possible to program these synchronizations using only the data types normally provided in a sequential language?

The simple answer to this question is 'yes'. Howwever, as we shall see over the next few pages, the solutions are inefficient and overcomplicated. The reader should be convinced that new primitives and abstractions are desirable.

3.4.1   Condition synchronization

Consider first the condition synchronization problem (Requirement 3.1a). This can be solved by introducing a second variable, a flag, which delays the reader process:

```
program passing2;
var value : integer;
    flag : boolean;

    process sender;
    var message : integer;
    begin
      . . .
      message := 42;
      value := message;
      flag := true;
      . . .
    end;
```

```
process receiver;
var data : integer;
begin
   . . .
   while not flag do
      sleep(0);
   data := value;
   write(data);
   . . .
end;

begin
   flag := false;
   cobegin
      sender; receiver
   coend
end.
```

With this solution the receiver process loops around and continually tests the flag until it can proceed. This will only occur when the sender has written a value. This algorithm is typical of those that use *busy waiting*: this means that a process that finds itself unable to proceed immediately remains executable and continues to execute instructions while it is waiting. In general such algorithms are extremely inefficient, as the process is using up valuable processor cycles even though it is doing no useful work. Even if receiver had its own hardware processor and there was nothing else for that processor to do, it would still produce excessive bus traffic. Note also that, in general, receiver must have a sleep statement in it: there is otherwise nothing to stop it from hogging the processor and so excluding sender from executing. If this were to happen, sender would never produce its value, and so receiver would never proceed beyond its busy wait. Without the sleep, proper execution of the program on a uniprocessor would rely on a run-time scheduler that does not permit receiver to be hoggish: we have already pointed out that any algorithm in a concurrent program must not be dependent on the scheduler in this way.

3.4.2   Mutual exclusion

Supporting mutual exclusion is more complicated. Indeed, Dijkstra (1968) noted that some of the people who had wrestled with this problem in the early years of concurrent systems had begun to doubt whether a solution was possible without the introduction of special-purpose communication and synchronization primitives. The following discussion is based on Dijkstra's, which first presented a series of unsuccessful attempts to illustrate the potential pitfalls in tackling the problem. Finally, he presented the solution known as **Dekker's algorithm**, which we shall present later in this section. Dekker's algorithm is not the only solution now known, and we shall also present one due to Peterson (1981).

Assumptions

The unsuccessful attempts and the solutions all rest on the following assumptions about the behaviour of the primitive read and write operations on shared variables:

- 'simultaneous' read operations do not interfere with one another;
- if two processes, P and Q, write 'simultaneously' to a variable, the result is either the value written by P or the value written by Q (but never a mixture of the two);
- if a process P writes to a variable 'simultaneously' with the reading of that variable by process Q, then Q sees either the old value or the new one (but never a mixture of the two).

These assumptions are reasonable for uniprocessor or shared memory multiprocessor systems, provided that the shared variable is a **scalar** type (for example, integer, char or boolean).

Requirements for a solution

Before examining the attempts, we should pause to ask what we require of a solution. To begin with, we shall make what will turn out to have been an incomplete specification of the requirements: the 'solutions' will serve to show why it was incomplete. For now, we shall state the requirements as follows:

> The number of processes in the critical section at any time must not exceed 1. (3.3)

Skeleton of a solution

Consider two processes (P1 and P2) that have mutual critical sections. To protect access to these critical sections we can assume that each process executes an **entry protocol** before the critical section and an **exit protocol** afterwards. Each process can therefore be considered to have the following form:

```
process P;
begin
    repeat
```

```
        entry protocol
          critical section
        exit protocol
        non-critical section
      forever
    end;
```

The non-critical section represents some set of actions that the processes can execute concurrently without danger of interference. We ignore it, because it presents no difficulties. It is the entry and exit protocols on which we focus attention. In general, non-critical sections are long in comparison with critical sections (though this will not be obvious from our rather abstract examples). This, then, is a model in which processes are able to proceed independently of one another for much of the time, and only comparatively rarely (and for short periods) need to coordinate their actions. Such processes are said to be **loosely coupled**.

Before attempting to solve the problem, we shall grant ourselves one luxury. The processes in our programs cannot fail in their critical sections or in their entry and exit protocols. This is a simplification, of course, but consideration of such failures would take us into the field of **fault-tolerant systems**, which is beyond the scope of this book.

First attempt

First consider a two-flag solution that is an (almost) logical extension of the busy-wait condition synchronization algorithm (flag1 and flag2 are initially false):

```
    process P1;
    begin
      repeat
        flag1:= true;        (* announce intent to enter *)
        while flag2 do
          null;              (* busy wait if the other process is in *)
                             (* its critical section *)
        CriticalSection;
        flag1:= false;       (* exit protocol *)
        NonCriticalSection
      forever
    end;

    process P2;
    begin
      repeat
        flag2:= true;
        while flag1 do
          null;
        CriticalSection;
```

```
            flag2:= false;
            NonCriticalSection
        forever
    end;
```

Both processes announce their intention to enter their critical sections and then check to see if the other has made a similar announcement. Because of this checking, the attempt fulfills the requirement on the number of processes in the critical section. Unfortunately it suffers from a not insignificant problem. Consider an interleaving that has the following progression:

P1 sets its flag (flag1 now true)
P2 sets its flag (flag2 now true)
P2 checks flag1 (it is true therefore P2 loops)
P2 enters its busy wait
P1 checks flag2 (it is true therefore P1 loops)
P1 enters its busy wait

The result is that both processes will remain in their busy waits. Neither can get out because the other cannot get out. This phenomenon is known as **livelock** and is a severe error condition. It is discussed in Section 3.7.

Now the reader will see why our specification of requirements was inadequate. We shall also need to ensure that the processes are not indefinitely prevented from *making progress*. Hence, we now add a new requirement to rule out 'solutions' that livelock:

If both processes are competing for entry into their critical sections, the decision as to which should succeed cannot be postponed indefinitely. **(3.4)**

Second attempt

The difficulty with the above approach arises because each process announces its intention to enter its critical section before checking to see if it is acceptable for it to do so. Another approach is to reverse the order of these two actions, and this is what is done in the second attempt:

```
    process P1;
    begin
      repeat
        while flag2 do
          null;          (* busy wait if the other process is in *)
                         (* its critical section *)
        flag1:= true;    (* announce intent to enter *)
        CriticalSection;
```

```
      flag1:= false;      (* exit protocol *)
      NonCriticalSection
    forever
end;

  process P2;
  begin
    repeat
      while flag1 do
        null;
      flag2:= true;
      CriticalSection;
      flag2:= false;
      NonCriticalSection
    forever
  end;
```

Now we can produce an interleaving that actually fails to give mutual exclusion:

P1 and P2 are in their non-critical section (flag1 = flag2 = false)
P1 checks flag2 (it is false)
P2 checks flag1 (it is false)
P2 sets its flag (flag2 now true)
P2 enters critical section
P1 sets its flag (flag1 now true)
P1 enters critical section (i.e. P1 and P2 are both in their critical sections).

Considerations of progress need not detain us, as this attempt is a clear failure!

Third attempt

The difficulty with the two structures given so far is that the setting of one's own flag and the check on the other's cannot be done as an indivisible action. One might therefore consider that the correct approach is to use just one flag that indicates which process should next enter its critical section. As this flag decides whose turn it is to enter, it will be called turn.

```
  process P1;
  begin
    repeat
      while turn = 2 do
        null;
      CriticalSection;
      turn:= 2;
```

```
        NonCriticalSection
     forever
  end;

  process P2;
  begin
    repeat
      while turn = 1 do
        null;
      CriticalSection;
      turn:= 1;
      NonCriticalSection
    forever
  end;
```

With this structure, the variable turn must have the value one or two. If it is one then P1 cannot be indefinitely delayed in its entry protocol and P2 cannot enter its critical section. Moreover, turn cannot become two while P1 is in its critical section, as the only place that turn can be assigned two is in the exit protocol of P1. A symmetric argument for turn having the value two implies that mutual exclusion is provided and livelock is not possible if both processes are cycling round.

Unfortunately this latter point is significant. If P1 is indefinitely postponed in its non-critical section, then turn will eventually obtain the value one and will stay with that value (i.e. P2 will be prohibited from entering its critical section even though P1 is no longer interested in doing so). Indefinite postponement in the non-critical section may be brought about, for example, by the failure of a process while in that section. Even when executing normally, the use of a single turn variable requires the processes to cycle round at the same rate. It is not possible for P1 (say) to enter its critical section three times between visits by P2. This constraint is unacceptable for autonomous processes. Again, the 'solution' is unsatisfactory because it can impair the progress of a process (though perhaps less spectacularly than was the case with the first attempt). Let us add another requirement, which rules out 'solutions' that lead to excessively close coupling between processes:

> If one process is in its non-critical section and the other requests entry into the critical section, the request should succeed.   (3.5)

We consider a process which fails in its non-critical section to be indefinitely *in* that section.

Peterson's solution

We now present an algorithm that does enforce mutual exclusion, whilst avoiding the other problems raised by the first and third attempts. This was originally proposed by Peterson (1981). His approach is to have two flags (flag1 and flag2) that are manipulated by the process that 'owns' them and a turn variable that is only used if there is contention for entry to the critical sections:

```
process P1;
begin
  repeat
    flag1:= true;      (* announce intent to enter *)
    turn:= 2;      (* give priority to other process *)
    while flag2 and (turn = 2) do
      null;
    CriticalSection;
    flag1:= false;
    NonCriticalSection
  forever
end;

process P2;
begin
  repeat
    flag2:= true;      (* announce intent to enter *)
    turn:= 1;      (* give priority to other process *)
    while flag1 and (turn = 1) do
      null;
    CriticalSection;
    flag2:= false;
    NonCriticalSection
  forever
end;
```

If only one process wishes to enter its critical section then the other's flag will be false and entry will be immediate. However, if both flags have been raised then the value of turn becomes significant.

Interestingly the above algorithm is fair in the sense that if there is contention for access (to their critical sections) and, say, P1 was successful, then P2 is bound to enter next. When P1 exits its critical section it lowers flag1. This could let P2 into its critical section but, even if it did not (because P2 was not actually executing at that time), then P1 would proceed, enter and leave its non-critical section, raise flag1, set turn to two and then be placed in a busy loop. There it would remain until P2 had entered and left its critical section and reset flag2 as its exit protocol.

Dekker's solution

Dijkstra presented a solution to the two-process mutual exclusion problem which was devised by Dekker. It is similar to Peterson's solution in that a turn variable is used to resolve contentions between the processes. When there is contention, one of the processes 'backs off': the other process does not proceed until this has happened (as indicated by the other's flag). We now use this algorithm to solve the Ornamental Gardens problem in Pascal-FC:

```
program dekker;
var turn : integer;
    flag1, flag2 : boolean;
    count : integer;

process turnstile1;
var
  loop : integer;
begin
  for loop := 1 to 20 do
  begin
    flag1 := true;
    while flag2 do
      if turn = 2 then
      begin
        flag1 := false;
        while turn = 2 do
          sleep(0);
        flag1 := true
      end;
    count := count + 1;
    turn := 2;
    flag1 := false
  end
end;

process turnstile2;
var loop: integer;
begin
  for loop := 1 to 20 do
  begin
    flag2 := true;
    while flag1 do
      if turn = 1 then
      begin
        flag2 := false;
        while turn = 1 do
          sleep(0);
        flag2 := true
      end;
    count := count + 1;
    turn := 1;
    flag2 := false
  end
end;
```

```
    begin
      flag1 := false;
      flag2 := false;
      turn := 1;      (* arbitrary value, could have been 2 *)
      count := 0;
      cobegin
        turnstile1;
        turnstile2
      coend;
      writeln('Total admitted: ', count)
    end.
```

3.4.3   More turnstiles

A problem often occurs when we produce a successful computer system: the client is so impressed with it that we are asked to build an even better one. In this case, the ornamental gardens prove to be so profitable that the management wish to add a third turnstile, with the prospect of yet more in the future. Can we produce a more general solution to the mutual exclusion problem?

Several such solutions have been published (for example, Dijkstra, 1968; Eisenberg and McGuire, 1972), but we shall present the **Bakery algorithm** devised by Lamport (1974). The algorithm is so called because it resembles the arrangements used in bakeries, delicatessens, and so on, for deciding which customer is to be served next. On entry to the shop, a customer takes a ticket which bears a number. When a shop assistant becomes free, he or she chooses the waiting customer whose ticket bears the smallest number. The ticket numbers must be unique if there are to be no disputes!

The Bakery algorithm is used to solve the Ornamental Gardens problem in the following program. Note that the selection procedure is a little more cooperative than the one described above: the customers decide amongst themselves who has the ticket giving the right to be served next.

```
    program bakery;
        (* Mutual exclusion with Lamport's bakery algorithm *)

    const
      nprocs = 3;
    var
      ticket: array[1. .nprocs] of integer;
      choosing: array[1..nprocs] of boolean;
      loop: integer;
      count: integer;

    process type turntype(thisproc: integer);
    var
```

```
        otherproc, loop: integer;

        function max: integer;
        var
          i, largest: integer;
        begin
          largest := 0;
          for i := 1 to nprocs do
            if ticket[i] > largest then
              largest := ticket[i];
          max := largest + 1
        end;    (* max *)

        function favoured(i, j: integer): boolean;
        begin
          if (ticket[i] = 0) or (ticket[i] > ticket[j]) then
            favoured := false
          else
            if ticket[i] < ticket[j] then
              favoured := true
            else
              favoured := (i < j)
        end;    (* favoured *)

  begin
    for loop := 1 to 20 do
    begin
      choosing[thisproc] := true;
      ticket[thisproc] := max;
      choosing[thisproc] := false;
      for otherproc := 1 to nprocs do
      begin
        while choosing[otherproc] do
          null;
        while favoured(otherproc, thisproc) do
          null
      end;
      count := count + 1;
      ticket[thisproc] := 0
    end
  end;    (* turntype *)

var
  turnstile: array[1..nprocs] of turntype;
begin
  count := 0;
  for loop := 1 to nprocs do
  begin
```

```
          ticket[loop] := 0;
          choosing[loop] := false
      end;
      cobegin
        for loop := 1 to nprocs do
           turnstile[loop](loop)
      coend;
      writeln('Total admitted: ', count)
  end.
```

Note that there is a potential problem when a process attempts to choose a ticket: if another process is choosing at the same time, then it is possible for them both to take the same number. In this event, Lamport's algorithm resolves the contention in favour of the process which has the smallest identification number (passed as a parameter in our program). Hence, this algorithm is not entirely fair, as lower-numbered processes will tend to receive better service than higher-numbered ones. The role of the choosing array is important: we leave it to the reader to consider its purpose.

Apart from favouring lower-numbered processes, this algorithm is satisfactory in that mutual exclusion is achieved and livelock is avoided. However, a great deal of busy waiting occurs and the algorithm becomes very inefficient when the number of contending processes is large.

Readers who run the above program may be surprised to find that the Pascal-FC system sometimes aborts it and asserts that livelock has occurred. Livelock is discussed in more detail in Section 3.7, and we have already seen an example in the first unsuccessful attempt to solve the mutual exclusion problem. Informally, we can say that it is a situation in which processes are busily doing something useless, in the sense that the processes involved will never make any further progress. Building a run-time system that infallibly detects this state of affairs would not be easy, since it takes a certain degree of intelligence to determine that what the processes are doing really *is* useless. Therefore, the Pascal-FC system uses a primitive method of 'detecting' livelock, which sometimes makes false positive errors. Simply, the number of instructions executed by the program is counted: when this reaches a certain limit, the system 'decides' that livelock must have occurred and aborts the program. Execution of the above program is one instance where it is in error: the program is always able to make progress, but *slowly*. Therefore, the user is advised to treat the 'livelock' warning with a little cautious scepticism whenever it is given.

3.4.4 Conclusions

This discussion has been given at length to illustrate the difficulties of implementing synchronization between processes using only shared variables and no additional primitives beyond those found in sequential languages. These difficulties can be summarized as follows:

- protocols that use busy loops may be difficult to design, understand and prove correct (particularly the more general *n*-process versions);
- testing programs may not examine rare interleavings that break mutual exclusion or lead to livelock;
- busy-wait loops are inefficient and do not allow a queue discipline (which can be used to ensure fair service to all waiting processes) to be programmed;
- an unreliable (rogue) task that misuses shared variables will corrupt the entire system.

No concurrent programming language relies entirely on busy waiting and shared variables; other methods and primitives have been introduced. The main ones are considered below and in the next four chapters.

3.5 Synchronization primitives for shared variable solutions

The above lengthy descriptions were included to convince the reader that new language features are needed. A number of primitives have been advocated for shared variable models. The two most important are **semaphores** and **monitors**: these are described in Chapters 6 and 7 respectively. A common feature of all synchronization primitives, whether they are based on the shared memory model or not, is that they are usually implemented so that, if a process cannot proceed, then it is considered non-executable. It does not continue to use processor cycles, but enters the *suspended* state introduced in Chapter 2 (in Figure 2.5). Only when conditions are appropriate for the process to proceed is it transferred back to the executable state.

Semaphores are low-level primitives that enable critical sections to be protected and condition synchronizations to be effected. Monitors more directly support the notion of a passive object, as they encapsulate the resource that needs protection. Both language features easily support simple mutual exclusion; other synchronizations, such as Readers and Writers, are more difficult to construct.

3.6 Message-based models

The more radical solution to the multiple update problem is to prohibit (in the language) the use of shared variables. If processes cannot communicate via such variables then they must pass data directly between them. The models are therefore **message based**. In its simplest form the transfer of data from one process to another can be accomplished by two operations: **send** and **receive**. For example:

> send (42, P)   (* send the value 42 to process P *)
> receive (X, Q)   (* receive into variable X a value from process Q *)

Many different models of message passing are available in languages – these are discussed in the next two chapters.

All message-passing models incorporate some form of condition synchronization, as the process that wishes to receive a message must wait until it has been sent. If the message is not there, the process is suspended (again see Figure 2.5). Once the message arrives, the process again becomes executable and will subsequently read the message.

Mutual exclusion is not an issue with message-based models as the shared variable of the passive model is replaced by a 'shared' process, which encapsulates the variable to be updated. Each process wishing to update the variable sends a message to the 'shared' process. As this process, internally, is a sequential piece of code, it can only be doing one thing at a time. Consequently, multiple updates are not possible.

3.7   The correctness of concurrent programs

We shall now try to draw together what has been learned while attempting to achieve mutual exclusion and condition synchronization. What we aim to do is to use this experience to elucidate what we mean by the 'correctness' of a concurrent program. What we shall say is that a correct program must fulfill certain **properties**: a property is some assertion that is true of *every* legal execution of that program. The properties we require will, in general, depend on the particular application at hand.

It is generally agreed that a correct concurrent program must satisfy two classes of property: **safety** and **liveness** (Owicki and Lamport, 1982). Informally, we may define these classes as follows:

> SAFETY PROPERTIES: assert that nothing 'bad' will ever happen during an execution (that is, that the program will never enter a 'bad' state).
>
> LIVENESS PROPERTIES: assert that something 'good' will eventually happen during the execution.

Liveness properties are concerned with whether the program is always able to make constructive progress. In order to prove that a program has liveness, it may be necessary to prove certain safety properties. As Owicki and Lamport (1982) point out, in order to prove that something good eventually happens, we may have to prove that nothing bad happens along the way.

One problem with our definition of liveness is the use of the word 'eventually'. How long should we have to wait? If we were concerned with real-time systems, then this question would be extremely important, since a defining characteristic of such systems is that they must be able to react within a *specifiable* delay. In a book on general concurrency, however, we are not concerned with such timing issues, and 'eventually' is good enough.

3.7.1 Safety properties

Examples of safety properties already seen in this chapter include mutual exclusion and the condition synchronizations necessary in the Producer–Consumer problem. Thus, the program must never enter a state in which two or more processes are in a mutual critical section, and a producer must never place a new item into a full buffer.

Another safety requirement is freedom from deadlock. We may define deadlock as follows:

> Deadlock is a state in which processes are blocked waiting for something that will never happen.

How such a state might occur may not be obvious to the reader: the only means we yet have of blocking a process in Pascal-FC is the sleep procedure. The blocking is always bounded in this case: eventually the time will run out because (in theory) time never stops. However, we have already said that language primitives for inter-process communication and synchronization usually use blocked waiting; the misuse of such tools provides rich opportunities to program unintended unbounded waiting!

Deadlock is a good illustration of what Owicki and Lamport meant when they wrote that proving liveness sometimes requires that we prove safety properties: if a program fails to avoid this bad state, then it is likely that some (even all) of the 'good' things are never going to occur. Deadlock is such a pervasive hazard that much research has been directed to it, and we devote Sections 3.8 and 3.9 to a consideration of the conditions that bring it about and to ways of coping with it.

3.7.2 Liveness properties

The most spectacular departure from liveness is livelock. We shall define this condition as follows:

> Livelock is a condition in which processes are executing instructions uselessly, in the sense that they will never make constructive progress.

One example of a liveness requirement was Requirement 3.5 for mutual exclusion. In effect, it stated that if both processes wanted to enter the critical section, then *eventually* a decision would be made as to which should succeed. Our first unsuccessful attempt failed to guarantee this, because executions were possible in which contention arose that would *never* be resolved.

The following question may have occurred to some readers:

> If livelock is a breach of liveness, why is deadlock considered a breach of safety rather than of liveness?

One answer to this is that deadlock is *both* a breach of safety and of liveness. Livelock, however, is not usually considered a violation of safety. One reason for this is that livelock is not an easily definable state in the way that deadlock is. One manifestation of this is that the Pascal-FC system is easily (and infallibly) able to determine that a deadlock has occurred because a point has been reached at which the scheduler has no executable processes from which to choose†, whereas the detection of livelock is far less straightforward.

There are other breaches of liveness, the effects of which are perhaps less spectacular than those of livelock. A common example is **indefinite postponement** or **starvation**. In this (more localized) condition, the system as a whole is always able to make progress, but some subset of the processes is being barred from access to required resources because competing processes are repeatedly 'overtaking' them. This could happen, for example, because processes have differing priorities. If resources are so limited that they are barely sufficient to fulfill the needs of high-priority processes, low-priority processes are never given a chance. One solution to such a problem would be to provide more (or more powerful) resources. In most cases, however, such an approach would do nothing to help a livelocked program.

In general, the liveness properties of programs are very dependent on the scheduling policy used. Further consideration is given to this in Section 3.10.

3.8 Deadlock

A fundamental feature of most concurrent systems is that processes will, from time to time during their execution, need to use **resources** of various types. Tape drives, printers, memory buffers and information stored in files

---

† Executing the sleep procedure cannot result in deadlock, however, because the system recognizes that processes blocked in this way will eventually awaken.

are common examples. A standard way of structuring systems is to place such resources in **pools**, and to put the pools under the supervision of a **resource controller** process. Processes must request an allocation from the resource controller when they reach a stage in their execution where (additional) resources are required. When they have finished using an allocated resource, they return it to the pool. A simple protocol would be as follows:

> request resource,
> use resource,
> release resource.

Protocols such as this may be executed many times during the lifetime of a process, as resources should only be attached to processes when they need to use them.

The task of a resource controller is complicated by the fact that many resources must be used under mutual exclusion. For example, once a process has been allocated a printer, that printer cannot be allocated to a second process until the first has released it: otherwise there would be an intermingling of output from the two processes. Hence, the 'request resource' operation may not succeed immediately, because there may not currently be enough free resources to satisfy the request. In such a case, it is usual to suspend the requesting process until its requirements can be fulfilled. Such protocols are a common cause of deadlocks. We must, therefore, know the conditions under which deadlock can arise and consider methods of dealing with the possibility of deadlock.

3.8.1 An example of a deadlock

Suppose that there are two processes P1 and P2 and two resources R1 and R2 which must be used under mutual exclusion. P1 has R1 allocated to it and has now reached a point where it can proceed no further until its request for R2 has been granted. However, R2 is allocated to P2 and P2 has reached a state in which it cannot continue until its request for R1 has been granted. In these circumstances, both processes will wait for their requested resource, but they will wait for ever!

3.8.2 Necessary and sufficient conditions for the occurrence of deadlock

Coffman *et al.* (1971) identified four necessary and sufficient conditions for the occurrence of deadlock:

- the processes involved need to share resources that must be used under mutual exclusion;

- processes hold on to resources already allocated to them while awaiting the granting of additional ones;

- the system has no way of pre-empting (forcibly withdrawing) resources from processes once they have been allocated to them (resources are only released voluntarily by processes when they have finished using them);

- a circular chain of requests and allocations exists (such as was described in the previous section).

3.9   Coping with deadlock

There are two different strategies for coping with deadlock:

- introduce components into the system that can detect when deadlock has occurred and, when it has, carry out some recovery action;
- design the system in such a way that deadlock *cannot* occur.

The first of these is called **deadlock detection/recovery**. The recovery phase can be done manually by computer operators, or automatically.

The second of the above strategies gives rise to two different approaches:

- deadlock *avoidance*
- deadlock *prevention*.

The principle with deadlock avoidance is to anticipate impending deadlock and to take avoiding action in advance. As deadlock occurs when a limited set of resources have to be shared among the processes, deadlock avoidance usually involves intercepting all the requests that processes make for further resources. If a request could possibly lead to deadlock, it is not granted.

Deadlock prevention makes the occurrence of deadlock logically impossible. There is no need to monitor requests for resources, because the system has been constructed in such a way that we know *a priori* that there are no circumstances in which deadlock could occur. This is possible because we know the necessary conditions for the occurrence of deadlock: if we ensure that, at all times, one of these conditions is denied, then no deadlock can occur.

Detection/recovery, avoidance and prevention are not mutually incompatible, and some systems use more than one of them: for any given type of resource, the strategy used is the one that best fits the characteristics of that resource type.

3.9.1 Deadlock detection and recovery

This approach differs from the other two in that it will permit deadlock to occur. Reliance is placed on the ability to detect the fact and recover from it. It is necessary to include in the concurrent system some data structure that records the current states of allocation of resources and of requests for resources that have not yet been fulfilled. One possible representation of this information is a **directed graph**.

A directed graph consists of a set of **nodes** (which in this case can be used to represent the processes and the resources) and a set of **edges** (which in this case can be used to represent requests and allocations).

An example is given in Figure 3.1. Circles have been used to represent processes and squares to represent individual resources. An edge from a process to a resource indicates a request for a resource that has not yet been fulfilled. An edge from a resource to a process indicates that the resource has been allocated to the process. (When a resource is granted, the 'request' edge is deleted.)

Figure 3.1 represents the deadlock described earlier. In general, if each individual resource and each individual process is represented by a single node, then a cycle in the graph indicates a deadlock. A deadlock detecting process could be included in a concurrent system to maintain the resource allocation graph and to look for cycles.

Once deadlock has been detected, recovery can be undertaken either manually (by computer operators) or automatically. The following approaches could be taken in such a recovery procedure:

- abort *all* processes involved in the deadlock;
- abort processes one by one until the deadlock is no longer present;
- pre-empt resources one by one from processes until the deadlock is removed.

If processes are aborted, the resources they held are returned to the pool and the process is re-started from the beginning.

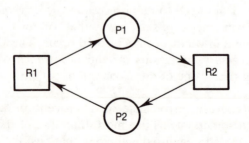

Figure 3.1 Resource allocation graph.

In all of these cases, the cost is that computing work that has already been done may be 'thrown away': some form of roll-back to a previous state is involved. There is also the possibility that, once having been rolled back, the processes simply proceed back to the same state of deadlock. However, the indeterminacy of concurrent systems can usually be relied upon to make the probability of this unfortunate occurrence acceptably low.

With this approach, 'victim' processes have to be selected, either for abortion or for the removal of some allocated resources. While this could be done on a random basis, it is usual to be more selective. Criteria that may be used include the following.

- Process priority: some processes might be considered more important than others and should not be selected as victims if this can be avoided.

- How long the process has been executing. The longer the time, the more work is likely to be thrown away.

- How long the process needs to complete its execution. It would appear pointless to abort a process that is very near to completion.

- How many resources the process requires. If a process needs (for example) only one more resource, then it may not be sensible to abort it.

- What kinds of resources are involved. Some resources are easier to pre-empt than others, or would necessitate throwing away less work.

3.9.2 Deadlock avoidance

The principle with deadlock avoidance is to anticipate that deadlock could occur if a request for a resource were granted, and therefore not to grant such requests. A naive approach to this would be to look one step ahead. Each time a request was made, the system could determine whether a state of deadlock would exist if the request were granted. If so, then the requesting process would, of course, have to wait. Unfortunately, this approach is too simple. We shall see that it is possible to identify system states in which deadlock, though not currently present, is dangerously likely to occur in the future. Hence, it is necessary to look more than one step ahead.

A common strategy in deadlock avoidance is known as the **Banker's algorithm**, because it resembles the way in which a bank might manage its deposits and loans. We consider here a simple example in which only one class of resource is involved.

Suppose that there are 12 instances of some resource class and that there are only three processes. In using the Banker's algorithm, each process must state its maximum *claim* before it begins using the resources: this is the maximum number of instances of the resource that it will ever need to hold simultaneously. Suppose that the claims are as set out in Table 3.1.

Table 3.1 Three processes and their maximum claims.

Process	Claim
A	4
B	6
C	8
Total	18

Note that the sum of the claims is greater than the 12 resources available. However, each process is unlikely to require its full claim throughout its execution: the number it needs will vary according to what it is currently doing.

Consider now that the processes have been running for some time and that the resources have been allocated as in Table 3.2. Note that there are still two resources left in the pool which are not allocated to any process. Process B now makes a request for one additional instance. Should the request be granted or should Process B have to wait?

The Banker's algorithm uses a two-part policy to answer such questions. The request is granted if, and only if, the following are both true:

- The sum of the requested instances and the number currently allocated to the process does not exceed that process's declared claim.
- If the request is granted, there would still be a way in which the various processes could eventually run to completion, even if they now all requested their full claim.

A system state that fulfills the second requirement is said to be **safe**. An **unsafe** state is one which, though not necessarily a deadlock, would result in

Table 3.2 Resource allocations after processes have been executing for some time.

Process	Claim	Allocated
A	4	1
B	6	4
C	8	5
Remaining		2

Table 3.3 An unsafe state.

Process	Claim	Allocated
A	4	2
B	6	4
C	8	5
Remaining		1

deadlock if the processes now all requested their full claims. As the system will always start in a safe state, the underlying strategy of the Banker's algorithm can be stated as follows:

> Never grant a request that takes the system from a safe to an unsafe state.

First, note that the position described in Table 3.2 is safe. If all processes now requested their full claim, they would not all be able to proceed immediately, but the following sequence would allow them all to complete eventually:

- the two remaining resources could be allocated immediately to Process B,
- on completion, Process B would return six resources to the pool,
- three resources could then be assigned to each of A and C.

Indeed, if the request for one additional resource from Process B were granted, the resulting state would still be safe. Hence, Process B *would* be granted its request.

Suppose, instead, that Process A had requested one additional resource. In that case, the position following the allocation would be as shown in Table 3.3. This is *not* a safe state and the request would therefore not be granted. Note, however, that Table 3.3 is *not* a deadlock. Moreover, deadlock is not inevitable: the processes may, for example, not request any further resources. The Banker's algorithm takes the cautious view that the danger of deadlock is too high and would not grant the request from Process A.

3.9.3 Deadlock prevention.

Because the necessary conditions for deadlock are known, an alternative to the problem is to build a system in which one of the conditions is not present. It is then logically impossible for deadlock to occur and there is no need to monitor requests for resources. This is the approach known as deadlock prevention.

Consider first the requirement that resources must be used under mutual exclusion. Often there is limited scope for removing this condition: the nature of the resources is such that the mutual exclusion requirement must be imposed. However, there is sometimes the possibility of making the resource *appear* as though it can be concurrently accessed. A common example is the way in which printers are used in multi-user operating systems. Output for the printer is *spooled*: instead of sending output from a user process directly to the printer, the operating system directs it to a file. A **printer spooler** process is given the task of taking the resulting files, one at a time, and printing them out. Individual users of the computer may be unaware that their output is treated in this way. What spooling does is to provide user processes with a **virtual printer** that *can* be simultaneously allocated to more than one process: this is because accesses to a high-speed disk (where the files are stored) from different processes can be rapidly interleaved.

The second necessary condition (hold-and-wait) can be denied in a number of ways. One way is to make processes request all their resources at once. Unless they are all available, no resources are allocated. A problem with this approach is that it tends to result in poor utilization of resources because they can be allocated to a process when not actually being used.

The third condition (no pre-emption) can be addressed by introducing a mechanism for withdrawing resources from a process. As this may result in the loss of some work that has already been done, this approach is not without disadvantages.

Finally, there is the 'circular wait' condition. One way of removing this condition is to give unique integers to each resource in the system. A process is then only allowed to request resources in order: if it will require resources i and j ($i < j$) during its execution, then it must request i before j, even if it needs to start using j before it requires i. Again, the price that is paid for this strategy is that processes may be holding resources when they are not actually making use of them.

An example of deadlock prevention will be seen in later chapters in connection with the problem of the Dining Philosophers, whose plight we introduce in Section 3.11.

3.10 Fairness

In Chapter 2 it was noted that some versions of Pascal-FC provide two different schedulers: the fair and the unfair. We shall now give further consideration to the concept of 'fairness'.

We have viewed a concurrent program as a set of processes, each running on its own logical processor. Each logical processor executes a sequence of atomic instructions from the process allocated to it. Consider the case in which several logical processors are mapped onto a single physical processor. Each time this processor is to execute an instruction, there may be several instructions among which a choice could be made: one instruction from each **executable process** is eligible for execution. The job of the scheduler is to select which one of the eligible instructions will be the next to be executed.

A fair scheduler is one which guarantees that every eligible instruction will eventually be chosen. A scheduler that is unfair discriminates in some way between the eligible instructions, so that some have a lower probability of being chosen than others (and may never be chosen). For example, a scheduler which takes into account process priorities is unfair. Pascal-FC's unfair scheduler discriminates according to the textual order of process activation. It is as though the system has implicitly given a unique priority to each process according to the textual order of its activation in the concurrent statement.

It would be an oversimplification to say that a scheduling scheme was either 'fair' or 'unfair': different degrees of fairness can be distinguished. Consider, for example, the following program:

```
program CoOp1;
var
  flag, finish: boolean;

  process one;
  begin
    flag := true;
    while not finish do
      null
  end;     (* one *)

  process two;
  begin
    while not flag do
      null;
    finish := true
  end;     (* two *)

begin
  flag := false;
  finish := false;
  cobegin
    one;
    two
  coend
end.
```

If this program is run with Pascal-FC's unfair scheduler, it will never terminate. With the fair scheduler, it quickly terminates. In fact, *any* scheduler that can guarantee that both processes will receive 'enough' processor time (for example, round robin) will allow the program to terminate eventually.

Consider the following, slightly different, program:

```
program CoOp2;
var
    flag, finish: boolean;

    process one;
    begin
      while not finish do
      begin
        flag := true;
        flag := false
      end
    end;     (* one *)

    process two;
    begin
      while not flag do
        null;
      finish := true
    end;     (* two *)

begin
  flag := false;
  finish := false
  cobegin
    one;
    two
  coend
end.
```

Again, this program will never terminate if run with the unfair scheduler, but it terminates quickly with the fair one. But even a scheduler that gave regular bursts of processor time to both processes might not enable this second program to terminate. For termination to occur, two has to 'notice' that flag has the value true. If the scheduler happened only to run two when flag was false, this would never occur. The probability of such an interleaving may be very low, but it is not necessarily zero (which is why the program usually terminates under the fair scheduler).

The scheduler is a low-level function of a concurrent system: it cannot be expected to 'understand' the requirements of every program run on the system. Its role is to make a choice among the eligible instructions. Hence it would not be reasonable to call a scheduler which only ran two in CoOp2 when flag was false 'unfair'. What is done instead is to distinguish various levels of fairness. One such distinction is that between **weakly fair** and **strongly fair** schedulers:

- A weakly fair scheduler is one that guarantees that *if a process continually makes a request*, eventually it will be granted.
- A strongly fair scheduler is one that guarantees that *if a process makes a request infinitely often*, eventually it will be granted.

(By 'continual', we mean that, once the request is made, it stays asserted and is never temporarily rescinded.)

To understand how these definitions apply to programs CoOp1 and CoOp2, consider process one to be making a request to terminate by setting flag to true. Process two is responsible for granting the request. In CoOp1, process one makes a continual request; in CoOp2, it makes an infinite series of short requests.

We can now say that a scheme such as round robin provides a weakly fair scheduler for the above programs. It would guarantee that the request of process one is eventually granted in CoOp1, but it could provide no such guarantee in the case of CoOp2. It is not, in fact, practical to design a scheduler that would be strongly fair for all possible programs.

If Pascal-FC's fair scheduler used strictly random numbers to decide among eligible instructions, it would be possible that it would choose process one (for example) every time. The probability of this is very low, but it is not zero. With strictly random determination, then, we could not guarantee that both processes would receive processor time. Hence 'fair' might be considered an inappropriate description of this scheduler. However, the random number generator used in Pascal-FC is designed to give a *balanced* distribution of numbers, so in practice we are justified in using the term 'fair' for this scheduler.

3.11   The Dining Philosophers problem

We conclude this chapter with an introduction to the famous Dining Philosophers problem. Although this problem has already been described in many books, no apology is given for including it here. It provides a (non-computer-oriented) system that illustrates many of the issues discussed in this chapter.

A number of philosophers are seated around a circular table. For illustration we shall assume that there are five female Chinese philosophers. Each philosopher involves herself in only two activities: eating and thinking. To eat she must sit at the table (at the place reserved for her). Between each pair of table positions there is a single chopstick (i.e. there are five chopsticks in total for the five philosophers). To eat, each philosopher must have two chopsticks (not even Chinese philosophers can eat with only one chopstick). Philosophers are too polite to reach across the table and pick up a spare chopstick, and hence they only use the two chopsticks on either side of them. As a consequence, a philosopher cannot be eating concurrently with her neighbour. Moreover, only two philosophers can eat at a time.

Each philosopher can be considered to be a process (active entity); the chopsticks are passive entities. Using the notation introduced in the previous chapter we can define the actions of each (non-terminating) philosopher:

$$\alpha P = \{think, eat, pickup, putdown\};$$
$$P = (think \rightarrow pickup \rightarrow pickup \rightarrow eat \rightarrow putdown \rightarrow putdown \rightarrow P).$$

The Dining Philosophers problem is of interest because, by attempting to solve it in a variety of ways, it can be used to illustrate many of the concepts of importance to concurrent programming:

- Mutual exclusion – each chopstick can only be used by one philosopher (process) at a time.

- Condition synchronization – a philosopher cannot eat until she has picked up two chopsticks.

- Shared variable communication – each chopstick can be represented by a variable that adjacent philosophers share.

- Message-based communication – the chopsticks could be passed directly from one philosopher to another.

- Busy-waiting – a philosopher denied a chopstick can loop round and continually watch to see if a dining neighbour is finishing her meal.

- Blocked waiting – a philosopher denied a chopstick can go to sleep and rely on her neighbour to wake her up when the chopstick is free.

- Livelock – a solution of the form 'pick up left chopstick and then busy wait on the availability of the right chopstick' will lead to livelock if all the philosophers simultaneously pick up one chopstick (the other chopstick will never become free). See the following example.

- Deadlock – a solution of the form 'pick up left chopstick and then sleep until the right one is free' will similarly lead to a complete lack of progress if all philosophers act simultaneously (they will all sleep for eternity).

- Indefinite postponement – two philosophers could starve (literally) a philosopher seated between them if at all times at least one of them is eating (the central philosopher will never get access to two chopsticks).

We conclude this chapter by giving an attempt to solve the Dining

Philosophers problem. This 'solution' is flawed as it can lead to livelock. Indeed, the average number of meals per philosopher before livelock (with the fair scheduler) was less than four when tested by one of the authors.

Each chopstick is represented by a boolean variable; the value *true* implies that the chopstick is free. To obtain a chopstick the philosopher must call the procedure pickup. The code for this procedure is not given, as it must support mutual exclusion over the chopstick variable. Dekker's algorithm (or one of the alternatives) could be used, but the primitives found in later chapters would be more effective. The activities of thinking and eating are simulated by the process calling sleep for a random time using the random function briefly introduced in the first chapter:

```
program philosophers;
const N = 5;
var chopsticks : array[1..N] of boolean;
    I : integer;

procedure pickup(var chop : boolean; var gotit : boolean);
begin
    (* pick up chop if available – under mutual exclusion *)
    (* if available then gotit := true; *)
    (* otherwise gotit := false *)
end;

procedure putdown(var chop : boolean);
begin
    (* put down chop *)
end;

process type philosophers(name : integer);
var I : integer;
    chop1, chop2 : integer;
    gotchop : boolean;
begin
  chop1 := name;
  if name = N then chop2 := 1 else chop2 := name + 1;
  repeat
    sleep(random(10));      (* THINK *)
    gotchop := false;
    repeat
      pickup(chopsticks[chop1], gotchop)
    until gotchop;
    gotchop := false;
    repeat
      pickup(chopsticks[chop2], gotchop)
    until gotchop;
    sleep(random(10));      (* EAT *)
    putdown(chopsticks[chop1]);
```

```
                putdown(chopsticks[chop2])
            forever
        end;

        var phils : array[1..N] of philosophers;

        begin
          for I := 1 to N do
            chopsticks[I] := true;
          cobegin
            for I := 1 to N do
              phils[I](I)
          coend
        end.
```

SUMMARY

For most of the time processes may proceed independently. However, it is inevitable that they must compete for resources and coordinate their activities in order to meet the program's requirements. They achieve these interactions by means of synchronizations and communications.

In this chapter we identified two classes of entities in a concurrent program: active ones, which must be represented as processes, and passive ones, which may also be coded as processes but may be encapsulated in a number of different ways. Passive entities have the important property that they must control how they are accessed.

We showed that even a single shared variable must be protected against concurrent access if the multiple update problem is not to lead to incorrect execution. Programming mutual exclusion over these passive entities is one of the chief difficulties of using concurrency. Without the help of further primitives, mutual exclusion can only be obtained via inefficient and error-prone structures. These difficulties form the motivation for the material in the following chapters.

A number of important terms were introduced and used in this chapter. They include multiple update, condition synchronization, livelock, deadlock, safety, liveness, fairness and busy waiting. We also introduced a number of classical problems, which are found in many treatments of concurrency and will be met again in later chapters.

FURTHER READING

Bernstein P.A., Hadzilacos V. and Goodman N. (1987). *Concurrency Control and Recovery in Database Systems*. Addison-Wesley

Deitel H.M. (1984). *An Introduction to Operating Systems*. Addison-Wesley

Hoare C.A.R. (1985). *Communicating Sequential Processes*. Prentice-Hall

Lamport L. (1986). The Mutual Exclusion Program. *Journal of ACM*, **33**(2), 313–26

Milner R. (1989). *Communication and Concurrency*. Prentice-Hall

Raynal M. (1986). *Algorithms for Mutual Exclusion*. MIT Press

Welsh J., Elder J. and Bustard D. (1988). *Concurrent Program Structures*. Prentice-Hall

Whiddett D. (1987). *Concurrent Programming for Software Engineers*. Ellis Horwood

Young S.J. (1982). *Real-Time Languages: Design and Development*. Ellis Horwood

EXERCISES

3.1   In Section 3.3, we said that the update of a variable would be accomplished on most current hardware by three separate operations. How many possible interleavings are there when two processes concurrently execute the update on a uniprocessor? How many of them lead to the 'loss' of an increment?

3.2   Given that the Pascal-FC compiler generates these three instructions when the counter is updated by a process in the gardens1 program of Section 3.2, what is the minimum value that you would expect the counter to have when the program completes? What is the maximum value for the counter?

3.3   In Section 3.4.1, we showed a solution to a 'primitive' version of the producer–consumer problem complying with Requirement 3.1a. Modify the program so that it meets Requirements 3.1b and 3.2a.

3.4   Adapt Peterson's algorithm so that three processes wish to gain access to the critical section.

3.5   The following attempts to show how two processes can pass data (without blocking) using two slots for the data:

```
program twoslots;
  type data = record
    A : integer;
    B : integer;
    C : integer
  end;
```

```
var twoslot : array[false..true] of data;
    slot : boolean;

process writer;
  var I : integer;
      D : data;
begin
  for I := 1 to 30 do
  begin
    twoslot[slot].A := I;
    twoslot[slot].B := I;
    twoslot[slot].C := I;
    slot := not slot
  end
end;

process reader;
  var I : integer;
      D : data;
begin
  for I := 1 to 40 do
  begin
    write(twoslot[not slot].A);
    write(twoslot[not slot].B);
    write(twoslot[not slot].C);
    writeln
  end
end;

begin
  slot := true;
  twoslot[false].A := 0;        (* initial value *)
  twoslot[false].B := 0;
  twoslot[false].C := 0;
  cobegin
    writer;
    reader
  coend
end.
```

The data is coded as a record so that atomic updates are clearly not possible. Boolean variables can, however, be assumed to be updated atomically. Does this program possess safety and liveness?

3.6   The following complete Pascal-FC program implements Simpson's 4-slot algorithm for information exchange between a single reader process and a single writer process. Neither process busy waits; instead the reader process will get immediate access to an old version if the writer process is currently updating the 'shared' data. Four slots for the data are needed so that no interleaving will break mutual exclusion on any copy of the data:

```
program simpson;
   type data = record
      A : integer;
      B : integer;
      C : integer
   end;
   var fourslot : array[false..true,false..true] of data;
       slot : array[false..true] of boolean;
       reading, latest : boolean;

   process writer;
      var I : integer;
          D : data;
          pair, index : boolean;
   begin
      for I := 1 to 30 do
      begin
         pair := not reading;
         index := not slot[pair];
         fourslot[pair,index].A := I;
         fourslot[pair,index].B := I;
         fourslot[pair,index].C := I;
         slot[pair] := index;
         latest := pair
      end
   end;

   process reader;
      var I : integer;
          D : data;
          pair, index : boolean;
   begin
      for I := 1 to 40 do
      begin
         pair := latest;
         reading := pair;
         index := slot[pair];
         write(fourslot[pair,index].A);
         write(fourslot[pair,index].B);
         write(fourslot[pair,index].C);
         writeln
      end
   end;

begin
   reading := false;
   latest := false;
   slot[false] := false;
   fourslot[false,false].A := 0;      (* initial value *)
```

```
        fourslot[false,false].B := 0;
        fourslot[false,false].C := 0;
        cobegin
           writer;
           reader
        coend
     end.
```

Study the algorithm. Does it possess safety and liveness?

3.7   In the game of chess, a series of moves can be repeated. Is this a livelock? How do the rules of chess deal with this problem?

3.8   In a crowded railway station, people trying to get off a train can be prevented from doing so by people getting on (who also cannot move). Is this a deadlock? What are the resources in contention? How is this deadlock potential usually dealt with?

4 Synchronous Message Passing

If shared variables are not to be used, then a language must employ message passing. One process will SEND a message and another process will WAIT for it to arrive. Surprisingly, the definition of these SEND and WAIT operations can be based on a variety of independent factors, giving rise to many different models of these message-passing primitives. In this chapter a basic rendezvous model is described. This model has been chosen as it closely resembles that found in the language occam (INMOS, 1984) and the formalism CSP (Hoare, 1985).

In order to increase the expressive power of this message-based model it is necessary to allow a process to choose between alternative communications. This non-deterministic language feature is discussed in detail in this chapter.

4.1 Alternative language models

A language designer wishing to incorporate message passing into a new language is faced with a variety of options. The main issues that we consider are:

- what form of synchronization, if any, to use;
- how to name source and destination processes.

4.1.1 Synchronization

The first, and most significant, factor concerns the behaviour of the process that executes the SEND. Three main alternatives exist:

- asynchronous send
- synchronous send (simple rendezvous)
- remote invocation (extended rendezvous).

If the sender is delayed until the corresponding WAIT is executed then the message passing is said to be synchronous. Alternatively, if the SENDing process continues executing arbitrarily then the communication is termed asynchronous. The drawback with the asynchronous method is that the receiving process cannot know anything about the present state of the calling process; it only has information on some previous state. Indeed, it is even possible that the calling process has terminated before its message is read. In addition, the sending process does not know directly if the message sent has ever been received.

Where a reply message is generated, it is possible for the process executing a synchronous SEND to be delayed further until this reply is received. This structure, known as remote invocation, is discussed in the next chapter.

To appreciate the difference between these approaches, consider the following analogy. The posting of a letter is an asynchronous send – once the letter has been put into the letter box the sender proceeds with his or her life. Only by the return of another letter can the sender ever know that the first letter actually arrived. From the receiver's point of view, a letter can only inform the reader about an out-of-date event; it says nothing about the current position of the sender. A fax machine is an appropriate analogy for synchronous communication. The sender waits until contact is made and the identity of the receiver verified before the message is sent. When transmission is complete, the sender continues. An analogy for remote invocation is the telephone. The sender waits not only for the message to be transmitted, but also for a reply to be returned.

Because the sender and receiver 'come together' for a synchronized communication it is often called a **rendezvous**. The remote invocation form is known as an **extended rendezvous**, as arbitrary computations can be undertaken before the reply is sent (i.e. during the rendezvous).

4.1.2 Naming

Another important issue in the design of a message-based programming language is how destinations and sources are designated. There are two independent decisions that the language designer may consider here:

- whether naming is direct or indirect;
- whether the naming scheme is symmetrical or asymmetrical.

The simplest form is for unique names to be given to all processes in the system; a SEND operation will then directly name the destination processes:

    SEND message TO ProcessName

A symmetric form for the receiving process would be:

    WAIT message FROM ProcessName

This symmetric form requires the receiver to know the name of any process liable to send it a message. By contrast, an asymmetric form may be used if the receiver is only interested in the existence of a message, rather than from where it came:

    WAIT message

This asymmetric form is particularly useful when the nature of the relationship between the two processes fits the client/server paradigm. The server process renders some utility to any client process that requires it (though usually only one client at a time). Clearly the client must name the server when sending a request message, but the server need not know the identity of the caller unless a reply message must be sent.

Where the unique naming of all processes is inappropriate, a language may define intermediaries (usually called mailboxes or channels) that are named by both partners in the communication. The naming is then said to be indirect:

    SEND message TO mailbox
    WAIT message FROM mailbox

Again there are a number of forms that a mailbox may take. A single mailbox could be defined to be used by many receivers and many senders, one receiver and many senders or one receiver and one sender. Moreover, it may be structured to pass information in both directions or in only one.

Finally, the message itself could be complex (such as a structured data type) or simple (such as a 16-bit word).

4.2 Selective waiting

With all of the above message structure the receiving process, by executing a WAIT, commits itself to the synchronization and will be suspended if no message is immediately available. This is, in general, too restrictive; the receiving process may wish to choose between a number of possible message sources. Within this structure it may also wish temporarily to restrict the sources over which it wishes to exercise this choice. These two properties lead to a language structure in which a process selects one of a set of alternative input or output messages, each of which may be guarded to impose a condition synchronization. For example, if a buffer process communicated with its clients via messages, then guards could be used to inhibit the processing of PLACE messages when the buffer is full or a TAKE message when it is empty. During normal operation (i.e. when the buffer is neither empty nor full) the buffer process will deal with either PLACE or TAKE messages, depending on which is outstanding.

4.3 Communication by channel

In this chapter we describe a model for synchronous message passing which resembles that found in occam (INMOS, 1984) and the formalism CSP (Hoare, 1985). Processes interact via named channels. The send and receive operations use the terse syntax found in these languages:

```
ch ! e    (* send the value of the expression e *)
          (* to the channel ch *)
ch ? v    (* receive from channel, ch, a value *)
          (* and assign it to variable v *)
```

The operations on the channel are synchronized. Whichever process arrives at the channel action first will be blocked until the other process arrives. When both processes are ready, a rendezvous is said to take place, with data passing from the expression e to the variable v. One way of considering this behaviour is to view it as a distributed assignment:

```
v := e
```

where the v is in one process and the e is in another. The named channel can only be used by a single sender and a single receiver; the communication is point-to-point.

More formally we can denote the use of a channel ch (for reading or writing) by the event 'ch'. For two processes (P and Q) to communicate via this channel, the ch event must be in both alphabets:

$$ch \in \alpha P$$
$$ch \in \alpha Q$$

We can denote the action of communication in two ways. To illustrate both, consider processes that have as their first action the channel operations:

$$P = (ch!e \rightarrow P')$$
$$Q = (ch?v \rightarrow Q'(v))$$

P, for example, first sends a value down channel ch and then behaves like P'. The expression Q'(v) merely notes that the behaviour of Q is potentially dependent on the value of the variable v, which it obtained from the channel.

If P and Q are composed by the concurrency operator, then the following laws apply:

$$P \parallel Q = (ch!e \rightarrow P') \parallel (ch?v \rightarrow Q'(v)) = ch!e \rightarrow (P' \parallel Q'(e))$$
$$P \parallel Q = ((ch!e \rightarrow P') \parallel (ch?v \rightarrow Q'(v))) \backslash ch = P' \parallel Q'(e)$$

The first law retains the channel write as the event that must occur before P' and Q' can proceed. The second law conceals the channel completely; it is of no concern to any process other than P and Q. Concealment is achieved by the '\ch' notation. In both laws the behaviour of Q' becomes dependent on e (as delivered by P).

In earlier chapters the problem of livelock was introduced. Previously it involved a number of processes all busy waiting for a shared variable to change. Now it is possible for processes to involve themselves in communications but still be unable to make constructive progress. For example, the following two processes are engaged in an endless (pointless) dance:

$$P = (ch1!e \rightarrow ch2?v \rightarrow P)$$
$$Q = (ch1?w \rightarrow ch2!f \rightarrow Q)$$

Note that the behaviour of P and Q is not dependent on the variables read down the respective channels. This is also true in the next, even simpler, example of livelock:

$$P = (ch1!e \rightarrow P)$$
$$Q = (ch1?w \rightarrow Q)$$

Clearly in both examples $P \parallel Q$ is useless.

4.4 Pascal-FC's channel model

In a strongly typed language like Pascal, an assignment is only legal if the expression and the variable are of the same type. This is also true with the message-passing primitive in Pascal-FC. The channel is declared at the beginning of the program (i.e. before the two processes that will use it) to have a *base type*. Example declarations are:

```
var link : channel of integer;

type packet =
  record
      (* some suitable structure *)
  end;
var network : channel of packet;

type IntChans = channel of integer;
var ch1, ch2 : IntChans;
```

The compiler will ensure that each channel is used correctly.

A single channel will only pass a single item of data (per rendezvous) between one sender process and one receiver process. The data item may be structured (a record or an array), but it is exchanged as a single logical operation. A sketch program which illustrates simple message passing between two processes follows:

```
program sketch;
type IntChan = channel of integer;
var ch1 : IntChan;
  process P;
  var item : integer;
  begin
    repeat
      ...
      ch1 ? item;
      ...
    forever
  end;

  process Q;
  begin
    repeat
      ...
      ch1 ! 42;
      ...
    forever
  end;
```

```
begin
    cobegin
        P; Q
    coend
end.
```

P and Q loop indefinitely with Q passing the value '42' to P on each iteration. The processes are synchronized at this point and hence must iterate at the same rate. The reader will recognize that this synchronization effects the simple producer–consumer relationship considered in the previous chapter.

To give a more complete example, a program for generating prime numbers will be developed. The program uses a pipeline of concurrent filter processes in order to implement a sieve. The structure of the algorithm is given in Figure 4.1. Before going into details it is worth noting the way a simple diagram can be used to represent the behaviour of a system of concurrent processes that interact using messages only. The boxes in Figure 4.1 define processes and the arrows indicate synchronous message passing. Obviously the direction of the arrow shows the direction of the information flow.

The process sieve works by the numbers process generating a series of integers starting at 2 (i.e. 2, 3, 4, . . .). Each of the filter processes obtains a prime number as the first integer it receives from its neighbour on the left. It is then passed a series of larger integers. If it can divide any of these integers exactly, it discards it: otherwise it passes it on. Each filter element uses a different divisor (the prime number it receives as the first message from its neighbour on the left). In this way the first process keeps the value 2 and subsequently discards all other even numbers. The second process gets the integer 3 and will discard 9, 15, 21, etc. (all even numbers having been filtered out by its neighbour to the left).

The above scheme allows N filter processes to store the first N prime numbers. They can then output these values to the outproc process, which will print the values. The consumer process will catch any integer passing through the sieve.

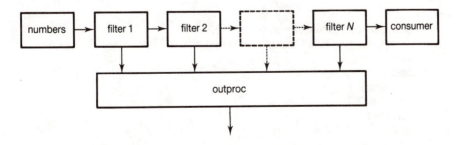

Figure 4.1 A prime number generator.

We shall construct the program by first considering what channels are needed and then the necessary process types. Figure 4.1 indicates that there are $N + 1$ channels needed in the pipeline that flows from numbers through each filter to consumer. In addition, N channels are needed for the filters to communicate their values to the concentrator (outproc). These declarations are as follows:

```
type chan = channel of integer;
     chans = array[0..N] of chan;
var pipeline : chans;
    output : chans;     (* 1 more channel than necessary! *)
```

Four process types are required, with N instances of the filter process being declared. Each of these processes needs initialization values to indicate which channels to use in the pipeline (i.e. which channels to interact with). Note that in this version of the program, the system of processes does not terminate when the prime numbers have been generated. To program termination requires a new language construct – the **select** statement. This will be introduced in the next section. It will then be left as an exercise to change the sieve program so that it terminates correctly.

The numbers process is straightforward, and is written as follows:

```
process numbers(var out : chan);
    (* produces a string of integers *)
var I : integer;
begin
  I := 2;
  repeat
    out ! I;
    I := I + 1
  forever
end;
```

The consumer process is similarly straightforward. It is needed because the program does not terminate, and hence some integers will pass through the sieve:

```
process consumer(var into : chan);
    (* consumes all integers passing through the sieve *)
var I : integer;
begin
  repeat
    into ? I
  forever
end;
```

The outproc simply loops round and prints out each integer it receives:

```
process outproc(var outs : chans);
    (* generates output for the program *)
var I, Num : integer;
begin
  for I := 1 to N do
  begin
    outs[I] ? Num;
    writeln(Num)
  end
end;
```

Finally, the process type for the important filter element can be developed; this is coded as a type, as *N* instances must be declared (as an array):

```
process type elements(var left, right, down : chan);
    (* implements one filter item *)
var p,q: integer;
begin
  left ? p;
  down ! p;
  repeat
    left ? q;
    if (q mod p <> 0) then
      right ! q
  forever
end;

var filters : array[1..N] of elements;
```

The complete program structure, including the **cobegin/coend** statement, can now be assembled. It is outlined below. All executions of this program produce the required number of prime numbers and then livelock (and eventually time out):

```
program primes;
const N = 10;

type chan = channel of integer;
     chans = array[0..N] of chan;
var pipeline : chans;
    output : chans;
    I : integer;

process numbers(var out : chan); ...
process consumer(var into : chan); ...
process type elements(var left, right, down : chan); ...
process outproc(var outs : chans); ...

var filters : array[1..N] of elements;
```

```
begin
  cobegin
    numbers(pipeline[0]);
    consumer(pipeline[N]);
    for I := 1 to N do
      filters[I](pipeline[I−1],pipeline[I],output[I]);
    outproc(output)
  coend
end.
```

The sieve program was developed in stages in the above description to illustrate the software development process. First a network of communicating processes is generated. From this the channel structures and process types can be defined. The **cobegin/coend** allows the complete network to be 'wired up' correctly. An examination of the data structures involved defines the type of the data that each channel must communicate. Having defined these top-level structures, each process type can be considered in isolation from any other process in the system. This isolation is a result of the fact that the only way a process can interact with another process is via the channels; there are no shared variables to complicate the process model.

In this example we have defined the interface to each process by using channel parameters. Alternatively we could have just passed an integer to each filter process and have it calculate which channels to use (see the Dining Philosophers example later in this chapter). Note that if channel parameters are used (which increases the readability of the programs), they must be **var** parameters.

4.4.1 Synchronous channels

The message-passing rendezvous is a single primitive that combines synchronization and data communication. In the situation in which only synchronization is needed, a dummy piece of data would have to be communicated. This can lead to confusion for someone reading the program at a later date. Pascal-FC allows the intention of the programmer to be clearly expressed by introducing a special base type for such *contentless* communication.

The type synchronous is predefined. The only operations allowed on the type are reads and writes on a 'channel of synchronous'. There are no values associated with the type. A variable called any, of type synchronous, is automatically declared by the compiler for every program. It is intended that this variable is used on the right hand side of all channel operations when the channel is of type synchronous. Although the programmer can declare and use other variables, the use of any is recommended for readability. The following sketch code illustrates how one process (starter) can be used to delay and then release two (worker) processes:

```
    program starters;
    type syn = channel of synchronous;
         barriers = array[1..2] of syn;

    var barrier : barriers;

    process starter;
      var I : integer;
    begin
      . . .
      for I := 1 to 2 do
        barrier[I] ! any;
      . . .
    end;

    process type worker(num : integer);
    begin
      . . .
      barrier[num] ? any;
      . . .
    end;

    var workers : array[1..2] of worker;
      . . .
```

Each worker will be delayed at the barrier until the starter process releases it.

4.5   The select construct

In this section we introduce the important selective wait construct. A message-based language without a **select** construct can be compared to a sequential language without an **if** statement: it is seriously impaired and severely limits the range of solutions the programmer can use. We shall illustrate the need for this construct by considering one solution to the Ornamental Gardens problem introduced in the previous chapter.

As all passive entities must be represented by processes in our message-based model, the visitor-counting variable must be embodied in a process that serializes accesses to it. The following program represents a solution to the problem. It is correct in the sense that the value of count is always correct. There is, however, a serious flaw in the system design (i.e. in the architecture of process interaction):

```
    program gardens3a;
    var path1, path2 : channel of integer;
```

```
process turnstile1;
var
  loop : integer;
begin
  for loop := 1 to 20 do
    path1 ! 1
end;     (* turnstile1 *)

process turnstile2;
var loop: integer;
begin
  for loop := 1 to 20 do
    path2 ! 1
end;     (* turnstile2 *)

process counter;
var count : integer;
    I, temp : integer;
begin
  count := 0;
  for I := 1 to 20 do
  begin
    path1 ? temp;
    count := count + temp;
    path2 ? temp;
    count := count + temp
  end;
  writeln('Total admitted: ',count)
end;

begin
  cobegin
    counter;
    turnstile1;
    turnstile2
  coend
end.
```

The (obvious) drawback is that the controller process (counter) insists that visitors enter at the same rate through the two turnstiles. Once a ticket has been sold at turnstile1 another cannot be issued until someone has bought a ticket at turnstile2. This is clearly, in general, an unacceptable solution. The problem is that the controller should interact with the other processes 'as required', not in an order predefined and embodied in the program. If more people come to turnstile1 then more tickets should be sold there: the controller needs to react dynamically to the incoming calls. To do this, a non-deterministic selective wait construct is needed. However, before giving the Pascal-FC version of this feature, a discussion on non-determinacy is needed, and this we shall present in the next section.

Note that the use of an array of channels and process types can reduce the code size of programs. The above (poor) program can be written equivalently as:

```
program gardens3b;
type path = channel of integer;
var paths : array[1..2] of path;

process type turnstile(name, num : integer);
var loop: integer;
begin
  for loop := 1 to num do
    paths[name] ! 1
end;     (* turnstile *)

var turnstiles : array[1..2] of turnstile;

process counter;
var count : integer;
    I, J, temp : integer;
begin
  count := 0;
  for I := 1 to 20 do
    for J := 1 to 2 do
    begin
      paths[J] ? temp;
      count := count + temp
    end;
  writeln('Total admitted: ',count)
end;

begin
  cobegin
    counter;
    turnstiles[1](1,20);
    turnstiles[2](2,20)
  coend
end.
```

4.5.1 Non-determinism

It was noted in Chapter 1 that a concurrent program only defines a partial ordering of the computational events defined in the program. By denoting process P and Q to be concurrent:

$$P \parallel Q$$

we indicate that the scheduler can choose which process to execute first (if, for example, only a single processor is available). The program can be considered to possess a level of non-determinism, as the order of executing is not fully defined. A program is also defined to be non-deterministic if the environment's behaviour is not fully predefined in terms of the expected order of inputs (interrupts). In both of these examples, however, each process is itself deterministic (it is, after all, just a sequence of instructions).

It is useful to extend the concept of non-determinism to the process level if, at some level of abstraction, the process seems to have a level of 'free choice'. For example, a process that must output two values may have a choice as to the order in which they are actually produced. The choice is made internally by the process itself, and is not directly controlled by the process environment. Indeed, if we view the process from the outside, we cannot predict which choice it will make on any one occasion.

The situation in which non-determinism is particularly important for a process is in process interaction. CSP uses the symbol $\square$ to signify non-deterministic choice. Consider the following:

$$P = X \ \square \ Y$$

This implies that P can act as X if the conditions for X are possible, or Y if it is possible. If both X and Y are possible then a non-deterministic choice will be made between X and Y. What is meant by X or Y 'being possible' is best explained with a more concrete example that is closer to our needs:

$$P = (ch1 \ ? \ a \rightarrow Q(a)) \ \square \ (ch2 \ ? \ b \rightarrow R(b))$$

This formalism is interpreted as follows. Process P has a choice: it can input a value down channel ch1 (into variable a) and then behave as process Q; or it can take a value from ch2 into b and proceed as R. (The parameters to Q and R indicate that their behaviour may depend on the value of the data received.) Whether it can input a value down ch1 (or ch2) is totally dependent on some other process wishing to write on this channel. If both alternatives are possible (i.e. a process wishing to write to ch1 and a process wishing to communicate down ch2), then a non-deterministic choice is made.

The formalism above is misleading in that it implies that the behaviour of P will diverge forever at the choice. Although this is theoretically possible, most 'real' processes converge again:

$$P = (ch1 \ ? \ a \rightarrow Q(a)) \ \square \ (ch2 \ ? \ b \rightarrow R(b))$$
$$Q = Q'T$$
$$R = R'T$$

Whatever path is taken P will eventually behave as T. If T is then defined recursively on P, a cyclic process has been defined:

$$T = T'P$$

As processes can interact with their environments either via channel input or channel output, the following are also possible:

$$P = (ch1 \ ! \ a \rightarrow Q) \ \square \ (ch2 \ ! \ b \rightarrow R)$$
$$P = (ch1 \ ! \ a \rightarrow Q) \ \square \ (ch2 \ ? \ b \rightarrow R)$$

To give a clear example of non-deterministic behaviour, consider the following:

$$P \ \| \ R$$
$$P = (ch1 \ ! \ a \rightarrow Q) \ \square \ (ch2 \ ! \ a \rightarrow Q)$$
$$R = (ch1 \ ? \ b \rightarrow S(b)) \ \square \ (ch2 \ ? \ c \rightarrow S(c))$$

P will end up behaving as Q, with the value of expression a having been communicated. R will similarly act as S, with S using the value of a. But which channel was used? Was it ch1 or ch2? There is, in fact, no way of knowing, nor should there be. Indeed, we can formulate the following rule:

> The correct behaviour of a concurrent program should not depend on the behaviour of any choice statements.

This rule is identical in spirit to the one given in Chapter 2 concerning the behaviour of the scheduler. Again it must be emphasized that the temporal behaviour of a real-time program will depend on all choice statements and scheduling decisions.

It is important to understand that non-determinism is only meaningful at the level of abstraction appropriate for considering process interactors. If one looked in detail at the actual implementation, then some form of deterministic behaviour would be apparent. In the above example it could be that ch1 is always chosen. Non-deterministic choice should not be confused with a random choice (or a 'fair' choice – whatever that might mean). It is merely a statement that, at the level of program semantics, the choice is not defined.

In this more formal treatment of language semantics we can observe that the choice operator is associative:

$$P \ \square \ (R \ \square \ S) = (P \ \square \ R) \ \square \ S = P \ \square \ R \ \square \ S$$

and symmetric:

$$P \ \square \ R = R \ \square \ P$$

In this way it is similar to the concurrency construct itself. Finally, we can note some useful relationships between both of these operators and the null (SKIP) process:

$$P \parallel SKIP = P$$
$$P \; \Box \; SKIP = SKIP$$

The latter is particularly important. It means that if there is a choice between some arbitrary process and the SKIP process, then it is totally acceptable for the SKIP (which is always ready) to be chosen.

4.6 Selective waiting in Pascal-FC

The select construct available to Pascal-FC is a very general one. It encompasses all the features found in different languages. As such it has a number of facets that will be introduced one at a time through this section. A full definition of the syntax is given in Appendix A.

We can first return to the Ornamental Gardens problem and allow the counter process to choose between the two input possibilities:

```
process counter;
var count : integer;
    I, J, temp : integer;
begin
  count := 0;
  for I := 1 to 40 do
  begin
    select
      paths[1] ? temp;      (* note ";" is needed *)
    or
      paths[2] ? temp
    end;    (* select *)
    count := count + temp
  end;
  writeln('Total admitted: ',count)
end;
```

The counter will respond to whichever process wishes to call it. If there is more than one outstanding call then one will be chosen. To emphasize the non-deterministic behaviour of the **select** statement, Pascal-FC uses a random algorithm to choose. This is to give illustrative behaviour and to help isolate incorrect programs that have assumed a particular behaviour on the part of the **select** (i.e. the errors have a good chance of manifesting themselves). However, the point about random *versus* non-deterministic behaviour made above must be borne in mind.

In general a **select** statement can have any number of alternatives (separated by **or**s). The execution of the **select** is synonymous with the execution of exactly one alternative. After the channel operation that distinguishes the alternative, any number of further statements can be given. For example, the **select** statement above could have been written as:

```
select
  paths[1] ? temp;
  count := count + temp;
or
  paths[2] ? temp;
  count := count + temp
end    (* select *)
```

Where the selection is between elements from an array of channels, an abridged syntax is supported by Pascal-FC. That is, rather than:

```
select
  chan[1] ? V[1];
or
  chan[2] ? V[2];
or
  chan[3] ? V[3];
or
  chan[4] ? V[4];
or
  chan[5] ? V[5];
or
  another ? T
end
```

the following can be written:

```
select
  for I := 1 to 5 replicate
  chan[I] ? V[I];
or
  another ? T
end
```

The selection of one message read alternative is the simplest form for the **select** statement. In general, each alternative within a **select** statement can be of one of four types:

(1)   message read alternative
(2)   message write alternative
(3)   **timeout** alternative
(4)   **terminate** alternative.

In addition there may be a default **else** alternative.

If, when a **select** is executed, there are no ready alternatives (for example, no customers in the Ornamental Gardens problem), then the process executing the **select** is suspended until one of the alternatives becomes ready (unless there is an **else** part).

4.6.1 Guarded alternatives

A **select** statement, although it has a number of alternatives, may not wish all alternatives to be available on every execution. To illustrate this requirement we shall look at a common process idiom: the buffer process. Figure 4.2 shows the interaction of two active processes: a producer and a consumer. As explained in Chapter 3, irregularities in the rates of production and consumption are often smoothed out by interposing a buffer between these active components.

Buffer processes are common in concurrent systems. They are, in general, passive entities (i.e. in our example they act only in response to the producer or consumer). In the current language model a buffer is represented as a process with a two-channel interface. We assume that only integers are being communicated in this example. The following gives a first (incomplete) attempt at the code for a buffer process:

```
type intchan = channel of integer;

process buffer(var put, get : intchan);
var BUFF : array[0..31] of integer;
    TOP, BASE : integer;
begin
  TOP := 0;
  BASE := 0;
  repeat
    select
      put ? BUFF[TOP];
      TOP := (TOP + 1 ) mod 32;
    or
      get ! BUFF[BASE];
      BASE := (BASE + 1 ) mod 32
    end
  forever
end;
```

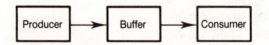

Figure 4.2 Producer/consumer system.

The **select** has two alternatives: one a channel input and the other a channel output. If the producer process wishes to write to the buffer, then the first alternative can be taken and the assignment into the buffer is made. Similarly, if the consumer wishes to extract an item, then the second alternative is chosen. If both consumer and producer are suspended waiting for the buffer, then a non-deterministic choice is made.

The buffer is constructed as a circular array. One pointer shows where the next free slot is; the other shows the next item to be extracted. The semantics of the buffer are FIFO (first in first out). An astute reader may have questioned why the buffer is programmed as a process. As the producer and consumer processes update different pointers there can be no multiple update problem. This is true for the code just given, but is not true for the refinement that must be made (see below). It is also not the case if the buffer has to deal with more than one producer or more than one consumer (as often occurs).

Although the buffer is a passive entity, it must protect itself against two forms of misuse:

- a consumer process attempting to read from an empty buffer;
- a producer process trying to write to a full buffer.

These both imply necessary condition synchronization on buffer usage.

A message-based language model caters for these condition synchronizations by avoiding process interactions when the conditions are not appropriate. This is accomplished by the use of **guards** on the **select** alternatives. A guard is a boolean expression that is evaluated (once) at the start of the execution of the **select** statement. If the guard evaluates to TRUE, then the alternative is said to be *open*; FALSE guards are termed *closed*. Any alternative for which the guard is closed is ignored for the remainder of that execution of the **select** statement. Note that an alternative without a guard is always open. A guard has the following syntax:

when *boolean_*expression =>

With the use of guards, the buffer process can now be coded correctly:

```
process buffer(var put, get : intchan);
var BUFF : array[0..31] of integer;
    TOP, BASE : integer;
    CONTENTS : integer;
begin
  TOP := 0;
  BASE := 0;
  CONTENTS := 0;
```

```
repeat
  select
    when CONTENTS < 32 =>
    put ? BUFF[TOP];
    TOP := (TOP + 1 ) mod 32;
    CONTENTS := CONTENTS + 1;
  or
    when CONTENTS > 0 =>
    get ! BUFF[BASE];
    BASE := (BASE + 1 ) mod 32;
    CONTENTS := CONTENTS − 1
  end
forever
end;
```

It is important to remember that each guard is only evaluated once per execution of the **select** (at the beginning). They are not re-evaluated when a call comes in. It must also be the case that at least one alternative is open, otherwise the process would be blocked for ever. In the buffer example, at least one guard will be true unless BUFF has no elements!

4.6.2   The terminate alternative

The buffer example is also useful in illustrating the application of the **terminate** alternative. Recall that a set of entities contained in a concurrent program can be classified as either active or passive. With the message-passing language model, all active and passive entities are encoded as processes. Where this distinction is particularly important is in programming termination (for programs that are required to terminate).

Active processes control their own execution and hence will terminate when their internal state requires it. The issue is more problematic with passive processes. Ideally they should terminate when 'no longer needed by any active process'. If this must be programmed, then each passive process must keep track of which other processes are using it and then be told by each of them that they guarantee never to call again. When each active process has signed off, the passive entity can terminate by branching to the end of its sequence of statements.

In the case of complicated programs, the programming of termination has been shown to be problematic (Burns, 1988). If the correct order of termination is not used, it is easy to introduce the error of a passive process terminating too early, with the result that an active process becomes blocked indefinitely and the program deadlocks.

To remove these problem areas, the **terminate** alternative has been introduced into the **select** construct. Passive processes incorporate this construct into their process interactions. Hence, rather than the simple channel read:

```
    in ? SomeVariable
```

the following code is used:

```
    select
        in ? SomeVariable;
    or
        terminate
    end
```

The semantics of the **terminate** alternative do not imply that the 'owner' task will terminate if there is no outstanding call – this is a common misunderstanding when first encountering this construct. The actual semantics are as follows:

> The process executing the **select** with the **terminate** alternative will terminate if, and only if, there are no outstanding calls and all the other processes that could call are either already terminated or are waiting on a **select** statement with a **terminate** alternative.

In Pascal-FC, with its flat process structure, the implementation of these semantics is easy. If the scheduler finds that there are no executable processes, then one of three situations must have arisen:

(1)   all processes have terminated;

(2)   some processes are suspended on channel operators or simple **select**s (those without the **terminate** alternative);

(3)   all non-terminated processes are suspended on **select** statements with **terminate** alternatives.

Condition 1 is clearly acceptable: the **cobegin/coend** structure can itself be terminated and the second sequential part of the program can proceed. Condition 2 corresponds to a system deadlock – the program must be abandoned (with an appropriate post-mortem dump). The third condition is not an error; all the suspended processes can be terminated and the sequential part of the program recommenced.

With the introduction of the **select** statement and its **terminate** alternative, it is now appropriate to extend the state diagram for a process. Figure 4.3 does this. There are now five ways to become blocked:

(1)   execute the sleep procedure;

(2)   execute a channel read when no other process currently wishes to write to that channel;

(3)   execute a channel write when no other process currently wishes to read from that channel;

(4)   execute a simple **select** statement in which no open alternative can immediately lead to a rendezvous;

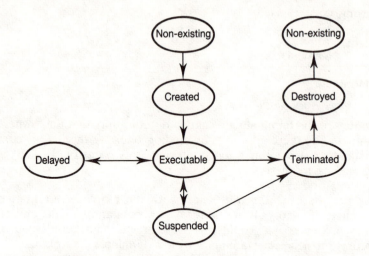

Figure 4.3 Complete state diagram for a process.

(5)   execute a **select** statement with a **terminate** alternative in which no open alternative can immediately lead to a rendezvous.

In Figure 4.3, 'suspended' has been used to refer to all but the first of these alternatives. Note that the possibility of direct movement from 'suspended' to 'terminated' is a result of alternative (5).

Our buffer process is a perfect example of a passive entity that should be terminated when no longer used:

```
process buffer(var put, get : intchan);
var BUFF : array[0..31] of integer;
    TOP, BASE : integer;
    CONTENTS : integer;
begin
  TOP := 0;
  BASE := 0;
  CONTENTS := 0;
  repeat
    select
      when CONTENTS < 32 =>
      put ? BUFF[TOP];
      TOP := (TOP + 1 ) mod 32;
      CONTENTS := CONTENTS + 1;
    or
      when CONTENTS > 0 =>
      get ! BUFF[BASE];
      BASE := (BASE + 1 ) mod 32;
      CONTENTS := CONTENTS − 1;
```

```
        or
           terminate
        end
     forever
  end;
```

If the producer and consumer both terminate, the buffer process will terminate even if there are still data in BUFF. At least this means that if the consumer has terminated too early, this error is not exacerbated by a deadlock ensuing.

As another example, consider the counter processes in the Ornamental Gardens program. Previously it had to know how many times it must loop round before terminating. This represents poor language structure, but without a **terminate** alternative each process would need to inform the counter that it had finished:

```
process type turnstile(name, num : integer);
var loop: integer;
begin
   for loop := 1 to num do
      paths[name] ! 1;
   closedown[name] ! any
end;     (* turnstile *)
```

where closedown is an array of synchronous channels. The counter process must terminate when it has received a synchronization down both closedown channels:

```
process counter;
var count : integer;
    I, J, temp : integer;
    continue : array[1..2] of boolean;
begin
   count := 0;
   continue[1] := true;
   continue[2] := true;
   while continue[1] or continue[2] do
      select
         paths[1] ? temp;
         count := count + temp;
      or
         paths[2] ? temp;
         count := count + temp;
      or
         closedown[1] ? any;
         continue[1] := false;
      or
         closedown[2] ? any;
```

```
              continue[2] := false
            end;     (* select *)
          writeln('Total admitted: ',count)
        end;
```

With a **terminate** alternative, the code is much more straightforward and less error-prone. It does not rely on programmed termination:

```
        process counter;
        var count : integer;
            I, J, temp : integer;
        begin
          count := 0;
          repeat
            select
              paths[1] ? temp;
            or
              paths[2] ? temp;
            or
              terminate
            end;     (* select *)
            count := count + temp
          forever;
          writeln('Total admitted: ',count)
        end;
```

However, the program now suffers from a significant problem. Although it terminates correctly it does not produce the correct result – in fact it does not produce any result at all! This is because the writeln statement is never reached. There is not, unfortunately, any opportunity for the process to execute a last rite. To circumvent this difficulty (for server processes that must produce a result just before terminating) with Pascal-FC requires the use of a **var** parameter to the process. By making count a **var** parameter its result will be returned to the main program after termination. There it can be output:

```
          ...
        process counter(var count : integer);
        var I, J, temp : integer;
        begin
          repeat
            select
              paths[1] ? temp;
            or
              paths[2] ? temp;
            or
              terminate
```

```
      end;      (* select *)
      count := count + temp
    forever
  end;

  begin
    number := 0;
    cobegin
      counter(number);
      turnstiles[1](1,20);
      turnstiles[2](2,20)
    coend;
    writeln('Total admitted: ',number)
  end.
```

4.6.3   Else and timeout alternatives

The above discussion has focused on the main uses and semantics of the selective waiting construct. There are, however, two other features that are useful in certain situations. In particular, there are applications for which a process willing to make a rendezvous on a channel may not wish to commit itself to waiting indefinitely for the partner in the communication. Two alternatives to such indefinite waiting are:

- if a rendezvous is not immediately possible (i.e. there is no pending call on any eligible channel), then abort the call and do something else instead;

- wait for a specified maximum period for a rendezvous, but abort the call and do something else if the period expires before such a rendezvous begins.

The **else** alternative (of which there can be at most one per **select**) caters for the first of these; the **timeout** alternative caters for the second.

The **else** part can play the role of the default alternative. It is not guarded and is taken immediately if none of the other open alternatives can lead directly to a rendezvous. As a consequence, a **select** statement with an **else** part can never lead to the executing process being blocked: it either takes one of the normal alternatives or it starts executing the **else** code. The form of a **select** with an **else** part is as follows:

```
  select
    inp ? SomeVariable;
  or
    out ! SomeValue
  else
      (* arbitrary sequence of statements *)
  end
```

An **else** alternative is only of use to processes that are hybrids of passive and active entities. They must respond to inputs, but have actions of their own to undertake if no input is available.

To give an example of the use of this construct, consider the numbers process in the prime number generator example given earlier. This is an active process that just generates an increasing series of numbers:

```
process numbers(var out : chan);
    (* produces a string of integers *)
var I : integer;
begin
  I := 2;
  repeat
    out ! I;
    I := I + 1
  forever
end;
```

One approach to getting the program to stop when all the *N* numbers have been generated is to tell this numbers process to cease its activities. This can be done by a synchronization-only communication from either consumer or outproc. The **else** alternative is needed for this:

```
process numbers(var out : chan; var stopchan : synchan);
    (* produces a string of integers *)
var I : integer;
    stopnumbers : boolean;
begin
  I := 2;
  stopnumbers := false;
  while not stopnumbers do
    select
      stopchan ? any;
      stopnumbers := true
    else
      out ! I;
      I := I + 1
    end     (* select *)
end;
```

where:

```
type synchan = channel of synchronous;
```

On each iteration of this process it 'looks' to see if there is a pending communication down the stopchan channel. If there is not, then it generates another integer and passes it down the pipeline.

The **timeout** alternative is more appropriate to real-time programming, but is described here for completeness. Indefinite waits are unacceptable in embedded systems where processes will be involved in real-time interactions with the external environment. Most languages designed for embedded work allow a timeout facility; it is usual to attach this facility to the **select** statement:

```
select
   inp ? SomeVariable;
or
   timeout 3;
   (* action to be taken if timeout *)
end
```

If a rendezvous down channel inp has not begun within three seconds, the **timeout** alternative is chosen. A typical application in real-time systems is to catch a failed or tardy process. An important control process can be structured to call a 'watchdog' timer process every five seconds (for example). If the call does not come in then the watchdog process will start some error-recovery action, or at least warn the operators that the system has failed. The following program simulates this activity. A sleeper process should call in on the watchdog process every five seconds. If the sleeper process is too slow (because of the random number it uses), a 'timed out' message will be produced:

```
program timer;
var coms : channel of synchronous;

process sleeper;
var I : integer;
begin
   for I := 1 to 10 do
   begin
      sleep(random(10));
      coms ! any
   end
end;

process watchdog;
var I : integer;
    count : integer;
begin
   count := 0;
   while count < 10 do
      select
         coms ? any;
         count := count + 1;
         writeln('received');
      or
```

```
        timeout 5;
        writeln('timed out')
      end
end;

begin
  cobegin
    sleeper; watchdog
  coend
end.
```

An example of the output from this program is:

```
Program timer ... execution begins ...
timed out
received
timed out
timed out
timed out
received
received
received
received
received
timed out
timed out
timed out
received
timed out
timed out
timed out
timed out
received
timed out
timed out
timed out
received
timed out
timed out
received

Program terminated normally
```

4.6.4 Priority select

The last feature of the **select** statement (the **pri select**) allows a deterministic choice to be programmed. Consider a process that is part of a pipeline and which outputs the values it receives from its input as long as they fall in the interval $[-K,K]$. This is shown in Figure 4.4. New values for K are input

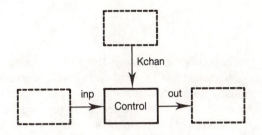

Figure 4.4 Control process.

down a 'control' channel. This basic structure for the process is typical of those found in control algorithms.

The body of the control process will contain a **select** inside an infinite loop:

```
Kchan ? K;      (* get initial K *)
repeat
  select
    Kchan ? K;
  or
    inp ? V;
    if (V <= K) and (V >=−K) then
      out ! V
  end
forever
```

The problem with this code is that the algorithm requires a new K to be taken immediately one is available. However, the semantics of the **select** statement do not define which alternative will be chosen if more than one is ready. It is possible for a valid execution of this program never to choose the Kchan alternative if the process that writes to inp is always ready to do so.

The use of the **else** alternative can help a little, but the following 'solution' is still not perfect:

```
Kchan ? K;      (* get initial K *)
repeat
  select
    Kchan ? K
  else
    null
  end;
  select
    Kchan ? K;
  or
    inp ? V;
    if (V <= K) and (V >=−K) then
      out ! V
```

```
        end
      forever
```

A new K will not necessarily be taken at the second **select**, although it will be taken at the first one during the next iteration. To give a more complete solution, a deterministic **select** is needed. The most straightforward form of this is to predefine an order to the **select** if there is more than one ready alternative. Pascal-FC supports a form of **select** that uses textual ordering. The above problem would be coded as:

```
Kchan ? K;      (* get initial K *)
repeat
  pri select
    Kchan ? K;
  or
    inp ? V;
    if (V <= K) and (V >=-K) then
      out ! V
  end
forever
```

Now if both channels are 'ready' then the Kchan alternative will be chosen. In all other respects the **pri select** acts identically to the ordinary **select**. In particular, if the process is suspended waiting for any call, then the first to arrive at an open alternative will be chosen. Some languages (e.g. Concurrent C) have even proposed a dynamic (i.e. run-time) method of determining the priority of each alternative. The static scheme, however, is adequate for our needs.

4.6.5 Consistent select statements

Pascal-FC enforces the rule that all **select** statements must have at least one channel alternative (input or output). An examination of the other three kinds of alternatives reveals that it is futile to mix them. An **else** alternative is taken immediately, and so no **timeout** alternative will ever be taken. Moreover, the **terminate** alternative assumes that the process is suspended (indefinitely): hence neither **timeout** nor **else** makes sense. Pascal-FC therefore prohibits mixing of the **else**, **timeout** or **terminate** alternatives in a single **select**.

4.7 Concurrency and non-determinism

In this section we again wish to look at the notions of concurrency and non-determinism. One way of looking at the selective wait construct is to view it as a low-level concurrency construct. Each of the alternatives represents a competing thread of control. At the start of the execution, certain threads are disqualified because of closed guards. The rest are ready to go. Unlike the true concurrency construct, the first thread to start execution cancels the others. For a channel input or output, this occurs when another process requests a rendezvous down that channel; for a **timeout** alternative it is when the delay expires. For the **terminate** alternative it is when conditions are right for termination. The only exception to this rule is the **else** alternative. As it is always ready to execute it must not compete on equal terms with the other alternatives. Remember one of the rules given for the choice operator:

P □ SKIP = SKIP

The **else** thread must only be allowed to win if none of the others makes an immediate start.

At this stage it is constructive to ask whether concurrency and non-determinism are equivalent. Both notions seem to embody the idea that the order of execution is not relevant to correct execution. If the notions are equivalent then, for two *atomic* events a and b, we are saying that:

a ‖ b = a → b □ b → a

A non-deterministic choice between executing a then b or b then a is the same as executing a and b concurrently. On a single processor there must be an interleaving for the execution of a and b and hence concurrency and non-deterministic ordering are equivalent. However, on a multiprocessor system there is an important distinction between the two ideas. We have defined concurrency to mean, essentially, independence. Hence a and b could be executed simultaneously. The notion of simultaneous events is missing from the notion of non-determinism. We can therefore draw a distinction between the more general term *concurrency* which is a property of sets of processes, and *non-determinism* which is the property of the choice structure *inside* a process. As we assume that all processes run on exactly one processor, the distinction is well founded.

4.8 Dining Philosophers with deadlock

Another version of the Dining Philosophers problem can now be given. In the (livelocking) version presented in Chapter 3, the chopsticks were represented by passive entities that used mutual exclusion synchronization to ensure that they were not used by two philosopher processes at the same time. We now present a version that is more in keeping with the pure process model described in this chapter. The chopsticks are now processes in their own right. This version is a direct translation of the earlier one and hence the livelock problem is transposed into a deadlock, that is, it is possible for all philosophers to have obtained only one chopstick and be suspended waiting for the other to become free.

The code is presented as it appears in the **listfile** produced by the Pascal-FC system. This is done to indicate the line numbers used in the post-mortem description of the program's execution (see below). Two numbers are given for each line. The first is just a simple line count; the second is a count of the executable instructions generated by each statement line. As one would expect, declarations do not generate run-time instructions. Statements produce various numbers: the channel write on source line 36, for example, has produced five. (The program counter is 62 at the beginning of the line and 67 at the beginning of the next one.) The global integer meals is used to keep an approximate track of the progress of the philosophers; it needs to be global and scalar for this purpose as the post-mortem description only notes the values of such variables.

```
 1     0    program philosophers;
 2     0    const N = 5;
 3     0    type synchchan = channel of synchronous;
 4     0
 5     0    var I : integer;
 6     0       leftget,leftdrop,
 7     0       rightget,rightdrop : array[1..N] of synchchan;
 8     0       meal : integer;
 9     0
10     0    process type chopstick(position : integer);
11     0    begin
12     0       repeat
13     0          select
14     0             leftget[position] ? any;
15    10             leftdrop[position] ? any;
16    15          or
17    16             rightget[position] ? any;
18    25             rightdrop[position] ? any;
19    30          or
20    31             terminate
21    31          end
22    32       forever
23    32    end;
24    33
25    33    process type philosophers(name : integer);
26    34    var I : integer;
27    34       chop1, chop2 : integer;
28    34
29    34    begin
30    34       chop1 := name;
31    37       if name = N then chop2 := 1 else chop2 := name + 1;
32    50       for I := 1 to 10 do
```

```
33   54    begin
34   54      sleep(random(5));     (* THINKING *)
35   57      leftget[chop1] ! any;
36   62      rightget[chop2] ! any;
37   67      meal := I;
38   70      sleep(random(5));     (* EATING *)
39   73      rightdrop[chop2] ! any;
40   78      leftdrop[chop1] ! any
41   83    end
42   83  end;
43   84
44   84  var phils : array[1..N] of philosophers;
45   85      chopsticks : array[1..N] of chopstick;
46   85
47   85  begin
48   85    cobegin
49   86      for I := 1 to N do
50   90      begin
51   90        chopsticks[I](I);
52   97        phils[I](I)
53  103      end
54  104    coend
55  105  end.
```

Each chopstick process is prepared to accept a call from either leftget or rightget. Having accepted one, it must then make a rendezvous with the same philosopher process when it returns the chopstick by calling the appropriate drop channel. Note that the read operations on the drop channels are not alternatives in the **select** statement: they just happen to be the statements to be executed once that particular alternative of the **select** is chosen. The chopstick processes are classic server processes: they terminate when all the philosopher processes have completed. This is easily programmed with the **terminate** alternative.

As indicated above, this code leads to deadlock. On 100 executions using the fair scheduler, two deadlocks were encountered. This illustrates the inadequacy of testing in the verification of concurrent programs: the program has a subtle bug that only leads to failure on rare occasions, and which can be missed during testing. Once deadlock has occurred, the Pascal-FC run-time system produces a post-mortem dump file that helps isolate the difficulty. For example, the following was produced by one of those two failed executions:

```
Pascal-FC post-mortem report on philosophe
Abnormal halt in process phils[2] with pc = 67
Reason: deadlock
```

Main program
Status: awaiting process termination

Process chopsticks[1]
Status: active
pc = 15
Process suspended on:
leftdrop[1] (channel)

Process phils[1]
Status: active
pc = 67
Process suspended on:
rightget[2] (channel)

Process chopsticks[2]
Status: active
pc = 15
Process suspended on:
leftdrop[2] (channel)

Process phils[2]
Status: active
pc = 67
Process suspended on:
rightget[3] (channel)

Process chopsticks[3]
Status: active
pc = 15
Process suspended on:
leftdrop[3] (channel)

Process phils[3]
Status: active
pc = 67
Process suspended on:
rightget[4] (channel)

Process chopsticks[4]
Status: active
pc = 15
Process suspended on:
leftdrop[4] (channel)

Process phils[4]
Status: active
pc = 67
Process suspended on:
rightget[5] (channel)

Process chopsticks[5]
Status: active
pc = 15
Process suspended on:
leftdrop[5] (channel)

Process phils[5]
Status: active
pc = 67
Process suspended on:
rightget[1] (channel)

————
Global variables

meal = 3
i = 5

As the dump indicates, each chopstick process is suspended waiting for the 'left' philosopher to drop it, and each philosopher process is suspended waiting to get its 'right' chopstick. The value of the variable meal is 3, showing that one of the philosophers was up to her 4th meal before being denied her utensils.

The Pascal-FC system indicates deadlock if, at any time, all extant processes are blocked waiting for communication from another process.† In such circumstances, the scheduler has no runnable process to choose, and it is obvious that the situation will remain thus indefinitely. Every process is awaiting an event (communication) that will never in fact occur.

---

† The only exception to this is that all the processes involved are blocked in **select** statements with **terminate** alternatives.

4.9   Occam's language model

The language model chosen for discussion in this chapter is based on the CSP formalism. As such it is very close to the general purpose programming language, occam. Practice with these features of Pascal-FC will develop appropriate skills for programming in this language. There are, however, some differences that should be borne in mind. The purpose of this section is to highlight them.

The most restrictive part of Pascal-FC is its flat process structure. Occam allows nested **cobegin/coend** constructs (called **PAR** in occam). It also uses an implicit process declaration; any code contained within a **PAR** is executed as a distinct process.

In terms of inter-process communication, however, occam is more restrictive. There are two major omissions from the occam language:

- the selective wait construct (called **ALT**) cannot have output (write) channel operations;
- there is no **terminate** alternative.

Both of these restrictions stem from perceived implementation overheads on distributed systems. These are important for occam because of its close association with the transputer.

In order to foster an understanding of the issues that shape the development of concurrent programming languages, the motivations behind the two restrictions will be outlined. First consider the non-symmetric **select**: the concern here is programs that have a selective wait construct at both ends of a channel. In Pascal-FC this would appear as follows:

```
var chan : channel of SomeType;
   ...
select     (* in process P *)
   chan ? variable;
or
   ...
end;
   ...
select     (* in process Q *)
   chan ! value;
or
   ...
end;
   ...
```

Now the choice made by one process's **select** cannot be made in isolation. Process P can choose to communicate down channel chan only if process Q also chooses the alternative involving the same channel. On a single processor system, this difficulty is not hard to solve as either P or Q gets to the **select** first – the other then makes the decision. On a multiprocessor system, P and Q can arrive at their **select**s simultaneously and hence a more elaborate protocol is needed. These protocols are known, but were considered too expensive (in time) for the transputer's language. The easiest way of making sure that no one channel is used by a **select** at each end is to restrict the **select**. As reading a message is seen in some sense to be the more 'natural' action, occam restricts selection to the read operation.

The **terminate** alternative was not considered important for the same reason – the overhead in a distributed environment. As processes are executing in parallel, it is not possible to get a snapshot of all the relevant processes to decide if termination is appropriate. Unfortunately the lack of this facility means that the programmer must program termination directly. As was pointed out earlier, this can be an error-prone activity.

Notwithstanding these differences, the basic language models are the same.† These represent the most natural form for a language based on one-directional point-to-point communication.

SUMMARY

The message-passing model described in this chapter represents an elegant, yet powerful, programming abstraction. All entities, both passive and active, are represented as processes, and all inter-process communication and synchronization is accomplished by a single primitive. For two processes to exchange data (or merely synchronize) a channel must be declared of the appropriate type. This channel will transfer a single data item from the sender process to the receiver process. The process which arrives first, whether sender or receiver, will be blocked until the rendezvous can take place. Each channel can only be used in one direction and cannot be shared between different senders (or receivers). To cater for situations in which synchronization only is needed, Pascal-FC supports a 'channel of synchronous'.

In order to increase the expressive power of this message-based model it is necessary to allow a process to choose between alternative communications. The language feature that supports this is called selective waiting. Here a process can choose between different alternatives; the execution of one alternative being synonymous with the execution of the **select**. On any particular execution of the **select** certain alternatives can be closed off by the use of boolean guards. In general a process can choose (at a **select**) between sending one or more messages or receiving one or more messages. It can also take an immediate alternative path if no other process is waiting to rendezvous on an open channel alternative. If, on execution of the **select**, more than one

† Occam also lacks a direct **else** alternative, although the equivalent semantics can be constructed.

channel alternative is ready (i.e. open and with a process waiting), then the choice is non-deterministic.

The other main feature of a general selective wait construct is that it allows effective termination to be programmed. A 'passive' process can be structured to terminate, when no longer callable, by placing a **terminate** alternative on the select statement, on which the process is suspended when not invoked by client processes. The absence of this feature makes program termination much more problematic.

The language model described in this chapter closely mirrors that found in occam. Occam, however, lacks a terminate facility and has a restricted select statement – only channel reads are allowed. Pascal-FC can easily be used in this mode to simulate the use of the occam language.

FURTHER READING

Burns A. (1988). *Programming in occam2*. Addison-Wesley
Hoare C.A.R. (1985). *Communicating Sequential Processes*. Prentice-Hall
Milner R. (1989). *Communication and Concurrency*. Prentice-Hall

EXERCISES

4.1   Consider again the drink dispensing process (see Exercise 2.1). Having received a coin, the process can then choose between dispensing tea or coffee. Although the choice is determined by the user's input, the behaviour of the process can be said to be non-deterministic. Define the alphabet and behaviour of this process.

4.2   As in Exercise 2.2, decompose the drink dispensing process into two processes. Use a synchronous message to allow the processes to communicate.

4.3   Complete the prime numbers program so that the entire program terminates correctly. First use occam language features only (e.g. no **terminate** alternative). Then, separately, program termination using the full Pascal-FC facilities.

4.4   Use occam's facilities (e.g. no symmetric **select**) to program the buffer process.

4.5   Write a Pascal-FC program in which a number of processes undertake read and write operations on a large array of integers. The array is visible to all processes, but another process or other processes must regulate access to the array so that concurrent reads are possible but a write operation precludes other writes and all reads (i.e. the Readers and Writers problem). Hint: a reader process may execute code such as:

Permission [i] ! any
(* read from array *)
Finished [i] ! any

where the channels Permission and Finished are read by the controller processes.

4.6   What is the difference between the behaviour of the following **select** statements?

```
select
   in ? v;
or
   timeout 0;
   P(. . .)
end;
```

and

```
select
   in ? v;
else
   P(. . .)
end.
```

4.7   Write a two-process program that splits a set of integers so that one process ends up with the highest integers and the other process gets the lowest. The processes should start with an array (say of 20 elements) which have arbitrary initial values (in the range 1 to 500). The processes then swap integers until they are split. Hint: sort the integers first.

4.8   Arrange $n*n$ (e.g. $3*3$) processes in a square grid. Each process can only communicate with its neighbour (either left, right, up or down). Those processes at the top of the grid are passed n integers (one at a time); these are then passed on to the process below. Similarly, those processes on the left of the grid are passed n integers which are passed on to the process on the right. Each process has a local variable (total), which is initially zero. As it gets an integer from the top and left, it executes:

total := total + leftvalue * rightvalue

Only when it has a pair of values are any passed on. It then passes both values on. Write a program that implements this arrangement and prints out the final values. The program is actually implementing matrix multiplication using a systolic algorithm.

4.9   Write a program to solve the Stable Marriage Problem. A collection of married men and women is stable unless there are two couples in which a man and a women prefer to be with each other rather than their partner. The program should contain n men and n women processes. Each process should hold an array in which the opposite gender is rated. Processes should then communicate to see if an unstable relationship exists.

4.10 Although the message-passing primitive described in this chapter is one-to-one, it is sometimes necessary to broadcast a value to a number of other processes. Write a server process that will enable a single client process to broadcast an integer value to a number of other clients. The server process should not dictate the order in which the receiving processes get their data. Moreover, the broadcasting process should be delayed if it wishes to send a second broadcast before all receivers have got the first.

4.11 Write a process that monitors the state of all other processes in a program. Three states should be considered: *executing*, *terminated* and *failed*. While executing, each process must send a regular *heartbeat* to the monitor process. If the monitor does not receive the heartbeat in a defined interval, then the process is deemed to have failed. A process can, however, indicate to the monitor that it is about to terminate; the monitor will then no longer expect heartbeats from that process. Test your process by adding it to one of your earlier programs.

4.12 Write a program that outputs a sorted set of integers. The set of integers should first be partitioned into *n* worker processes that sort their subsets. The sorted output is obtained by merging the outputs of each worker process. The worker processes should communicate with each other to agree on which of them should output the next value.

5 Remote Invocation

The message-based language model presented in the previous chapter is characterized by:

- point-to-point communication
- one-direction data flow.

That is, each channel is used to pass information, in one direction only, between a single receiver process and a single sender process. In this chapter we consider a different language model: one that is used in the Ada programming language. Communication is now many-to-one and data can pass in either (or both) directions; no intermediary channel is used. This language model is more in keeping with the client–server paradigm of process interaction. Selective waiting is, however, still required.

5.1 Basic model

To understand the motivation for this model we shall first consider the familiar relationship between a procedure and its callers. The following points are apposite:

- a single procedure can be called from many different places;
- a procedure call can involve information passing into, or out of, the procedure (or both);
- a procedure embodies a series of computational events that are executed on behalf of the caller (before information is returned).

In Pascal-FC it is possible to define a procedure that is called (concurrently) by two or more processes. Indeed, this structure is used constructively in Chapter 7. The procedure is, however, a neutral entity and is not in itself a form of inter-process communication.

The **remote invocation** model *is*, however, a message-passing formalism that has many of the characteristics of a procedure call. Informally the model allows one process to call a 'procedure' that is owned and controlled by another process. To minimize confusion, the term procedure is not used; rather a process that is prepared to accept calls defines one or more 'entries'. The following are examples of entries that do not involve data exchange:

    entry HALT;

    entry CALL;

    entry SYNCHRONIZE;

If all the entries in a program had unique names then a calling process need only name the entry (in a similar way to naming only the channel). However, to emphasize that an entry is owned by a process, it is required that entries are defined within the context of a process. A calling process names the process *and* the entry. Given the process:

    process RUNNING;
        entry START;
        entry HALT;
        entry CONTINUE;
        . . .

an example call would be:

    RUNNING.HALT

As a consequence, entry names do not have to be unique (except within a process).

In keeping with the procedure analogy, a process entry can be called by any other process that has access to the process's name (i.e. has it in scope). The communication structure is no longer point-to-point but many-to-one. This is more appropriate with the client–server programming paradigm. Active processes act as clients to the passive processes that merely serve the interests of the clients. Typically, server processes define entries while active client processes do not – they call the entries of others.

To complete this introduction, it is necessary to contrast remote invocation and the technique known as remote procedure call (RPC). Both appear to involve the external execution of a procedure; they are, however, quite distinct activities.

RPCs are a way of gaining parallel execution by placing one of the procedures that a process uses on a different processor. In order for the process to call its procedure, the execution environment (operating system) must allow a call from one processor to another. This technique is known as an RPC. To obtain parallel execution, an implementation of RPC will often allow the calling process to give up its processor while the remote call is being undertaken. RPCs are particularly effective and useful in distributed systems.

To make the distinction between RPCs and remote invocation clear, the following points should be understood. They should help to remove a common misconception with the terms:

- Remote invocation is a concurrent language construct; RPC is a technique for implementing procedure calls in a distributed system. They are not at the same level of abstraction. The 'remote' in remote invocation means another process; the 'remote' in RPC implies another processor.

- The entry called during remote invocation belongs to another process; the procedure called during RPC either belongs to the calling process or is a general in-scope procedure.

- The entry called during remote invocation will only execute when the process that owns the entry allows; the procedure called during RPC is immediately executable (as is an ordinary procedure). Only the time needed to make the call itself moderates the meaning of 'immediate'.

- The entry called during remote invocation is executed by the owner process; the procedure called during RPC is executed on behalf of the calling process by a surrogate process created by the execution environment (operating system).

- The entry called during remote invocation, and the caller, can execute on the same processor (indeed, on a single processor system they always do); it makes no sense for an RPC to be local!

- If the process called during remote invocation is actually on a different processor, then RPCs may be used by the execution environment to implement the remote invocation.

5.2 Entry definitions and entry queues

In Pascal-FC entries are defined with the process type, as in the following two examples:

```
process P;
   entry E1;
   entry E2;
   . . .
   entry En
var
      (* internal declarations for the process *)
begin
      (* statement part *)
end;

process type Q;
   entry E1;
   entry E2;
   . . .
   entry En;
var
      (* internal declarations for the process *)
begin
      (* statement part *)
end;
```

In the second case, declaration of process variables is the same as for process types without entries:

```
var
   Q1, Q2: Q;
```

To allow two processes to call each other, a form of forward declaration is supported:

```
process P provides
   entry E;
end;
```

```
process Q;
  entry F;
begin
  . . .
  P.E;
  . . .
end;

process P;
  entry E;
begin
  . . .
  Q.F;
  . . .
end;
```

A common use of this facility is when we have an array (or pipeline) of processes that wish to call each other, that is, process *i* needs to call process *i + 1*. The following outline code gives the structure of this type of program:

```
process type ELEM(NUM : integer) provides
  entry CALL;
end;

var
  ELEMENTS : array[1 .. PIPELENGTH] of ELEM;

process type ELEM(NUM : integer)
  entry CALL;
begin
  . . .
  if NUM <> PIPELENGTH then
    ELEMENTS[NUM+1].CALL;
  . . .
end;
```

Whereas a channel can have at most one process waiting on it, an entry (because calling is many-to-one) can have a number of calls outstanding. For each entry there is, therefore, a possible queue of calling processes. Ada currently defines a default FIFO discipline on entry queues, but Pascal-FC makes the discipline a priority queue.

Data is communicated between processes via the parameters of the entry definition. The parameter-passing model used for procedure calls is reused in our entry definition. Hence an entry can have any number of parameters; each parameter has a type and is either passed by value (the default) or is defined to be a variable. In the latter case, this allows data to be communicated back to the calling process. The following are four example declarations:

```
    entry PLACE(C : char);
    entry TAKE(var C : char);

    entry COUNT(I : integer);

    entry EXCHANGE(InData : integer; var OutData : integer);

    entry LOTS(A,B : integer; var C,D : integer; E : boolean);
```

A process can define any number of entries.

5.3   The accept statement

For each entry defined, the process must embody at least one **accept**
statement that corresponds to that entry and which defines the code to be
executed when an entry call is accepted. An **accept** statement will
correspond to an entry declaration only if it has the same name and the
same parameter profile. The typical function of an **accept** statement is to
save the values of any input data and to undertake whatever actions are
needed to generate any defined output data. For example:

```
process P;
  entry EXCHANGE(InData : integer; var OutData : integer);
var
  D1, D2 : integer;
begin
  . . .
  D2 := SomeValue;
  accept EXCHANGE(InData : integer; var OutData : integer) do
  begin
    D1 := InData;
    OutData := D2
  end;
  . . .
end;
```

When some other task calls this entry, data will be exchanged. For instance,
the following will pass 42 into process P and obtain some new value for X
(where X is a local variable in the calling process):

```
P.EXCHANGE(42,X);
```

The general form of the **accept** statement in Pascal-FC is similar to other
structured Pascal statements, such as the **for** and **while** loops:

accept_statement ::=

    accept *entry*_identifier[formal_part] **do**
       statement

The above example had a compound statement following the **do**, but any single Pascal-FC statement is legal. Note that the name of the formal parameters of the entry are in scope throughout the statement following **do**.†
    It is important to appreciate the major distinction between a procedure and an **accept** statement. Whereas a procedure is passive, is always available for execution and is executed by the calling process, an **accept** statement is part of another process: it is only executed when that process allows it to be, and is executed by the owner process not the caller. As a first example, consider the Ornamental Gardens program. With remote invocation, a **select** construct is not necessary in this case, as all the gates can call in on the same entry:

```
program gardens;

process counter;
  entry path(temp : integer);

var count : integer;
    I : integer;
begin
  count := 0;
  for I := 1 to 40 do
    accept path(temp : integer) do
      count := count + temp;
  writeln('Total admitted: ',count)
end;

process type turnstile(name, num : integer);
var loop: integer;
begin
  for loop := 1 to num do
  counter.path(1)
end;    (* turnstile *)

var turnstiles : array[1..2] of turnstile;

begin
  cobegin
    counter;
    turnstiles[1](1,20);
    turnstiles[2](2,20)
  coend
end.
```

† Unless we nest another **accept** for an entry which has a parameter of the same name as one of the parameters of the outer **accept**.

The interaction between an entry caller and its acceptor is a rendezvous, in the sense that the party that arrives first at the point of communication is blocked until the other arrives. The process making the call will, in fact, *always* be blocked, even if the acceptor is immediately ready to process its call: it remains blocked until completion of the **accept** statement. If a process attempts to execute an **accept** and there are no outstanding calls (the entry queue is empty), then it is suspended. Only when two processes are prepared to rendezvous with each other is the code of the **accept** statement executed. When this is completed the rendezvous is terminated and the two processes can then continue their executions independently and concurrently.

It is important to note that the code inside an **accept** can be arbitrarily complex. Indeed it can involve an entry call to another process, as is illustrated in the following contrived program:

```
program complex;

process P;
   entry E(var I : integer);
var T : integer;
begin
  T := 42;
   accept E(var I : integer) do
    I := T
end;

process Q;
   entry E(var I : integer);
var T : integer;
begin
   accept E(var I : integer) do
   begin
     P.E(T);     (* while accepting E a call to P.E is made *)
     I := T
   end
end;

process S;
var T : integer;
begin
   Q.E(T)
end;

begin
   cobegin
     P;Q;S
   coend
end.
```

At the other extreme, an **accept** statement can be entirely empty, being used for synchronization only:

> **accept** START **do;**
> ...

or

> **accept** START **do**
> **null;**
> ...

It is necessary to consider the behaviour of **var** parameters as they are used in data communication. Consider the following simple calling relationship:

```
process Q;
  entry GET(var I : integer);
var
  STORE : integer;
begin
  ...
  accept GET(var I : integer) do
    I := STORE;
  ...
end;

process P;
var
  LOCAL : integer;
begin
  ...
  Q.GET(LOCAL);
  ...
end;
```

The first thing to note is that when process P calls process Q, the effect is for information to flow from Q to P, i.e. the direction of communication is the opposite of the direction of call. This can be confusing when using terms such as 'message passing', 'sender' and 'receiver'. Hence the term 'remote invocation' is preferred: *remote* because it involves another process and *invocation* because a request has been made. Another term used is 'extended rendezvous'. The distinction between data flow and direction of call can also be confusing in diagrams. Any convention using arrows (which they almost all do) must clearly define what the arrow actually means.

The second issue concerns the parameter itself. If P and Q, in the above example, are on the same processor and use the same memory partition, then Q can directly manipulate the location at which P's variable LOCAL is stored. If this is not the case, then the value of the parameter must be copied across to Q at the start of the rendezvous and copied back at the end. This can lead to one more copy than is necessary (when the initial value of the variable parameter is not used), but this is inevitable with Pascal's parameter-passing model. Ada's more sensible model, in which a parameter can be defined as 'output only', removes this source of inefficiency.

5.4 Remote invocation and selective waiting

There is always a need for a selective wait construct with message-passing semantics. In the remote invocation model this takes the form of a (possibly guarded) **accept** alternative to a **select** statement. This behaves in an equivalent way to the channel alternatives described in the previous chapter. As an example, consider a passive process, the role of which is to protect access to a single shared variable. This variable can be written to or read from:

```
process share;
  entry read(var I : integer);
  entry write(I : integer);
var
  value : integer;
begin
  accept write(I : integer) do
    value := I;
  repeat
    select
      accept write(I : integer) do
        value := I;
    or
      accept read(var I : integer) do
        I := value
    end
  forever
end;
```

There are two important points that even this simple example illustrates. Firstly, the body of a process can have more than one **accept** statement for an entry. In the particular code above, the first **accept** for write ensures that an initial value is assigned into the variable. After this has been done the process loops around and accepts (in an arbitrary order) calls to read or write. In general an entry can have any number of **accept**s associated with it. Moreover, the code executed in each **accept** need not be the same.

The second characteristic of this example is the reversal of the direction of call associated with the read operation. As data can flow in the opposite direction to the call, the read request is also programmed as a 'call-in'. This has a number of advantages:

- an asymmetric **select** is adequate (i.e. selecting between **accept**s rather than between **accept**s and entry calls);
- it is more in keeping with the abstraction of a passive entity (the server process never calls out), it just accepts incoming calls.

All passive processes can be programmed in this way. It is left as an exercise to program the finite buffer process.

The **select** statement was discussed in detail in the previous chapter. All the various features introduced there are applicable to the language model discussed in this chapter, except that only **accept** statements are allowed (i.e. no entry calls) and that the **replicate** alternative is not applicable. As indicated above, the asymmetric **select** is adequate with remote invocation. However, **timeout** alternatives, **else** parts and **terminate** alternatives are all valid, as are guards.

To illustrate some of these features, consider a resource controller that allocates a collection of 16 objects. Clients obtain one of these objects by calling ALLOCATE; the object is returned by calling REPLACE. The following gives an outline to the structure of the CONTROLLER. Omitted from the code are details of how the object is actually passed out to the client (and returned). Rather, a simple integer is returned that indicates which object number has been allocated:

```
program control;

process CONTROLLER;
  entry ALLOCATE(var NUM : integer);
  entry REPLACE(NUM : integer);
const
  SIZE = 16;
var
  OBJECTS : array[1..size] of boolean;
  I : integer;
  FREE : integer;     (* number of free objects *)

procedure GetObj(var OB : integer);
    (* find the first free object *)
var
  J : integer;
begin
  J := 1;
```

```
          while J <= SIZE do
          begin
            if not OBJECTS[J] then
            begin
              OBJECTS[J] := true;
              OB := J;
              J := SIZE + 1     (* terminate search *)
            end;
            J := J + 1
          end;
          if J = SIZE + 1 then      (* no free object found *)
            writeln ('Error on GetObj')
        end;

        begin     (* process controller *)
          for I := 1 to SIZE do
            OBJECTS[I] := false;
          FREE := SIZE;
          repeat
            select
              when FREE > 0 =>
              accept ALLOCATE(var NUM : integer) do
              begin
                GetObj(NUM);
                FREE := FREE − 1
              end;
            or
              accept REPLACE(NUM : integer) do
              begin
                FREE := FREE + 1;
                OBJECTS[NUM] := false
              end;
            or
              terminate
            end     (* select *)
          forever
        end;     (* CONTROLLER *)

        process type CLIENT;     (* example client structure *)
        var
          OB : integer;
          I : integer;
        begin
          for I := 1 to 10 do
          begin
            CONTROLLER.ALLOCATE(OB);
            sleep(random(5));                    (* Use the resource *)
            CONTROLLER.REPLACE(OB)
          end
        end;
```

```
var
  CLIENTS : array[1..20] of CLIENT;
  COUNT : integer;

begin     (* main program *)
  cobegin
    CONTROLLER;
    for COUNT := 1 to 20 do
      CLIENTS[COUNT]
  coend
end.
```

With this number of clients, the FREE variable soon drops to zero (which can be illustrated by adding a write statement to the CONTROLLER).

A point of useful detail can be observed in this code by considering the **accept** statement for the ALLOCATE entry. In general the code inside the **accept** should be the minimum required for the rendezvous, so that the potential for concurrency can be fully exploited. The assignment to FREE is therefore inappropriately placed; it should be done after the rendezvous, as it only affects a local variable:

```
when FREE > 0 =>
accept ALLOCATE(var NUM : integer) do
  GetObj(NUM);
FREE := FREE − 1
```

Before continuing, the reader should consider how this code can be changed so that each client can request a number of objects (say between one and six). A solution to this extended problem is given at the end of this chapter.

5.5   Solution to the Dining Philosophers problem

Two attempts to solve this problem have already been given; one suffered from potential livelock and the other from deadlock. To illustrate further the remote invocation model, a correct solution will now be given. The essence of the solution is to restrict the number of possible eaters. This strategy is an example of deadlock prevention (see Chapter 3). In particular, it removes the 'circularity' of requests and allocations, which is one of the four necessary conditions for the occurrence of deadlock.

The previous attempts both got into difficulty when the N philosophers all wished to eat at the same time and each obtained access to a single chopstick. If only $N - 1$ philosophers can try to eat simultaneously, then there must exist one philosopher with two chopsticks. She can proceed and will eventually free both chopsticks. The solution is modelled as follows: although there are N places at the table and N chopsticks, there are only

$N - 1$ chairs. As everyone knows, philosophers are too polite to eat while standing: to eat, a philosopher must first sit down. The code for this model follows. Note that the chopstick processes are simpler than in the previous program: they now have two entries rather than four channel interactions. This is because both philosophers who use a particular chopstick can call the same entry:

```
program philada;
const N = 5;
var
  I : integer;

process type chopstick;
  entry pickup;
  entry putdown;
begin
  repeat
    select
      accept pickup do
        null;
      accept putdown do
        null;
    or
      terminate
    end
  forever
end;

var
  chopsticks : array[1..N] of chopstick;

process chairs;
  entry getchair;
  entry replacechair;
var freechairs : integer;
begin
  freechairs := N - 1;
  repeat
    select
      when freechairs > 0 =>
      accept getchair do
        null;
      freechairs := freechairs - 1;
    or
      accept replacechair do
        null;
      freechairs := freechairs + 1;
    or
      terminate
```

```
        end
      forever
    end;


    process type philosophers(name : integer);
    var I : integer;
        chop1, chop2 : integer;
    begin
      chop1 := name;
      if name = N then chop2 := 1 else chop2 := name + 1;
      for I := 1 to 10 do
      begin
        sleep(random(5));      (* THINKING *)
        chairs.getchair;
        chopsticks[chop1].pickup;
        chopsticks[chop2].pickup;
        sleep(random(5));      (* EATING *)
        chopsticks[chop2].putdown;
        chopsticks[chop1].putdown;
        chairs.replacechair
      end
    end;


    var phils : array[1..N] of philosophers;

    begin
      cobegin
        for I := 1 to N do
        begin
          chopsticks[I];
          phils[I](I)
        end;
        chairs
      coend
    end.
```

5.6 Process idioms

An important distinction has been made in this book between active and passive processes. In general, passive processes can be classified into a number of process idioms. A partial list is as follows:

(1)   buffer
(2)   stack
(3)   mailbox
(4)   forwarder.

Buffer processes have already been considered. A stack process merely implements a LIFO (Last In First Out) data store. The other two idioms introduce agent processes that act on behalf of other entities. Each will now be considered.

5.6.1 Mailbox

A mailbox is a process that acts as a temporary buffer between two other processes. It allows the active processes to pass data asynchronously (via the mailbox). The mailbox type simply has two entries for capturing and releasing the message (which is of type integer in the following examples):

```
process type MAILBOX;
  entry PUT(Mess : integer);
  entry GET(var Mess : integer);
var
  temp : integer;
begin
  repeat
    select
      accept PUT(Mess : integer) do
        temp := Mess;
      accept GET(var Mess : integer) do
        Mess := temp;
    or
      terminate
    end
  forever
end;
```

The users of this process simply call the appropriate entry. Note that if a message is still 'in' the mailbox, then a subsequent call of PUT will block.

5.6.2 Forwarder

A forwarder acts as a direct intermediary between two processes. Consider a program in which process P calls entry E in process Q, and deposits an integer. If P calls Q directly it will block if Q is not able to accept the call immediately. This synchronous communication can be altered by P using an agent that calls Q on its behalf, so that P and Q become less tightly coupled. The following code outline illustrates this:

```
program FORWARDER;

process Q;
  entry E(Mess : integer);
begin
  . . .
end;
```

```
process type FORWARDER;
  entry PUT(Mess : integer);
var
  temp : integer;
begin
  repeat
    select
      accept PUT(Mess : integer) do
        temp := Mess;
      Q.E(temp);
    or
      terminate
    end
  forever
end;

var F, . . . : FORWARDER;

process P;
var V : integer;
  . . .
begin
  . . .
  F.PUT(V);
  . . .
end;
  . . .
```

P calls F and then F calls Q. Note that the structure of Q is unaffected by this use of the agent.

5.7   A reactive example

Many concurrent systems are driven by the arrival of data at the system's interface. These systems are often called **reactive**. In the following example an output value is produced in response to a new input value. There are three sources of input which are intended to be three alternative measures of the same environmental quantity: for example, they might come from three different devices that estimate altitude in an aeroplane. As each of the devices might give different data representations, the program uses three distinct processes for input (even though only integers are passed in the example). Whenever a new input value is registered, the output process can run, get a new weighted average of the inputs and produce an appropriate output. However, it is important that if a number of new inputs arrive before the outputting process gets around to reading the input values, then it is given an up-to-date average; some data may be lost but the average always uses the latest values from the three input sources.

One way to accommodate the freshness requirement (and to minimize the number of times the averaging activity is performed) is to call the average procedure only when a request for data is made. This requires the procedure to be called from within the **accept** statement, thus illustrating why it is often useful to be able to execute code within an **accept** body:

```
program control;

process server;
   entry A(I : integer);
   entry B(I : integer);
   entry C(I : integer);
   entry GET(var I : integer);
var newvalue : boolean;
    tempA, tempB, tempC : integer;
procedure average(X,Y,Z : integer; var result : integer);
begin
   (* form a weighed average of the input values *)
end;
begin
   newvalue := false;
   repeat
     select
       accept A(I : integer) do
         tempA := I;
       newvalue := true;
     or
       accept B(I : integer) do
         tempB := I;
       newvalue := true;
     or
       accept C(I : integer) do
         tempC := I;
       newvalue := true;
     or
       when newvalue =>
       accept GET(var I : integer) do
         average(tempA,tempB,tempC,I);
       newvalue := false;
     or
       terminate
     end
   forever
end;
```

```
process inputA;
var V : integer;
begin
  repeat
      (* Wait for input *)
      (* Obtain input value V *)
    server.A(V)
  forever
end;

process inputB;
var V : integer;
begin
  repeat
      (* Wait for input *)
      (* Obtain input value V *)
    server.B(V)
  forever
end;

process inputC;
var V : integer;
begin
  repeat
      (* Wait for input *)
      (* Obtain input value V *)
    server.C(V)
  forever
end;

process output;
var V : integer;
begin
  repeat
    server.GET(V);
      (* Use V to produce output *)
  forever
end;

begin     (* main *)
  cobegin
    inputA;
    inputB;
    inputC;
    output;
    server
  coend
end.
```

5.8 Ada's language model

The importance of remote invocation is highlighted by its use in the Ada language. Ada calls processes 'tasks'. These are hierarchically related, but have remote invocation as their model of message passing. The model is as defined in Pascal-FC except for the restriction that there is no **pri select** statement. The **select** statement can, however, have 'timeout' alternatives (called **delay** alternatives), **else** parts and **terminate** alternatives.

The motivation for using remote invocation rather than simple message passing was as follows:

- The client/server paradigm is a rational one for program construction. In this paradigm the server does not need to know the identity of the clients or indeed how many there will be.

- Most interactions between processes are more complex than simple message passing.

- 'Var' parameters (**in out** parameters in Ada) to entries allow data to pass in the opposite direction to the call, thereby removing the need for a symmetric **select**.

It is perhaps useful to consider the second point in more detail. In the absence of a remote invocation, the client must make two calls: one to pass in data and the other to receive the reply after the input data has been processed:

```
process SERVER;
  entry REQUEST(D : SomeData);
  entry REPLY(var D : SomeOtherData);
var
  . . .
begin
  repeat
    select
      accept REQUEST(D : SomeData) do
        SomeVar := D;
      (* calculate Some Result *)
      accept REPLY(var D : SomeOtherData) do
        D := SomeResult;
    or
      terminate
    end
  forever
end;
```

```
process CLIENT;
begin
  ...
  SERVER.REQUEST(DATA);
  SERVER.REPLY(ANSWER);
  ...
end;
  ..
```

Apart from the inelegance of this solution, it suffers from a further structuring problem. In general a server process should not be affected by an unreliable client. If it were, the error in one client would soon propagate throughout the entire system. With the above code, a client that failed to make the second call would prevent the server from passing beyond the second interaction. The difficulty stems from the representation of a single logical transaction as two separate communications. Remote invocation allows the transaction to be represented as a single process interaction:

```
process SERVER provides
  entry REQUEST(D1 : SomeData; var D2 : SomeOtherData);
  ...

process CLIENT;
begin
  ...
  SERVER.REQUEST(DATA,ANSWER);
  ...
end;
  ..
```

Of course, where data communication is only in one direction, the Ada model is equivalent to that of occam.

5.9 Resource control problem revisited

Earlier in this chapter a program was given that showed how a resource CONTROLLER process can control access to a set of objects that are needed by a group of competing clients. The program restricted each client to obtaining only one object at a time and the ALLOCATE operation was thus programmed as a single entry. If we now extend the problem to allow each client to ask for a variable number of objects, the guard structure (as described so far) is inadequate. To know whether an outstanding request can be satisfied, the CONTROLLER must accept the call to ALLOCATE so that the number of objects requested can be ascertained. However, having accepted the call, if it cannot be satisfied (because there are not enough free objects) then it must be terminated with no resources being allocated. The client has no option but to request again and hope for better luck next time – a solution that is, in effect, polling. This inadequacy with the Ada synchronization model was first discussed by Wellings *et al.* (1984); a detailed description has been given by Burns *et al.* (1987). The essence of the problem is that message-based languages use the guard to provide condition synchronization via *avoidance* of communication. This is arguably not as expressive as other forms of condition synchronization such as that employed in monitors – see examples in Chapter 7 and the discussion in Chapter 8.

In this section we will give the best solution that can be obtained to the resource allocation problem using the Ada language model. The model used in the language SR is then outlined.

The CONTROLLER process will again control access to 16 objects. A client can request between 1 and 16 objects. If a request is successful, the actual objects returned are represented by booleans set in an array.† To stop clients busy-waiting, if their call to ALLOCATE fails, they are required to call on one of two RETRY entries; these will only be accepted after some objects have been returned. When a call to REPLACE increases the number of FREE objects, all outstanding clients who are waiting for a RETRY are woken up and checked. If there are now enough objects, then they are released; if there are not, then they must call again on RETRY. Two entries are needed to manage the retries. At any one time a single queue is open and retries must enter that queue. When objects are returned, all members of the queue are checked (as just described); unsuccessful ones are put into the other queue, which now becomes the open queue. This technique must be used because otherwise a rejected RETRY could loop round, re-enter the same queue and be checked a second time. The program follows:

```
program control;

const SIZE = 16;

type ObjectFlags = array[1..size] of boolean;

process CONTROLLER;
  entry ALLOCATE(NUMBER : integer; var OK, queue : boolean;
                 var ObF :ObjectFlags);
  entry RETRYA(NUMBER : integer; var OK, queue : boolean;
                 var ObF :ObjectFlags);
  entry RETRYB(NUMBER : integer; var OK, queue : boolean;
                 var ObF :ObjectFlags);
  entry REPLACE(NUMBER : integer; var ObF :ObjectFlags);
var
  OBJECTS : ObjectFlags;
  I : integer;
```

† Pascal-FC does not have a predefined set type.

```
    FREE : integer;     (* number of free objects *)
    OUTSTANDING : integer;
        (* number of processes queued on RETRYs *)
    SWITCH : boolean;     (* which RETRY queue is current *)

procedure GetObjs(NUMBER : integer; var ObF :ObjectFlags);
    (* find the first NUMBER free objects *)
var
  J : integer;
  FOUND : integer;
begin
  J := 1;
  FOUND := 0;
  while J <= SIZE do
  begin
    if not OBJECTS[J] then
    begin
      OBJECTS[J] := true;
      ObF[J] := true;
      FOUND := FOUND + 1;
      if FOUND = NUMBER then
        J := SIZE + 1     (* terminate search *)
    end;
    J := J + 1
  end;
  if J = SIZE + 1 then     (* not enough free objects found *)
    writeln ('Error on GetObjs')
end;

procedure ReturnObjs(var ObF :ObjectFlags);
var
  J : integer;
begin
  for J := 1 to SIZE do
    if ObF[J] then
    begin
      ObF[J] := false;
      OBJECTS[J] := false
    end
end;

begin     (* process controller *)
  OUTSTANDING := 0;
  switch := true;
  for I := 1 to SIZE do
    OBJECTS[I] := false;
  FREE := SIZE;
  repeat
    select
      when FREE > 0 =>
```

```
            accept ALLOCATE(NUMBER : integer; var OK, queue : boolean;
                           var ObF :ObjectFlags) do
         begin
           if FREE >= NUMBER then
           begin
             OK := true;
             queue := switch;
             GetObjs(NUMBER,ObF);
             FREE := FREE - NUMBER
           end else
           begin
             OUTSTANDING := OUTSTANDING + 1;
             queue := switch;
             OK := false
           end
         end;
       or
         accept REPLACE(NUMBER : integer; var ObF :ObjectFlags) do
         begin
           ReturnObjs(ObF);
           FREE := FREE + NUMBER
         end;
         for I := 1 to OUTSTANDING do
           if switch then
             accept RETRYA(NUMBER : integer;
                 var OK, queue : boolean; var ObF :ObjectFlags) do
             begin
               if FREE >= NUMBER then
               begin
                 OK := true;
                 GetObjs(NUMBER,ObF);
                 FREE := FREE - NUMBER;
                 OUTSTANDING := OUTSTANDING - 1
               end else
               begin
                 queue := not switch;
                 OK := false
               end
             end else
             accept RETRYB(NUMBER : integer;
                 var OK, queue : boolean; var ObF :ObjectFlags) do
             begin
               if FREE >= NUMBER then
               begin
                 OK := true;
                 GetObjs(NUMBER,ObF);
                 FREE := FREE - NUMBER;
                 OUTSTANDING := OUTSTANDING - 1
               end else
```

```
                    begin
                       queue := not switch;
                       OK := false
                    end
                  end;
              switch := not switch;
          or
            terminate
          end      (* select *)
        forever
      end;

      process type CLIENT;
      var
        OB : ObjectFlags;
        NEEDS : integer;
        CONTINUE, WHICH : boolean;
        I : integer;
      begin
        for I := 1 to SIZE do
          OB[I] := false;
        for I := 1 to 10 do
        begin
          NEEDS := random(5) + 1;
          CONTROLLER.ALLOCATE(NEEDS, CONTINUE, WHICH, OB);
          while not CONTINUE do
            if WHICH then
              CONTROLLER.RETRYA(NEEDS, CONTINUE, WHICH, OB)
            else
              CONTROLLER.RETRYB(NEEDS, CONTINUE, WHICH, OB);
          sleep(random(5));
          CONTROLLER.REPLACE(NEEDS,OB)
        end
      end;

      var
        CLIENTS : array[1..20] of CLIENT;
        COUNT : integer;

      begin      (* main program *)
        cobegin
          CONTROLLER;
          for COUNT := 1 to 20 do
            CLIENTS[COUNT]
        coend
      end.
```

It is clear when examining the code for each client that it must follow a precise behaviour if the server process is not to be corrupted (e.g. a call to the wrong queue would cause the CONTROLLER to deadlock). The program illustrates a lack of expressive power in the Ada rendezvous model.

We shall conclude this chapter with an extended model of remote invocation. This is supported in the language SR (Andrews, 1981) but not in Pascal-FC, although we shall use Pascal-like syntax to illustrate the facility. The added feature of SR is that guards can contain parameters to the call that is being guarded:

accept (I : integer) **when** I > 0 **do**

This extends the expressive power of the language but at the cost of increased run-time complexity. In the Ada model, guards need only be evaluated once (per execution of the **select** statement); in the SR model they must be re-evaluated each time a call is made on the process with the **select**. Nevertheless, the increase in run-time complexity is compensated by a reduction in program complexity. The resource controller process is much simplified, and the RETRY entries are not required:

```
process CONTROLLER;
  entry ALLOCATE(NUMBER : integer; var ObF :ObjectFlags);
  entry REPLACE(NUMBER : integer; var ObF :ObjectFlags);
var
  OBJECTS : ObjectFlags;
  I : integer;
  FREE : integer;    (* number of free objects *)

procedure GetObjs(NUMBER : integer; var ObF :ObjectFlags);
  (* AS BEFORE *)

procedure ReturnObjs(var ObF :ObjectFlags);
  (* AS BEFORE *)

begin    (* process controller *)
  for I := 1 to SIZE do
    OBJECTS[I] := false;
  FREE := SIZE;
  repeat
    select
      accept ALLOCATE(NUMBER : integer; var ObF :ObjectFlags)
            when FREE >= NUMBER do
      begin
        GetObjs(NUMBER,ObF);
        FREE := FREE - NUMBER
      end;
    or
      accept REPLACE(NUMBER : integer; var ObF :ObjectFlags) do
      begin
        ReturnObjs(ObF);
        FREE := FREE + NUMBER
      end;
```

```
  or
    terminate
  end      (* select *)
 forever
end;
```

This example illustrates one of the two ways in which the expressive power of the guards (i.e. avoidance synchronization) can be enhanced. In Chapter 8 a **requeue** primitive is introduced within the context of a unified language model. This primitive is supported in Pascal-FC. The motivation for this language model comes from an appreciation of not only message-based languages but also those that use shared memory-based synchronization. The next two chapters illustrate and discuss this latter group of language features.

SUMMARY

Remote invocation represents a high-level language abstraction for inter-process communication and synchronization. A single request in this language model can involve the movement of any number of data items in either (or both) directions. Moreover, the receiver process can undertake whatever computations are necessary during the extended rendezvous. The result of using this abstraction is that programs require fewer communications and have simpler inter-process interactions. By using a similar syntactical form for procedure calls and remote invocation, a straightforward language model is defined. Removal of the channel intermediary also simplifies the language and leads to programs that more readily support the client–server paradigm of programming.

As with all message-based languages, a selective wait primitive is needed. However, the asymmetric model is adequate with remote invocation as data can pass in the opposite direction to the call. The incorporation of this language model into Ada indicates that it does form an appropriate base for a software enginnering language. A number of examples have been included in this chapter that illustrate its wide applicability; the resource control problem, however, showed that certain requirements are not easily satisfied with message passing.

FURTHER READING

Burns A. (1985). *Concurrent Programming in Ada* (Ada Companion Series). Cambridge University Press

Burns A., Lister A.M. and Wellings A.J. (1987). A Review of Ada Tasking. In *Lecture Notes in Computer Science*, vol 262. Springer-Verlag

Burns A. and Wellings A.J. (1990). *Real-Time Systems and Their Programming Languages*. Addison-Wesley

Gehani N.H. (1984). *Ada Concurrent Programming*. Prentice-Hall

---

EXERCISES

5.1 Distinguish between the channel and the entry.

5.2 Implement the standard circular buffer.

5.3 Program the readers and writers problem using the Ada style of inter-process communication.

5.4 Write a Pascal-FC program that emulates a simple terminal handler. One process should read characters from 'input'. Lower case characters are the normal ones; upper case letters represent control characters. Each normal character must be passed on to a buffer process before another is read. Four control characters should be recognized and acted upon (others should be ignored):

    B – erase last character from buffer
    L – put end-of-line marker into buffer
    U – remove current incomplete line from buffer
    C – remove contents of buffer

A third process should be coded to read lines of characters from the buffer. This process should then 'output' these lines. The buffer process should only allow the reader process access to complete lines of characters. You can assume that a line will have a maximum of 20 characters.

5.5 Write a program that implements a lift (elevator) control system. A server process accepts calls on floor buttons and moves the lift to the requesting floor. The lift is very small and so can only take a single person at a time. In the lift are buttons that allow the passenger to choose the destination floor. The program should contain a number of passenger processes that make calls on the lift.

5.6 Modify the previous example so that there are now *m* lifts (each only carrying a single person). Hint: use a single server process to accept all calls from the floor buttons, and one process to represent each lift.

5.7 Consider a collection of *n* processes. Each has a unique identity and an arbitrary integer value (in the range 1 to 5, say). By communicating with every other process, each process is able to find out how many other processes have the same integer value. Construct a program that implements these communications (without deadlock!).

5.8 In the previous exercise, is it possible to order the processes so that a full
$(n - 1)*(n - 1)$ set of communications is not necessary?

5.9 In Pascal-FC, processes can be given unique identities by the parameter-passing
mechanism of initialization. If this facility were not present, then each process
would have to be communicated with as soon as it started its execution:

```
program name;
  const N = 9;

  process type TASK;
    entry ID(M : integer);
    var MYID : integer;
  begin
    accept ID(M : integer) do
      MYID := M;
    repeat
        (* code *)
    forever
  end;

  var clients : array[1..N] of TASK;

  process namer;
    var I : integer;
  begin
    for I := 1 to N do
      clients[I].ID(I)
  end;

begin
  cobegin
    for I := 1 to N do
      clients[I];
      namer
  coend
end.
```

For a large number of processes this naming sequence gives poor concurrency.
Write a program that implements distributed naming, that is, each process takes
responsibility for calling other processes and passing on naming information. Hint:
consider the process set to be a binary tree.

5.10 In a hardware fault-tolerant environment, processes are replicated. Consider a
program in which there are three client processes and one server process. The only
interactions in the program are between the clients and the server. The fault-
tolerant program has each software process replicated on different hardware. The
hardware is assumed to be 'fail stop'. In order for the program to execute correctly,
the replicated servers must interact with the clients in the same order. On program

start-up, one of the servers is considered to be the *leader*. It interacts with its clients using a standard **select** statement. However, whenever it interacts with a client it must communicate with the *follower* servers to say which process they must talk to. Write a program in which each client and the server is duplicated. The clients and server should be written to constitute a single-producer, one-buffer, dual-consumer relationship. Each client follows a deterministic path. The servers can ignore the problems that would arise in their communications (with each other) if one of them is on failed hardware. The program will be seen to be working correctly if each duplicated consumer client gets the same data from the buffer when the fair scheduler is used.

5.11 Timeouts can be used to take account of communication failure (when a process has failed). It may be assumed that a timeout of five seconds will extend beyond normal quiet periods. Is it possible to modify your solution to the previous exercise so that the leader server will not be affected by a failed follower, and vice versa? Would this have been easier with the facilities provided with synchronous message passing (i.e. symmetric selective waiting)? The failure of a server can be simulated by it terminating after a fixed number of cycles, rather than interacting indefinitely.

5.12 Write a program in which a number of customer processes interact with a bank cash dispensing process. A customer can ask for balance information or request money; however, the account must not go negative. A maximum of 100 pounds can be withdrawn in a one-hour period.

5.13 Modify the previous exercise so that there are now three cash dispensers. A customer may go to any dispenser. Note that more than one customer may share an account.

6 Semaphores

In Chapter 3, we asked whether it was possible to solve problems of mutual exclusion and condition synchronization without recourse to specialized language features. A lengthy discussion of the implementation of a critical section suggested that this was possible, but rather uncomfortable: some additional facilities appear desirable. Chapters 4 and 5 have introduced two such sets of features, based on the idea of message passing. These were not historically the first synchronization primitives, however. That honour falls to Dijkstra's (1968) semaphores.

In this chapter, we introduce the semaphore as a data type and then see its application in a number of familiar problems: mutual exclusion, Producer–Consumer, Readers and Writers and the Dining Philosophers. During the course of solving these problems, we shall use two kinds of semaphore, usually known as 'binary' and 'general'. We shall also ask whether it is actually necessary to have two kinds, or whether binary semaphores are sufficient.

Semaphores are rather low-level primitives compared with the message-passing models of Chapters 4 and 5. This is one of their primary disadvantages, recognition of which led to the more structured shared-memory facilities described in Chapter 7.

6.1   Definition of semaphores

Semaphores are an example of a **data type**. For the computer scientist, a data type has two attributes:

- a set of **permissible values**
- a set of **permissible operations** on objects of the type.

6.1.1   Permissible values of semaphores

In general, the permissible values for semaphores are the non-negative integers. However, it is common to distinguish between **general** (or **counting**) semaphores (which can take an arbitrary non-negative integer value) and **binary** semaphores (for which values are restricted to 0 and 1). Binary semaphores have the advantage that only a single bit of storage is required to code their value. Applications of both types of semaphore will be seen later in this chapter.

6.1.2   Permissible operations on semaphores

There are only two operations which concurrent processes can carry out on semaphores. Dijkstra referred to these as the P and V operations, using the initial letters of two Dutch words. In many English texts, the operators are called **wait** (Dijkstra's P) and **signal** (Dijkstra's V). Pascal-FC and this text both use the English names. The operations would usually be provided as predefined procedures.

The action of the wait operation can be described as follows:

- wait (S): decrease the value of S as soon as the result would be non-zero.

Clearly, this involves testing the value of S and (when appropriate) modifying its value. These two actions are to be implemented as a single indivisible operation.

The action of the signal operation is:

- signal (S): increment the value of S.

This is also to be implemented as a single indivisible action.

It is important to understand the consequences of the indivisibility of these operations. Suppose, for example, that the value of S is currently 1 and that two processes 'simultaneously' attempt to execute a wait on S. Only *one* of these operations will be able to complete before the next signal on S. In general, for any two arbitrary semaphore operations, op1 and op2, on a given semaphore, the following must hold:

$$\forall e \bullet (\text{op1} \rightarrow \text{op2}) \quad \text{or} \quad (\text{op2} \rightarrow \text{op1})$$

We are not stipulating the order in which the two instructions are carried out, but we are insisting that there is no overlap. The reader will recognize this as the mutual exclusion requirement.

The wait operation has the potential to delay a process. An implementation of semaphores *could* accomplish this by busy-waiting, but one of the advantages of semaphores over the techniques used in Chapter 3 is that busy-waiting is not the only method that can be used to hold up a process. Because busy-waiting is inefficient, **blocked waiting** would normally be preferred; this is what we shall usually assume in the rest of this chapter.

The actions of the semaphore operations when blocked waiting is used can be described as follows:

```
wait(s)
if s > 0 then
  s := s − 1
else
  block this process on s

signal(s)
if processes are blocked on s then
  unblock one of them
else
  s := s + 1
```

Again, an essential characteristic of these operations is that they are indivisible.

It is possible for a signal operation to be carried out when there are several processes blocked on the semaphore concerned. Notice that the definition of signal does not specify *which* process should be unblocked in such circumstances, but merely stipulates that *one* of them should be. An implementor of semaphores is free to choose any scheme: FIFO, process priority and random choice are all legitimate policies to use, for example. We shall return to this question in Section 6.4, when we consider the notion of fairness in relation to semaphores.

Another issue with the signal operation concerns what should happen if an attempt is made to signal on a binary semaphore which already has a value of 1. Three possible approaches are:

- the signal becomes a 'no-operation' (that is, it has no effect);
- the implementation generates an error message and aborts the process executing the signal;
- the calling process is blocked until the semaphore value becomes 0, at which point the operation may be completed.

The last of these is an unusual approach, and will be ignored in this book.

As we have decided to ignore the possibility of a blocking signal, it is only the wait operation that has the potential to block a process. Even then, blocking will only occur when a wait is carried out on a semaphore whose value is zero. For this reason, it can be argued that 'wait' is a somewhat misleading name for the operation: in everyday English, wait always implies some delay, whereas the semaphore operation will not delay a process if the semaphore value is currently greater than zero.

6.2 Pascal-FC's semaphores

In Pascal-FC, a new standard type, semaphore, has been introduced. Declaration of semaphore variables is as for any of Pascal's unstructured data types, so the following are valid declarations:

```
type
  semtable = array[1..10] of semaphore;

var
  s1, s2: semaphore;
  stab: semtable;
  semarray: array[1..10] of semaphore;
  semrec:
    record
      i: integer;
      s: semaphore
    end;
```

Note that Pascal-FC does not make any distinction between binary and general semaphores: it is the programmer's responsibility to ensure that a signal is never carried out on a (logically) binary semaphore with a value of 1.

There are two restrictions on the declaration of semaphores (including any structured object having a semaphore as an element at any level):

- they may only be declared in the main program declaration part;
- they may be parameters of processes, procedures or functions, but they must always be formally declared as **var** parameters.

The rationale for both restrictions is the same, and it is left as an exercise for the reader to consider why these restrictions have been imposed.

The two semaphore operations have been implemented as procedures in Pascal-FC. Calls have the form:

```
wait(s)
```

and

    signal(s)

The single parameter in either of these procedure calls *must* be a semaphore. Pascal-FC does not specify any particular queue discipline on semaphores (i.e. choice is non-deterministic), but we shall usually assume in this book that if a signal is carried out on a semaphore on which several processes are blocked, a random choice determines which one of them is unblocked. Section 6.4 briefly considers the possible effects of the queuing discipline in use.

The wait and signal operations are not quite all that we require to write programs using semaphores: there is also the question of providing initial values. We shall return to this issue in the next section. A final facility which is useful in a teaching language is to *output* the current value of a semaphore. To permit this, Pascal-FC allows semaphores to be parameters of the write(ln) procedure.

6.3   Mutual exclusion with semaphores

Solving the two-process mutual exclusion problem is trivially easy using semaphores: the entry and exit protocols are implemented by wait and signal operations, respectively, on a binary semaphore. In fact, the generalization to N processes ($N \geq 2$) is so simple that we consider it straight away. Below is the outline of the required process declarations:

```
const
  N = 3;     (* for example *)

process type proc;
begin
  repeat
    wait(s);
    CriticalSection;
    signal(s)
  forever
end;

var
  P, Q, R: proc;
```

The definitions of wait and signal show the importance of the semaphore value, and we must find an appropriate initial value for s in the above. Consider what might occur when the program containing these processes begins its execution: s still has its initial value. Suppose that P wants to enter its critical section, but that Q and R do not. Requirement 3.5 of Chapter 3 demands that P should be allowed to proceed. This means that when it executes wait(s), it should not be blocked. This, in turn, means that the initial value of s cannot be 0.

Suppose that Q requests entry to its critical section while P is in its critical section. As processes must have mutually exclusive access to this section, the request cannot be granted before P has left the critical section. This implies that the value of s must be zero while a process is inside its critical section. As a process must pass the wait(s) operation in order to enter its critical section, we now see that the initial value for s in the above example can only be 1. Any other value will cause incorrect program behaviour.

The reader may now wonder whether semaphores must *always* have an initial value of 1. If this were so, then an implementation of semaphores could automatically assign this value to each semaphore as part of its declaration. We shall see, however, that 1 is *not* the appropriate value in some other applications. Hence, the programmer must have some means of providing an arbitrary (non-negative) initial value. In Pascal-FC, this is done by the initial procedure, a call to which has the form:

```
initial(s,v)
```

Here, s must be a semaphore, and v must be a non-negative integer expression. The semantics of this procedure are simply described as follows:

```
s := v
```

There is an important restriction on the use of initial. It should be clear that it would be dangerous for a concurrent process to use this procedure. As it simply gives a value to the semaphore, it would cause havoc, for example, if executed when processes were already blocked on the semaphore. Hence, only the main program is allowed to perform semaphore initialization. As the semaphores in a program must have the appropriate initial values before the processes begin concurrent execution, the only meaningful place for calls to initial is before the **cobegin** of the main program body.

A suitable body for a Pascal-FC program using the above process outlines can now be written as follows:

```
begin
  initial(s,1);
  cobegin
    P;
    Q;
    R
  coend
end.
```

6.4   Fairness and semaphores

The definitions of wait and signal provided above do not commit the implementor of semaphores to any particular queuing discipline, but the choice made can have a very marked effect on the liveness properties of a program. In this section, we consider two different disciplines:

- FIFO. Any process attempting a wait on a semaphore with a value of 0 is blocked on a FIFO queue. When a signal is executed on that semaphore, the first process in the queue is unblocked (allowed to complete its wait).

- RANDOM. Any process that attempts a wait on a semaphore with a value of 0 joins an unordered set of processes. When a signal is carried out, one member from the set is chosen at random and completes its wait.

Note that these are both examples of semaphore implementations using blocked waiting.

As an illustration of the effects that the queuing discipline might have, consider the N-process mutual exclusion example outlined above. Consider a scenario in which Q and R are both blocked on s when P leaves its critical section. P executes a signal. Suppose that this unblocks R. When will Q be unblocked?

The answer will depend on the queuing discipline used in the semaphore implementation. If FIFO queues are in use, then we can certainly say that Q will be unblocked by the next signal operation. The reason that it was not unblocked this time must be that R was ahead of it in the queue. As the only other process in the program (P) is not blocked, then Q must now be at the head of the queue. If the random discipline is in use, we cannot be so sure: we can say this only if Q is still the only process blocked on s when the next signal is executed. With this random discipline, processes blocked on a semaphore can be overtaken by later arrivals. This could continue for ever, with Q repeatedly being unlucky.

The FIFO discipline is an example of what is usually called a **strongly fair semaphore**. With a strongly fair semaphore, no matter how long the queue of blocked processes, a new arrival will eventually be unblocked provided that enough signal operations are carried out. (If N processes are already blocked when the newcomer arrives, it will need $N + 1$ signals to unblock it.) No such guarantee can be given with the random discipline, which is an example of what is usually called a **weakly fair semaphore**. With a weakly fair semaphore, a process could remain permanently blocked even if an infinite number of signal operations was carried out.

Hence, the liveness properties of our mutual exclusion program will be affected by the semaphore implementation. If $N > 2$, then processes can suffer indefinite postponement (starvation) if weakly fair semaphores are in use. If $N \leq 2$, this cannot occur with either of the disciplines we have considered. Starvation will not occur, with strongly fair semaphores, no matter how many processes there are.

Note that, in this section, we have concentrated on the influence of the semaphore implementation on liveness. We have not been discussing the general process scheduling policy of the language implementation. Even if the latter is fair, processes can still experience lockout if the semaphores are not strongly fair.

6.5   Semaphore invariants

In analysing the behaviour of semaphore programs, it is useful to know that two relations are satisfied at all times during the execution of a program. They are:

(1) $s >= 0$, and

(2) $s = s0 + \#signals - \#waits$

where s0 is the initial value of the semaphore, #signals is the number of signal operations carried out to date, and #waits is the number of *completed* waits (note the importance of this qualification).

As an illustration of the application of semaphore invariants, consider again the mutual exclusion problem. The following proof of the correctness of our semaphore solution follows Ben Ari (1990). The semaphore invariants are used to show that:

$$\#CS + S = 1$$

is invariant. Here, #CS is the number of processes currently executing the critical section and S is the current value of the semaphore. Since we know from invariant (1) that:

$$S => >= 0$$

it would follow that $\#CS <= 1$, which is what we want to prove.

The following steps use the semaphore invariants:

(1) $\#CS = \#wait(S) - \#signal(S)$, which can be shown by examination of the program text;
(2) $S = 1 + \#signal(S) - \#wait(S)$, which is semaphore invariant (2);
(3)   From (1) and (2), it follows that $S = 1 - \#CS$;
(4)   Hence, $\#CS + S = 1$.

6.6   Condition synchronization with semaphores

Semaphores are not only useful for implementing mutual exclusion, but can also be used for general condition synchronization. We shall, over the next few pages, consider a number of illustrative applications, starting with the now familiar Producer–Consumer problem.

6.6.1   Producer and consumer – unbounded buffer

We first make the simplifying assumption that the buffer used to decouple the producer and the consumer has an infinite capacity. In this case, we have to meet Requirement 3.1b, which we repeat for convenience:

$$\forall e \bullet \text{produce}^i \rightarrow \text{consume}^i \qquad \qquad \textbf{(3.1b)}$$

The requirement implies that:

(1)   the producer may produce a new item at any time;
(2)   the consumer may only consume an item when the buffer is not empty.

In addition, we would want to impose the following requirements:

(3)   the order in which items are placed in the buffer is the same as the order in which they are taken from it;
(4)   all items produced are eventually consumed.

Actually, (3) is a property which we require of the buffer, rather than a requirement of inter-process communication. We shall assume that we have an implementation of a buffer, with the two operations place and take, which guarantee a FIFO discipline on buffer accesses. Requirement (4) is a liveness requirement.

Our problem is to ensure that the consumer is never allowed to 'overtake' the producer. Clearly, it must be possible to block the consumer so that it never attempts to take when the buffer is empty. The only means of blocking a process using semaphores is to have that process execute a wait on a semaphore with a value of 0. We must ensure, then, that the semaphore has a value of 0 whenever the buffer is empty, including initially before the producer has become active. When the producer has executed place, it should signal on this semaphore. If the consumer is already blocked, it will be unblocked by this operation; otherwise the semaphore value will be incremented and the consumer will not block when it next attempts to take an item. In outline, then, the producer and the consumer will be as follows:

```
process producer;
var
  item: sometype;
begin
  repeat
    produce(item);
    place(item);
    signal(ItemsReady)
  forever
end;

process consumer;
var
  item: sometype;
begin
  repeat
    wait(ItemsReady);
    take(item);
    consume(item)
  forever
end;
```

The initial value of ItemsReady must be 0.

It is clear from the above code that the following would have to hold in order for the consumer to overtake the producer:

#wait > #signal

or, equivalently:

#signal − #wait < 0

Hence, from semaphore invariant (2), we have:

ItemsReady < 0

since the initial value in this case is 0. This clearly violates invariant (1), and we conclude that the consumer cannot overtake the producer with the above code.

The version we have now produced may not yet be entirely satisfactory, however. When the buffer is not empty, there is nothing to stop overlapping of a place and a take. We might have assumed that these two operations could be safely overlapped, but this is not necessarily so: it depends on how the buffer has been implemented. Moreover, if we consider the more general case in which there may be multiple producers and consumers, then we may very well expect that overlapping buffer operations would be undesirable. Finally, then, we make our solution more general by introducing a binary semaphore MutEx to enforce mutual exclusion on buffer accesses. Its initial value is 1.

```
process producer;
var
  item: sometype;
begin
  repeat
    produce(item);
    wait(MutEx);
    place(item);
    signal(MutEx);
    signal(ItemsReady)
  forever
end;

process consumer;
var
  item: sometype;
begin
  repeat
    wait(ItemsReady);
    wait(MutEx);
    take(item);
    signal(MutEx);
    consume(item)
  forever
end;
```

6.6.2 Producer and consumer – bounded buffer

Of course, any practical concurrent program requiring buffered communication between producers and consumers will require the use of a buffer of finite size. We shall use the constant BuffSize for this. We must now add Requirement 3.2b, as follows:

$$\forall e \bullet \text{consume}^i \rightarrow \text{produce}^{i + \text{BuffSize}}$$

Another way to express this requirement is that the producer must never attempt to place an item into the buffer when there is no free space. This leads to an easy implementation of the new requirement: we need to introduce a semaphore that will block the producer whenever there are no free spaces. Hence, this semaphore must have a value of zero when this condition obtains and, in general, the value of the new semaphore should equal the number of free spaces remaining. Its initial value, therefore, is BuffSize. A full Pascal-FC program is given below. It is structured so that the producer produces all the lower-case letters from 'a' to 'z': the consumer terminates when it has processed the 'z':

```
program pcsem;
(* Producer-Consumer – semaphore version *)

const
  BuffSize = 5;
  BuffInxMax = 4;     (* must be BuffSize – 1 *)
var
  MutEx: semaphore;       (* binary *)
  SpacesLeft: semaphore;      (* general *)
  ItemsReady: semaphore;       (* general *)
  Buffer: record
            Products: array[0..BuffInxMax] of char;
            NextIn: integer;
            NextOut: integer
          end;

procedure place(ch: char);
begin
  Buffer.Products[Buffer.NextIn] := ch;
  Buffer.NextIn := (Buffer.NextIn + 1) mod BuffSize
end;     (* place *)

procedure take(var ch: char);
begin
  ch := Buffer.Products[Buffer.NextOut];
  Buffer.NextOut := (Buffer.NextOut + 1) mod BuffSize
end;     (* take *)

process producer;
var
  item: char;
begin
  for item := 'a' to 'z' do
    begin
    wait(SpacesLeft);
    wait(MutEx);
    place(item);
    signal(MutEx);
    signal(ItemsReady)
    end
end;     (* producer *)

process consumer;
var
  local: char;
begin
  repeat
    wait(ItemsReady);
    wait(MutEx);
    take(local);
    signal(MutEx);
```

```
      signal(SpacesLeft);
      write(local)
    until local = 'z';
    writeln
end;      (* consumer *)

begin
    initial(SpacesLeft,BuffSize);
    initial(ItemsReady,0);
    initial(MutEx,1);
    cobegin
        producer;
        consumer
    coend
end.
```

6.7 Are general semaphores necessary?

The Producer–Consumer problem provides a good example of the application of general semaphores. But do we really need general semaphores, or are binary semaphores sufficient? How could we answer such a question? One possibility might be to take all known programs using general semaphores and to attempt to re-write them using only the binary type. If we found one case where this was not possible, then we would have established a requirement for general semaphores.

This is not a promising approach. A huge number of semaphore algorithms would need to be translated. More importantly, it is difficult to see how we could *ever* convince ourselves of the necessity of counting semaphores in this way. Showing that all existing algorithms could be converted would tell us nothing about the one that someone may invent the next day.

If, however, we could simulate the action of a general semaphore using only binary ones (and whatever ordinary variables proved necessary), then we could be certain that there was no problem that could be solved with general semaphores that could not be solved using binary ones. We would say that they have the same expressive power. A simulation would require:

- a data structure to represent a general semaphore;
- wait and signal procedures to implement the required operations on general semaphores.

Below, we present such a simulation (Barz, 1983):

```
type
  GenSemaphore =
  record
    MutEx: BinSemaphore;
    delay: BinSemaphore;
    count: integer
  end;
```

The MutEx component, as its name suggests, is used to provide mutual exclusion over the operations on GenSemaphore. It therefore has the initial value of 1. The integer count holds the value of the semaphore and the delay binary semaphore is used to block any process that calls a wait operation when the count value is 0. The operations below require the initial value of delay to be 0 if count is initially 0, or otherwise 1:

```
procedure GenWait(var s: GenSemaphore);
begin
  wait(s.delay);
  wait(s.MutEx);
  s.count := s.count - 1;
  if s.count > 0 then
    signal(s.delay);
  signal(s.MutEx)
end;      (* GenWait *)

procedure GenSignal(var s: GenSemaphore);
begin
  wait(s.MutEx);
  s.count := s.count + 1;
  if s.count = 1 then
    signal(s.delay);
  signal(s.MutEx)
end;      (* GenSignal *)
```

The reader should be able to see how these operations work.

The above simulation shows that, theoretically, general semaphores are redundant. In practice, having to simulate the effect of a general semaphore may be inconvenient for efficiency reasons.

6.8 Further illustrative examples of the use of semaphores

6.8.1 Readers and writers

We have met the problem of readers and writers earlier in this book. The requirements for a solution state that any number of readers can be concurrently active while write accesses to the data concerned must exclude *all* other accesses. Given that readers can operate concurrently without interference with one another, then a solution to the problem must allow them to do so. Hence, simply placing all accesses within a single critical section protected by a binary semaphore will not suffice.

We shall present a solution to this problem in the form of OPEN and CLOSE procedures. Any process requiring access to the data must first call OPEN, indicating whether the access is for reading or writing. When the process finishes its access, it must call CLOSE, again indicating whether it had been reading or writing. We ignore the details of how the data is given its initial values. Hence, the following are the outlines of reader and writer processes:

```
process type reader;
var
   local: SomeType;
begin
   repeat
      OPEN(ReadAccess);
      (* access data, copying to local *)
      CLOSE(ReadAccess);
      (* use local data *)
   forever
end;    (* reader *)

process type writer;
var
   local: SomeType;
begin
   repeat
      (* produce new local data *)
      OPEN(WriteAccess);
      (* write new local values to data *)
      CLOSE(WriteAccess)
   forever
end;    (* writer *)
```

Courtois *et al.* (1971) suggested the following protocols for the OPEN and CLOSE operations:

```
OPEN:
if mode = ReadAccess then
begin
   wait(MutEx);
   readers := readers + 1;
   if readers = 1 then
      wait(writing);
   signal(MutEx)
end else
   wait(writing)
```

```
CLOSE:
if mode = ReadAccess then
begin
    wait(MutEx);
    readers := readers − 1;
    if readers = 0 then
        signal(writing);
    signal(MutEx)
end else
    signal(writing)
```

This solution uses two binary semaphores, MutEx and writing, which must both have initial values of 1. The variable readers is an integer initialized to 0.

The following points will help the reader to understand the operation of the above procedures:

(1)   A reader executes a wait on writing (thereby making itself susceptible to blocking on that semaphore) only if there are no readers already active in the data.

(2)   If there are readers active in the data, the first one of them must have passed the wait on writing, and the value of this semaphore will therefore be 0.

(3)   Points (1) and (2) above combine to ensure that, if there is at least one active reader, then no writer can open the data (because writing is zero), but that any additional reader can.

(4)   Any writer active in the data must have passed the wait on writing, and its value must be 0.

(5)   If there is an active writer and a reader attempts to open the data, then the reader will block on writing because its value is 0.

(6)   A reader that blocks on writing must have passed the wait on MutEx, and its value must be 0.

(7)   If there is a reader blocked on writing, then any subsequent reader that attempts to open the data will block on MutEx.

(8)   Points (4) to (7) combine to ensure that there is at most one writer, and that if there is a writer there can be no reader.

(9)   A writer that closes the data will either awaken a process blocked on writing (which may be another writer or a reader), or increment its value to 1.

(10) If a writer awakens a reader blocked on writing, then the reader will be able to continue with the signal on MutEx. Either this will awaken a blocked reader or, if there is none, the value will be incremented to 1. In either case, the reader executing the signal has completed the OPEN procedure and is now active in the data.

(11)   Any reader that was unblocked by the signal on MutEx will now, in turn, also execute a signal on that semaphore. If there are any further blocked readers, one of them will be awakened. Readers, therefore, take part in what is called a **cascaded wake**.

The above procedures enforce the necessary safety requirements, but they can be criticized on liveness grounds. This is because readers can conspire to lock out writers indefinitely: as long as a single reader is active, no writer can gain access, but other readers are allowed in. A Readers-and-Writers algorithm with these characteristics is called a **readers' preference** protocol. In applications where there are frequent read accesses and it is important to make frequent updates, these simple procedures might be unsuitable.

As an alternative to the above procedures, Courtois *et al.* (1971) presented an algorithm in which incoming readers become blocked when a writer is waiting to access the data: their solution uses five binary semaphores. The following variable declarations are made:

```
var
    readers, writers: integer;      (* initially 0 *)
    MutEx1,
    MutEx2,
    MutEx3,
    writing,
    r: semaphore;      (* initially 1 *)
```

The algorithm is given below:

```
OPEN:
if mode = ReadAccess then
begin
    wait(MutEx3);
    wait(r);
    wait(MutEx1);
    readers := readers + 1;
    if readers = 1 then
        wait(writing);
    signal(MutEx1);
    signal(r);
    signal(MutEx3)
end else
begin
    wait(MutEx2);
    writers := writers + 1;
    if writers = 1 then
        wait(r);
    signal(MutEx2);
    wait(writing);
end
```

```
CLOSE:
if mode = ReadAccess then
begin
  wait(MutEx1);
  readers := readers − 1;
  if readers = 0 then
    signal(writing);
  signal(MutEx1)
end else
begin
  signal(writing);
  wait(MutEx2);
  writers := writers − 1;
  if writers = 0 then
    signal(r);
  signal(MutEx2)
end
```

These procedures should be studied carefully: they will not only challenge the reader's grasp of semaphores, but also illustrate the non-trivial design task that faces anyone using semaphores to implement even fairly simple requirements. The following points will facilitate an understanding of the operation of the algorithm:

(1)   The role of MutEx1 is the same as that of MutEx in the first version, and writing also plays its previous role.

(2)   A writer that attempts to open the data when no other process wishes to do so will succeed. When it leaves the OPEN procedure, writing and r will both be zero, MutEx2 will be 1, and writers will be 1.

(3)   Because of (1) and (2), as long as there is a writer active in the data, further requests to open for writing will result in the calling process being blocked on writing. This is so regardless of any pending requests to open for reading.

(4)   Because of (1), once a writer is active in the data, any requests to open for reading will result in blocking on r (first reader) or MutEx3 (subsequent ones). This is so whether or not there are additional writers already waiting to open.

(5)   Because a writer that closes the data executes signal(writing), if both readers and writers are waiting to open the data, one of the writers will be unblocked.

(6)   If readers are active in the data, any writer requesting entry will block on writing, because the first reader executed wait(writing). Before doing so, it will have executed wait(r) and its value will be zero. Any further applications to open for reading will now block on r (first reader) or MutEx3 (subsequent ones).

One of the exercises at the end of this chapter requires further exploration of this algorithm.

6.8.2 The dining philosophers

We pointed out in earlier chapters that the Dining Philosophers problem is a useful allegory because it can illustrate a number of pitfalls, including deadlock. We shall first see how easy it is to produce a deadlocking 'solution' using semaphores, and then present a deadlock-free version.

Recall that each philosopher must pick up two chopsticks in order to eat and that she must have exclusive use of them. We can model each chopstick as a binary semaphore with an initial value of 1. Picking up a chopstick is implemented by executing a wait, while putting it down is effected by a signal. Hence the following might be proposed as a solution:

```
repeat
    wait(LeftChop);
    wait(RightChop);
    eat;
    signal(LeftChop);
    signal(RightChop)
forever
```

A full Pascal-FC program using this outline is given below:

```
program philsem1;
(* Dining Philosophers – semaphore version 1 *)

const
    N = 5;
var
    chopsticks : array [1..N] of semaphore;    (* binary *)
    I : integer;

process type philosophers(name : integer);
begin
    repeat
        sleep(random(5));       (* THINKING *)
        wait(chopsticks[name]);
        wait(chopsticks[(name mod N) + 1]);
        sleep(random(5));       (* EATING *)
        signal(chopsticks[name]);
        signal(chopsticks[(name mod N) + 1]);
    forever
end;    (* philosophers *)
```

```
var
   phils : array[1..N] of philosophers;

begin
   for I := 1 to N do
         initial(chopsticks[I],1);
   cobegin
         for I := 1 to N do
               phils[I](I)
   coend
end.
```

This attempt is susceptible to deadlock for the same reason that the version presented in Chapter 3 could livelock (and that in Chapter 4 also deadlocks). If all philosophers 'simultaneously' pick up their left chopstick, none of them will be able to take the one to the right, and they will all starve.

We can prevent deadlock by removing one of the four necessary conditions for its occurrence. In the following program, the 'circular' pattern of requests and allocations is broken by ensuring that no more than $N - 1$ philosophers are ever simultaneously seated at the table. To do this using semaphores requires only the addition of a general semaphore (freechairs) with an initial value of $N - 1$. Hence a deadlock-free solution to the problem is as follows:

```
program philsem2;
(* Dining Philosophers – semaphore version 2 *)

const
   N = 5;
var
   chopsticks : array [1..N] of semaphore;      (* binary *)
   freechairs : semaphore;      (* general *)
   I : integer;

process type philosophers(name : integer);
begin
   repeat
         sleep(random(5));      (* THINKING *)
         wait(freechairs);
         wait(chopsticks[name]);
         wait(chopsticks[(name mod N) + 1]);
         sleep(random(5));      (* EATING *)
         signal(chopsticks[name]);
         signal(chopsticks[(name mod N) + 1]);
         signal(freechairs)
   forever
end;      (* philosophers *)
```

```
var
   phils : array[1..N] of philosophers;

begin
   for I := 1 to N do
       initial(chopsticks[I],1);
   initial(freechairs, N − 1);
   cobegin
       for I := 1 to N do
           phils[I](I)
   coend
end.
```

Informally we can say that the above program prevents deadlock because, if only four philosophers can sit down and compete for the five chopsticks, then at least one of them will be able to pick up two. The assumption is made that a philosopher who starts to eat will eventually finish and return her chopsticks. We should also like to know whether individual philosophers could suffer starvation. Does the semaphore implementation affect the answer to this question? If we assume that the underlying process scheduler is fair and that semaphores are implemented using blocked waiting, then this question amounts to asking whether there can ever be more than one process blocked on any of the semaphores in the program. It is left as an exercise to answer this question.

6.9   Implementation of semaphores

The applications programmer who needs to write a concurrent program in a language that supports semaphores needs only to know the syntax and semantics necessary to use them to implement whatever synchronization is required. Certainly, he or she can take for granted that the wait and signal operations have been implemented in such a way that they are indivisible (otherwise one would not have reliable semaphore invariants). However, the implementation of these operations is fairly straightforward, and we shall now consider some possible methods. In particular, we focus on the way in which the operations might be guaranteed to be indivisible.

What we must do is to make the wait and signal operations into critical sections. We need to enforce lock and unlock operations to protect these critical sections, as follows:

```
WAIT:
lock;
if s > 0 then
    begin
    s := s − 1;
    unlock
    end
else
    block_and_unlock

SIGNAL:
lock;
if processes are blocked on s then
    unblock one of them
else
    s := s + 1;
unlock
```

Let us clarify the indivisibility requirements. We must ensure that operations on a given semaphore s cannot be overlapped. It is not necessary to ensure that an operation on a semaphore t does not overlap with an operation on a semaphore s, and any mechanism that did so would potentially reduce efficiency by limiting the degree of concurrency that could be achieved. We shall see that one common method of achieving indivisibility does, in fact, prevent overlapping of any two semaphore operations, even though the semaphores involved are different.

We shall now consider three approaches to the implementation of the lock and unlock operations. They are:

(1)   a software method relying on the ordinary memory access operations included in the instruction set of any CPU;

(2)   disablement of interrupts;

(3)   use of special instructions provided by the CPU designer specifically for the solution of synchronization problems.

Whilst looking at these different approaches, we shall assume that we want to implement semaphores either on a uniprocessor or a tightly-coupled multiprocessor.

6.9.1   Software method

We saw in Chapter 3 that it is possible to solve the mutual exclusion problem without special language features; the lock and unlock operations we now require could be implemented by the entry and exit protocols of one of the n-process solutions we presented. The assumptions that they rested on apply equally to uniprocessors or to multiprocessors, so that this approach could be used on either type of architecture.

6.9.2 Disabling interrupts

Unlike the software solutions, this method is only applicable to a uniprocessor system, for reasons that will be stated later. As we saw in Chapter 1, parallel logical processors are implemented on a hardware processor by interleaving instructions from the various processes: the run-time support system switches the CPU from one process to another from time to time. The two main occasions for a process switch are:

(1) in a time-sharing system, the system clock indicates that the process currently running has now used its current time quantum;

(2) in a system recognizing differences in process priorities, an event occurs that unblocks a process of higher priority than the one currently running in the processor.

In practice, both events would be signalled to the system by the occurrence of interrupts. It follows that disabling interrupts (temporarily) will prevent any process switches from taking place and will make any code between the disable and enable instructions indivisible. Hence the lock operation is simply 'disable interrupts' and unlock is 'enable interrupts'. Each of these is a single instruction at the machine-code level.

It is important to understand that, in a multiprocessor, a process that executes the disable interrupts instruction only inhibits interrupts on the processor on which it is running: it exercises no control over what is happening on any other processor, and therefore this method (alone) is not suitable for such a system.

This approach to the problem, while simple, is more drastic in its effects than it needs to be. Since *all* process switches are temporarily abolished while a process is executing an operation on semaphore s, the system cannot respond to any urgent events during this period. This might be a serious problem in a real-time control system, where the occurrence of such events will generally require that a high-priority process be run in order to maintain the safety of the controlled system. It may be that the high-priority process would not want to use the same critical section as is being protected by the ongoing semaphore operation, so the process is being prevented from running by a lower-priority process for no good reason. This is clearly not ideal but, as the wait and signal operations can be coded into a fairly small number of instructions, the interrupt lockout is unlikely to last more than a few tens of microseconds on a modern processor.

6.9.3 The use of 'special' instructions

Whereas the processors of the early 1960s were not designed to provide any special support for concurrent programming, today's often are. CPU designers, therefore, usually now provide special-purpose atomic instructions to implement a lock operation (unlock does not have to be specially provided for, as it can be implemented by a single write operation). Moreover, their CPU designs often anticipate multiprocessor applications, so that these instructions will work in such configurations. Various versions of these 'special' instructions have been provided by different manufacturers, but one of the most common is the Test and Set (TAS) operation, as provided (for example) on the Motorola 68000 family of microprocessors. We shall focus on the TAS instruction in this section. (We describe general principles, rather than the TAS instruction of any specific processor family.)

The assembly language programmer would see the instruction as an operation with one operand. The operand would be some suitable storage unit, such as a byte, word or bit. The instruction carries out the following as an indivisible step:

(1)   TEST the operand and set the CPU status flags so that they reflect whether it is currently zero or non-zero;

(2)   SET the operand, so that it is non-zero.

The effect on the operand is therefore always the same: it is non-zero on completion of the instruction. However, the processor status flags always reflect the value that the operand had *when the instruction began*. A lock may, therefore, be implemented as follows:

```
LOOP:
        TAS lockbyte
        BNZ LOOP        ; branch back if non-zero
        CriticalSection
        CLR lockbyte    ; set lockbyte to zero
```

The implementors of a TAS instruction will have ensured that, even on a tightly-coupled multiprocessor, it is carried out as an atomic action. On the Motorola 68000 processor, the TAS instruction is implemented at the bus level with what is called a **read–modify–write** cycle. This means that any processor executing the instruction is granted exclusive use of the data bus for the entire time that it takes to access a storage location and to write a new value into it: no other processor can 'sneak in' between the reading and writing.

Suppose that two processes, running on different processors, simultaneously attempt to execute the TAS instruction for the same lockbyte. Suppose also that the value of this byte is initially zero. One of the processes will be granted exclusive use of the bus to execute the instruction. When it has finished, the other may be granted exclusive use. The result is that one process will complete TAS with the CPU flags indicating that lockbyte was zero and the other with its CPU flags indicating that the value was non-zero. One process will enter its critical section and the other will busy-wait on the loop.

6.9.4 Priority and busy waiting

Methods (1) and (3) for making semaphore operations indivisible (see beginning of Section 6.9) both rely on busy waiting. We now consider a problem that can arise in *any* situation in which busy waiting is used and in which processes with different priorities share a hardware processor. This problem will illustrate once more the pitfalls that await the designer of concurrent systems!

Suppose that processes running on a hardware processor have different priorities and that a low-priority process has just passed a lock operation and is now executing the semaphore operation protected by it. Now a high-priority process assigned to the same processor becomes executable. The scheduler should switch to this process. Assume that it now attempts to enter the locked section. It will not succeed, because the section is locked: hence it will busy-wait until the low-priority process has cleared the protected section. However, if the scheduling is strictly based on process priority, the low-priority process will not be given the CPU because a high-priority process is running! One of the exercises in this chapter explores a solution to this problem.

6.10 Why semaphores?

If critical sections can be implemented in any of the three ways just described, why do we need semaphores? We know, after all, that once we can achieve mutual exclusion, we can implement any algorithm that uses general semaphores. However, as we pointed out in Chapter 3, methods that rely on busy-waiting, as our first and third approaches did, make inefficient use of processor instruction cycles: while a processor is executing a busy-waiting loop, it cannot be performing any useful work. It might be acceptable to allow such busy waiting for very short periods, but sometimes we might need to hold up a process for fairly long intervals. A buffer, for example, might remain empty for many seconds if the computational effort involved in producing items was significant. It would be profligate to have busy waiting continue for such a long period. Nor would the method using disablement of interrupts be suitable in such circumstances: to be unable to respond to potentially urgent interrupt requests for such a protracted time would be disastrous in real-time control systems.

The problem is that the applications programmer needs to be provided with a synchronization method which is applicable in a wide variety of circumstances: sometimes processes may be blocked for a few microseconds, but seconds or even minutes of blocking may be needed in other cases. A practical implementation of semaphores would achieve blocking not by busy waiting, but by making the blocked process unrunnable, so that it does not contend for (and therefore use) processor cycles.

The implementor of semaphores is in a different position from the applications programmer: the range of circumstances he or she has to deal with is very restricted. It is simply necessary to provide a lock that will protect the wait and signal operations. Both of these can be coded into a comparatively small number of instructions, so that the implementor knows that any busy-waiting (or interrupt lockout) which is involved will always be for an acceptably short period of time. What would not be appropriate for general use, then, is quite suitable for this very restricted application.

6.11   Evaluation of semaphores

Semaphores are beautifully simple and can be efficiently implemented, but they have received extensive criticism. The principal complaint is that they are at too low a level of abstraction and, therefore, that they are difficult to use reliably. Omitting a single signal, for example, is likely eventually to lead to deadlock. Omitting a single wait may lead to a violation of safety requirements, such as mutual exclusion. Placing wait and signal operations in the wrong places, rather than omitting them, can equally lead to erroneous program behaviour. All of this is made worse by the fact that semaphores are an unstructured programming tool, so that synchronization code is likely to be widely dispersed in a program which uses them, rather than localized in well defined regions. Fault finding and maintenance of such software is likely to be difficult. Hence, while semaphores are adequate for simple concurrent systems, it would be very difficult to ensure the reliability of a large system that depended on them. In the next chapter, while remaining with the shared-memory model, we shall investigate inter-process communication and synchronization with more structured language features.

SUMMARY

Semaphores have been introduced as a data type for which the permissible values are non-negative integers and the permissible operators are wait and signal. For reasons of efficiency and code readability, it is useful to have general semaphores, but we have seen that binary semaphores (with permissible values of 0 and 1) are, in principle, sufficient.

A number of familiar problems were successfully tackled with semaphores. However, though semaphores are elegant and simple, it is not always easy to devise an appropriate algorithm or to understand an existing one. Moreover, mistakes can fairly easily be made. These problems arise from the low-level nature of semaphores.

Though we do not, in general, focus on methods of implementing communication and synchronization primitives in this book, we have made an exception with semaphores, as their implementation is fairly straightforward. The essence of the implementor's problem is to make the wait and signal operations indivisible. Three possible ways of doing this were outlined.

FURTHER READING

Andrews G.R. (1991). *Concurrent Programming: Principles and Practice*. Benjamin/Cummings

Dijkstra E.W. (1968). Co-operating Sequential Processes. In *Programming Languages* (Genuys F., ed.). Academic Press

Hsieh C.S. (1989). Further Comments on Implementation of General Semaphores. *Operating Systems Review*, **23**(1), 9–10

Lister A.M. and Eager R.D. (1988). *Fundamentals of Operating Systems*. Macmillan

EXERCISES

6.1   Can a process be simultaneously blocked on more than one semaphore? Give reasons for your answer.

6.2   If a semaphore has a non-zero value, is it possible for processes to be currently blocked on it?

6.3   Generalize the solution to the mutual exclusion problem so that the programmer can specify for k, the number of processes that can be simultaneously in their 'critical' section, any positive integer.

6.4   In attempting to solve the Producer–Consumer problem (bounded buffer), suppose that the consumer process had been written as follows:

```
process consumer;
var
   item: sometype;
begin
   repeat
      wait(MutEx);
      wait(ItemsReady);
      take(item);
      signal(MutEx);
      signal(SpacesLeft);
      consume(item)
   forever
 end;      (* consumer *)
```

Would this then have been a satisfactory solution? What about the following?

```
process consumer;
var
   item: sometype;
begin
   repeat
      wait(ItemsReady);
      wait(MutEx);
      take(item);
      signal(SpacesLeft);
      signal(MutEx);
      consume(item)
   forever
end;     (* consumer *)
```

6.5   In the second algorithm for Readers and Writers, can a reader ever become blocked on writing?

6.6   Consider the implementation of semaphores on a tightly-coupled multiprocessor. Suppose that processes will be allowed to have different priorities. How can the problem introduced in Section 6.8.3 be solved by combining the use of the TAS instruction with one of the other methods for making the semaphore operations indivisible?

6.7   In Section 6.7.2 we presented a solution to the Dining Philosophers problem (philsem2) which prevented deadlock by removing the circular wait condition. Another possible approach is to remove the hold-and-wait condition, whereby processes hold on to resources already allocated to them while waiting for others. This can be done by allowing a philosopher to acquire both chopsticks, or none at all. Use semaphores to solve the problem using this strategy. In what ways might the fairness of the semaphore implementation affect the possibility of individual starvation?

6.8   In the program philsem2, can any semaphore have more than one process simultaneously blocked on it?

6.9   If semaphores were implemented with busy waiting, rather than blocked waiting, would individual starvation be possible in philsem2? (Assume that the underlying process scheduling is fair.)

6.10   A set of processes have *precedence* relationships if there are restrictions on the order in which they can execute. Consider six processes. P1 and P2 must both run before P3; P3 runs before P4 and P5; and P6 runs after all other processes. Use semaphores to enforce these precedence relationships. Allow each process to be cyclic so that, for example, the first execution of P6 can be concurrent with the second execution of P1 and P2.

6.11 Exercises 5.5 and 5.6 concern a lift control system. Solve these problems using semaphores.

6.12 Quantity semaphores have wait and signal operations that have two parameters: one is a semaphore and the other a positive integer Q. The signal operation adds Q to the semaphore value; the wait operation will only succeed when Q can be taken away from the current value of the semaphore without it going negative. Implement quantity semaphores using ordinary counting semaphores.

6.13 Use quantity semaphores (see previous question) to program the resource control problem outlined in Section 5.9.

7 Conditional Critical Regions and Monitors

Semaphores may be an elegant primitive for process synchronization, but they are at such a low level of abstraction that it is difficult to design and understand semaphore algorithms and serious mistakes are very easily made. Following the introduction of semaphores by Dijkstra, language designers explored more structured approaches. Hoare and Brinch Hansen were particularly influential in this, investigating first the idea of conditional critical regions, which are introduced in the early part of this chapter, and then monitors, to which the bulk of the chapter is devoted.

7.1 Beyond semaphores

In the previous chapter we saw that semaphores have significant limitations: being rather low-level primitives they leave too much for the applications programmer to do. As a result, semaphore algorithms can be difficult to design and to understand. This not only decreases programmer productivity, but also gives too much scope for programming errors.

Common errors in semaphore programming include the following:

- Even though the programmer understands the synchronization required on a data object, a wait or a signal may be omitted accidentally. In general, omitting a wait is likely to lead to an eventual breach of safety requirements, such as mutual exclusion, while omitting a signal is likely to lead to deadlock.

- The necessary semaphore operations are included but put in the wrong places.

- A programmer who has to modify existing software may misunderstand the synchronization required on a data object. With typical semaphore facilities (such as those provided in Pascal-FC), there is no means of providing a programmer with access to the data structure and at the same time forcing all such accesses to include the required semaphore protocols.

In the early seventies, attempts were made to make such errors less likely by providing language constructs which, being at a higher level of abstraction, allowed compilers partially to automate the necessary controls on access to shared data objects. In this chapter we shall look at two such constructs: **Conditional Critical Regions** (Brinch Hansen, 1972) and **monitors** (Hoare, 1974). Conditional critical regions can be seen as a precursor to monitors, but they are not merely of historical interest. Brinch Hansen (1981), for example, included them in his language Edison in preference to monitors. More recently, the Ada 9X **protected type**, which will be introduced in Chapter 8, has been influenced by conditional critical regions.

Pascal-FC provides an implementation of monitors, but not of conditional critical regions: the examples of these will, therefore, not be executable Pascal-FC programs.

7.2 Critical regions

Before looking at conditional critical regions, we shall consider a slightly simpler (and less powerful) construct: the **Critical Region** (CR). Note a point of terminology here: in previous chapters we used the term *critical* *section* to refer to a piece of code that *should* be executed under mutual exclusion if the algorithm is to work correctly. A programming error may result in a violation of this requirement. A critical *region* is a piece of code that, by definition, always *is* executed under mutual exclusion.

The CR construct provides a secure way of implementing mutual exclusion, because:

- a variable which should be accessed only under mutual exclusion can be declared in such a way that the compiler can flag as an error any attempt to access it outside designated critical regions;
- in effect, the wait and signal operations that would be required to guard a critical section when using semaphores are automatically generated by the compiler, so that they cannot be overlooked.

Though Pascal-FC does not include an implementation of critical regions, it is worthwhile to see how a solution to the Ornamental Gardens problem might look in a Pascal-like language. In the following program, we have used a programming notation similar to the one originally proposed by Brinch Hansen (1972). This comprises two components:

- a special form of declaration for variables which must be accessed under mutual exclusion;
- a new structured statement which is used to code the required operation on the variable.

One possible form for the declaration is:

```
var
   V: shared T;
```

where V is the variable name and T is a type. The structured statement could have the following form:

```
region V do
   S
```

where V is the name of the variable to be accessed in the critical region and S is an arbitrary statement (including structured statements) which implements the required action. *All* critical regions tagged with the same variable name execute under mutual exclusion, but the following statements may be allowed to execute concurrently:

```
region V1 do
   S1
region V2 do
   S2
```

Mutual exclusion could be implemented by some form of busy waiting but, as with semaphores, blocked waiting would usually be preferred on efficiency grounds, and this is what we shall assume from now on.

Any process that attempts to enter a critical region for V must first obtain a mutual exclusion lock on V. If it cannot, because another process already has the lock, it becomes blocked on a queue associated with V.† When a process leaves any critical region for V, it releases mutual exclusion over V. This will unblock one of the processes waiting on the queue, if there are any.

The following program illustrates how such facilities could be used to solve the Ornamental Gardens problem:

```
program GARDENS;
    (* Ornamental Gardens with Critical Regions *)
    (* NOT valid Pascal-FC *)
var
  COUNT: shared integer;

process TURNSTILE1;
var
  LOOP: integer;
begin
  for LOOP := 1 to 20 do
    region COUNT do
      COUNT := COUNT + 1
end;    (* TURNSTILE1 *)

process TURNSTILE2;
var
  LOOP: integer;
begin
  for LOOP := 1 to 20 do
    region COUNT do
      COUNT := COUNT + 1
end;    (* TURNSTILE2 *)

begin    (* main *)
  region COUNT do
    COUNT := 0;
  cobegin
    TURNSTILE1;
    TURNSTILE2
  coend;
  (* output final value of COUNT *)
end.
```

† Note that the queue is associated with V and not with the critical region: there may be several regions naming V, but there will only be one queue.

Because a special form of declaration has been introduced for shared variables, it is straightforward to build a compiler that can detect any attempt to access such a variable from outside a critical region. A variable declared as **shared** is only in scope inside critical regions tagged with its name. Note that this means that the initialization of COUNT in the above example must be coded as a critical region, even though mutual exclusion is not required at this point. An alternative would be to permit initial values to be given to **shared** variables as part of their declaration.

7.3   Conditional critical regions

Critical regions provide a more structured and secure way of implementing mutual exclusion than semaphores. However, we need something more powerful if we want critical regions to be as widely applicable as semaphores: critical regions, as described above, are not capable of simulating semaphores. Some provision is required for condition synchronization. **Conditional Critical Regions** (CCRs) were introduced to meet such requirements. In a language with CCRs, the declaration of **shared** variables may be done as before, but the structured statement needs to be extended to allow for a condition to be expressed. The following is one possible form:

> **region** V **when** B **do**
>   S

Here B is a boolean expression (which will usually refer to V), the evaluation of which is considered part of the critical region.

The execution of a CCR proceeds as follows:

(1)   A process wishing to enter a CCR for V must first obtain a mutual exclusion lock on V. Again, a queue can be provided to implement blocked waiting.

(2)   Once the mutual exclusion lock has been obtained, the boolean expression B can be evaluated. If it evaluates to true, the process can proceed to execute S under mutual exclusion. Otherwise it must release the mutual exclusion and become blocked. It cannot execute S until it has again obtained mutual exclusion on V and found B to be true.

(3)   A process that completes the execution of S must release its mutual exclusion on the **shared** variable.

The eventual release of processes blocked at the second stage above is considered further in Section 7.3.1. For the present, it is sufficient to understand that some arrangement will be made so that when a process leaves a CCR there is the potential for a process whose B is now true to inherit the mutual exclusion.

Bearing in mind again that Pascal-FC does not include conditional critical regions, we can now see how a CCR solution to the Producer–Consumer problem might look:

```
program PCON;
    (* Producer-Consumer with Conditional Critical Regions *)
    (* NOT valid Pascal-FC *)
const
  BUFFSIZE = ... ;
type
  ITEM = ...;
  BUFFTYPE =
    record
      NEXTIN,
      NEXTOUT,
      COUNT: integer;
      ELEMENTS: array [1..BUFFSIZE] of ITEM
    end;
var
  BUFF: shared BUFFTYPE;

process PRODUCER;
begin
  repeat
      (* produce item *)
    region BUFF when BUFF.COUNT < BUFFSIZE do
        (* put new item *)
  forever
end;    (* PRODUCER *)

process CONSUMER;
begin
  repeat
    region BUFF when BUFF.COUNT <> 0 do
        (* take next item *)
  forever
end;    (* CONSUMER *)

begin    (* main *)
    (* Initialize BUFF *)
  cobegin
    PRODUCER;
    CONSUMER
  coend
end.
```

7.3.1 Releasing blocked processes

Brinch Hansen (1972) suggested that, in implementing CCRs, two queues be associated with each **shared** variable. The first (the 'main' queue) is joined by any process that finds the relevant variable already locked. The second (the 'event' queue) is joined by a process that, having gained the mutual exclusion lock, finds the boolean condition false. Again note that there will be one main queue and one event queue per **shared** variable.

Whenever a process completes the execution of a CCR, it may have changed the value of B for some (or all) of the processes blocked on the event queue. Brinch Hansen therefore proposed that whenever a process leaves a CCR for V, *all* processes blocked on V's event queue be transferred to the main queue. Such processes then compete for re-entry into the CCR. When a process gains entry, it re-evaluates B.

The following pseudocode outlines the actions of a process finishing the CCR.

```
if not empty event_queue then
    transfer all processes from event queue to main queue;
if not empty main queue then
    release one process from main queue
else
    unlock the shared variable
```

With this scheme, condition synchronization is in effect implemented by polling since a process that finds B false will evaluate the expression repeatedly until it finally yields true. However, as Brinch Hansen (1972) points out, this is a *controlled* polling because retesting only takes place when there is reason to believe that the condition may have changed. This is less inefficient than the kind of busy waiting seen in Chapter 3, where a 'blocked' process continues to test a variable regardless of the actions of other processes.

Not everyone has accepted Brinch Hansen's argument. Process switches, as we noted in Chapter 2, are costly in CPU time, and releasing a process only to find that it blocks again (almost) immediately is not very satisfactory. One possible optimization would be to have the process which has completed the CCR evaluate B on behalf of the processes blocked on the event queue: one for which B now evaluated true would be released and would inherit mutual exclusion. However, while this is, in principle, an attractive optimization (because it eliminates unnecessary process switches), it may be difficult to implement. For example, the boolean expression B may contain variables local to a process: with some implementations, it may not be feasible for one process to 'see' the values of local variables of another. In such a case, there may be no alternative to releasing all processes blocked on the event queue.

7.3.2 Limitations of conditional critical regions

Though conditional critical regions are an improvement on semaphores, they still suffer from shortcomings. In particular:

- They may be dispersed in the program text. Ideally, all code that manipulates a particular shared variable should be collected together in one place.

- The integrity of a shared data structure is easily damaged because there is no control over what operations are carried out by the applications programmer inside a critical region. Ideally, a set of approved operations on the data structure should be provided and all processes should be restricted to those operations.

- They are difficult to implement efficiently, as outlined in the previous section. By contrast, semaphores can easily be implemented efficiently.

The second point is perhaps best illustrated with a simple example. Suppose that a data structure represents the accounts of customers in a bank. The data structure might, for example, be an array of records, as below:

```
const
  CUSTOMERMAX = ... ;

type
  ACCOUNTNUMBER = 1..CUSTOMERMAX;
  ACCOUNTREC =
  record
    ...
    BALANCE: integer;
    ...
  end;
var
  ACCOUNTS: shared array[1..CUSTOMERMAX] of ACCOUNTREC;
```

This data structure would be shared by processes running on behalf of customers at automatic service machines, clerks in branches, the manager at the customer's home branch, and so on, and would clearly need controls for concurrent access.†

The accounts are manipulated by various forms of transaction. Each transaction could be modelled as a procedure; one would be the procedure to transfer funds from one customer to another.

---

† We have naively assumed that this is achieved by locking the whole structure when an access is to be made, which would not in practice provide adequate performance. Nevertheless, the same principles would apply if locking were done at the level of individual records.

```
procedure XFER(FROMACC, TOACC: ACCOUNTNUMBER; SUM: integer);
begin
  region ACCOUNTS do
  begin
    with ACCOUNTS[FROMACC] do
      BALANCE := BALANCE – SUM;
    with ACCOUNTS[TOACC] do
      BALANCE := BALANCE + SUM
  end
end;    (* XFER *)
```

This procedure could be provided so that all parts of the program that needed to perform transfers could call it. However, we cannot prevent a programmer from writing code elsewhere which attempts to carry out the operation. Suppose that a programmer did this and by mistake (or malice) omitted the debit of the first customer's account. We have now lost the integrity of the data structure: its state is inconsistent.

The problem is that it is necessary to give *carte blanche* in order to allow programmers to have any access at all to the accounts data. We should really like some means of forcing a programmer to use the official procedure for funds transfer (which would have been written by senior personnel and very carefully validated).

Monitors can be seen as an improvement on CCRs because they provide a way of localizing *all* the code that operates on a data structure in one place: there is no way of side-stepping the official operations. They can also be efficiently implemented.

7.4   Monitors for mutual exclusion

The description of monitors will be based largely on the facilities available in Pascal-FC. These are essentially the same as those described by Hoare (1974). Other languages that have incorporated monitors include Concurrent Pascal (Brinch Hansen, 1975), Pascal Plus (Welsh and Bustard, 1979), Mesa (Mitchell *et al*, 1979) and Turing Plus (Holt and Cordy, 1988).

7.4.1   Basic outline of a monitor

The outline of a monitor declaration in Pascal-FC is as follows:

```
monitor_declaration ::=

    monitor identifier;
        export_list
        {
        constant_declaration
      | type_declaration
```

```
                      | variable_declaration
                      | procedure_declaration
                      | function_declaration
                      }
              [monitor_body]
              end;

       export_list ::=

              export procedure_identifier_list;
              {export procedure_identifier_list;}

       monitor_body ::=
              begin
                  statement_sequence
```

The declarations may include constants, types, variables, procedures and functions, but not processes or other monitors. Most of the declarations are only in scope within the monitor: the exception is that identifiers appearing in the **export** list are visible outside the monitor. In Pascal-FC, only the names of procedures can be exported. An exported procedure can be called from outside the monitor by a statement of the form:

*monitor_*identifier.*exported_procedure_*identifier[actual parameters]

Examples are provided later in this chapter.

Because of the visibility rules described above, access to data declared in a monitor is only possible by calling one of the exported procedures; this gives complete control over the operations processes are allowed to carry out. Moreover, all the code that manipulates monitor data is declared in the monitor itself, thus providing a neat structuring method.

The monitor body, which is optional, is provided to give initial values to variables declared within the monitor. It is executed once for every entry to the block in which the monitor is declared. Because of Pascal-FC's flat process structure (see Chapter 2), monitors may only be declared in the main program, so that any monitor bodies are executed just once during the execution of a program. Though the order in which the different monitor bodies in a program are executed is not defined, it is guaranteed that they will all have been executed before the first statement of the main program itself.

The compiler guarantees that access to the code within a monitor is done under mutual exclusion. As usual, busy waiting could be used to implement this, but we shall assume blocked waiting in this description. A process that tries to execute a monitor procedure when there is already a process executing one of the procedures in the same monitor becomes blocked on what we shall call a monitor **boundary queue**. In general, several processes may be blocked on this queue by the time an occupying process completes its monitor procedure call. Mutual exclusion is then passed to *one* of the blocked processes. Monitor boundary queues are often defined to be FIFO, as is the case in Pascal-FC.†

The following points outline the way in which the features of monitors allow the programmer to implement secure mutually exclusive access to a data structure:

- The data structure is declared inside a monitor; the code in the body may be used to give it initial values before processes begin to call on the monitor.

- The data structure is not directly visible from outside the monitor; it can only be accessed by executing one of the 'official' operations implemented by the exported procedures. Hence the unwary or malicious programmer cannot compromise the integrity of the data because he or she cannot manipulate it directly. (It is assumed that the monitor has been written by senior personnel of unimpeachable competence and trustworthiness.)

- Mutually exclusive access is enforced automatically by the compiler when it generates code for a call to an exported monitor procedure: it is not possible to access the data except under mutual exclusion. (The compiler writer, of course, is infallible!)

- In comparison with conditional critical regions, monitors are more structured, since all the code that manipulates a given data structure must be located in one place.

7.4.2 The Ornamental Gardens with monitors

The solution of a problem such as the Ornamental Gardens is trivial using monitors. A Pascal-FC program for this is given below.

```
program GARDMON;
(* Ornamental Gardens – monitor version *)

const
  MAX = 10;    (* number of turnstiles *)
monitor TALLY;
  export
    INC, PRINT;
  var
    COUNT: integer;
```

† Strictly, the queue is a priority queue, but we have already said that we shall assume that all processes have the same priority in this book.

```
procedure INC;
begin
  COUNT := COUNT + 1
end;      (* INC *)

procedure PRINT;
begin
  writeln(COUNT)
end;      (* PRINT *)

begin     (* body of TALLY *)
  COUNT := 0
end;      (* TALLY *)

process type TURNSTILETYPE;
var
  LOOP: integer;
begin
  for LOOP := 1 to 20 do
    TALLY.INC
end;      (* TURNSTILETYPE *)

var
  TURNSTILE: array [1..MAX] of TURNSTILETYPE;
  PROCLOOP: integer;

begin
  cobegin
    for PROCLOOP := 1 to MAX do
      TURNSTILE[PROCLOOP]
  coend;
  TALLY.PRINT
end.
```

This program should be self-explanatory. Note that it is necessary to call the monitor procedure PRINT from the main program in order to view the final result. As the concurrent phase of execution has been completed by this point, the monitor's mutual exclusion property is not required here, but the variable COUNT is, of course, only accessible by calling a monitor procedure.

It is worth noting that numerous languages include a structure with the data hiding capabilities of monitors, but without the mutual exclusion. Such structures are designed to facilitate the modular implementation of reliable sequential† software. Examples are the **module** of Modula–2 and the **package** of Ada.

---

† They can, of course, be used in concurrent programs, but the programmer must remember that no concurrency control is incorporated into them.

7.5 Condition synchronization with monitors

Just as plain critical regions needed to be extended to conditional critical regions, so we need to enhance monitor facilities to make them as generally applicable as semaphores. Pascal-FC follows Hoare's (1974) suggestion that condition synchronization be provided by condition variables. Variables of this type have no values accessible to the programmer but instead are FIFO queues (initialized automatically to the empty queue on declaration). Declarations of conditions in Pascal-FC are exemplified below:

```
var
    C: condition;
    CARRAY: array [1..10] of condition;
```

Such variables will be declared inside a monitor and are used to block and unblock processes which, having entered the monitor, find that the state of the enclosed data is such that they must not at present proceed with their call. (For example, a consumer might discover an empty buffer on entry to a monitor.)

Two principal operations are defined on condition variables; they are described in the next two sections. In Pascal-FC, the operations are called delay and resume, but many discussions of monitors use the terms wait and signal, respectively. We have reserved these names for the semaphore operations.

7.5.1 The delay operation

This operation is the counterpart of the semaphore wait, though there are important differences. In Pascal-FC, it is implemented as a procedure, which is called in the following way:

```
delay(C)
```

C must be a condition variable.

A first attempt at describing the semantics of this operation is as follows:

```
block the calling process on C
```

An important difference between this operation and the semaphore wait is immediately obvious: delay always causes the calling process to be blocked, whereas the semaphore wait only does so if the value of the semaphore is 0.

In fact, something more is required. If a process executes this operation while executing code inside a monitor, it must release mutual exclusion. This is necessary because otherwise no further process could gain access to the monitor and change the state of its variables. Yet such access must take place if the process currently calling delay is ever to become runnable again. (For example, a producer needs to place another item to change the state of an empty buffer and thereby make a blocked consumer runnable.)

A fuller definition of delay is as follows:

```
release the monitor
block the calling process on C
```

The first part of this operation provides another contrast with Pascal-FC's semaphore wait: wait does not release the current monitor when blocking a process, because semaphores were not designed for use with monitors.

A condition variable in Pascal-FC may have an arbitrary number of processes blocked on it at any time.

7.5.2 The resume operation

This is the counterpart of the semaphore signal, but once more there are important differences. The operation is again a procedure in Pascal-FC, and is called as follows:

```
resume(C)
```

A first pseudocode description of the semantics of this operation is:

```
unblock the first process waiting on C
```

The question naturally arises: what happens if *no* processes are blocked on C when resume is executed? The resume is then defined to be a null operation. A contrast with the semaphore signal is now clear: signal always has some effect. Either it unblocks a process or it increments the semaphore value. Note also that Pascal-FC's condition variables are defined to have a FIFO† unblocking discipline, in contrast to the arbitrary discipline on semaphores.

There is a potential problem with the operation as described above. A process that is unblocked by way of a resume (call it the 'resumed process') originally became blocked by executing a delay. When it is unblocked, it will re-enter the monitor. However, the process that executed the resume (call it the 'resumer') is already inside the monitor. To have both processes in the monitor would violate the rule of mutual exclusion, so we cannot permit this to happen. Two potential solutions to this problem might be considered:

(1) The resumed process must wait until the resumer leaves the monitor (by completing its call to the monitor procedure or by executing a delay) before re-entering the monitor.

† Again, strictly a priority queue.

(2)   If resume unblocks a process, the resumer must immediately 'step outside' the monitor, handing mutual exclusion to the resumed process. This is called **immediate resumption**.

The first alternative is called resume-and-continue semantics (taking the point of view of the resumer). The second can be accomplished in a variety of ways, each with a different name. Both variants have been used in existing languages, but we shall see later that Pascal-FC uses the immediate resumption approach.

The question of the semantics of resume is further considered in Section 7.7. For the present, we side-step the issue by using some self-discipline. Calls to resume will only be placed at the end of a path through a monitor procedure. In effect, this is a voluntary adoption of the principle of immediate resumption.

7.5.3   The empty function

Hoare (1974) proposed one further operation on condition variables: a function to determine whether the condition queue was empty. Such a function has been included in Pascal-FC: it returns a boolean result. An example of its use will be given in Section 7.6.2.

7.6   Illustrative examples of the use of monitors

7.6.1   The bounded buffer

The first executable Pascal-FC program using condition variables is a solution to the Producer–Consumer problem with a bounded buffer. The program should require no further explanation:

```
program PCMON;
(* Producer-Consumer problem – monitor version *)

monitor BUFFER;
  export
    PLACE, TAKE;
  const
    BUFFSIZE = 5;
    BUFFMAX = 4;      (* Must be BUFFSIZE – 1 *)
  var
    STORE: array[0..BUFFMAX] of char;
    COUNT: integer;
```

```
              NOTFULL, NOTEMPTY: condition;
              NEXTIN, NEXTOUT: integer;

           procedure PLACE(CH: char);
           begin
             if COUNT >= BUFFSIZE then
               delay(NOTFULL);
             STORE[NEXTIN] := CH;
             COUNT := COUNT + 1;
             NEXTIN := (NEXTIN + 1) mod BUFFSIZE;
             resume(NOTEMPTY)
           end;     (* PLACE *)

           procedure TAKE(var CH: char);
           begin
             if COUNT = 0 then
               delay(NOTEMPTY);
             CH := STORE[NEXTOUT];
             COUNT := COUNT - 1;
             NEXTOUT := (NEXTOUT + 1) mod BUFFSIZE;
             resume(NOTFULL)
           end;     (* TAKE *)

        begin     (* body of BUFFER *)
          COUNT := 0;
          NEXTIN := 0;
          NEXTOUT := 0
        end;     (* BUFFER *)

        process PRODUCER;
        var
          LOCAL: char;
        begin
          for LOCAL := 'a' to 'z' do
            BUFFER.PLACE(LOCAL)
        end;     (* PRODUCER *)

        process CONSUMER;
        var
          CH: char;
        begin
          repeat
            BUFFER.TAKE(CH);
            write(CH)
          until CH = 'z';
          writeln
        end;     (* CONSUMER *)
```

```
begin     (* main *)
  cobegin
    PRODUCER;
    CONSUMER
  coend
end.
```

7.6.2 Readers and writers

A monitor solution to this problem is presented below. As in the semaphore versions of Chapter 6, we have provided OPEN and CLOSE operations for the data structure. These are implemented as monitor procedures. Possible outlines for the reader and writer processes are as follows:

```
process type reader;
begin
  repeat
    READANDWRITE.OPEN(TRUE);
    (* access data *)
    READANDWRITE.CLOSE(TRUE);
    (* use returned data *)
  forever
end;     (* reader *)

process type writer;
begin
  repeat
    (* produce new data *)
    READANDWRITE.OPEN(FALSE);
    (* modify data *)
    READANDWRITE.CLOSE(FALSE)
  forever
end;     (* writer *)
```

The parameter to the OPEN and CLOSE procedures is a boolean indicating whether the request is from a reader.

Two solutions to the Readers and Writers problem were presented in Chapter 6. Courtois *et al.* (1971) showed that it was comparatively straightforward to devise a semaphore algorithm that satisfied safety requirements, but their first version could lead to lockout of writers. Their second solution avoided this liveness problem, but it was fairly complex. We shall now see that a monitor solution treating both readers and writers fairly is reasonably simple.

Hoare (1974) proposed that:

● a new reader should not be permitted to start if there is a waiting writer;

- at the end of a write operation, waiting readers are given preference over waiting writers.

The need to determine whether there are processes waiting can be easily served by using Pascal-FC's empty function.

The monitor given below incorporates Hoare's scheduling proposals. Note that, as in the semaphore solutions presented in Chapter 6, readers take part in a **cascaded wake**:

```
monitor READANDWRITE;
  export
    OPEN, CLOSE;
  var
    READERCOUNT: integer;
    ACTIVEW: boolean;
    OKTOREAD, OKTOWRITE: condition;

  procedure OPEN(READING: boolean);
  begin
    if READING then
    begin
      if ACTIVEW or not empty(OKTOWRITE) then
        delay(OKTOREAD);
      READERCOUNT := READERCOUNT + 1;
      resume(OKTOREAD)
    end else
    begin
      if ACTIVEW or (READERCOUNT <> 0) then
        delay(OKTOWRITE);
      ACTIVEW := true
    end
  end;    (* OPEN *)

  procedure CLOSE(READING: boolean);
  begin
    if READING then
    begin
      READERCOUNT := READERCOUNT - 1;
      if READERCOUNT = 0 then
        resume(OKTOWRITE)
    end else
    begin
      ACTIVEW := false;
      if not empty(OKTOREAD) then
        resume(OKTOREAD)
      else
        resume(OKTOWRITE)
    end
  end;    (* CLOSE *)
```

```
begin
  ACTIVEW := false;
  READERCOUNT := 0
end;    (* READANDWRITE *)
```

7.6.3   A simple alarm clock

The following example was given by Hoare (1974). A set of SLEEPER
processes wish to SLUMBER for various times and set an alarm clock to wake
them when it is time to get up. Unfortunately, their alarm clock is a little
primitive: every hour it squirts cold water at the nearest sleeper, who
immediately prods the next sleeper. Each sleeper checks the time: if it is not
time for him/her to go to work, then he/she goes back to sleep. To
understand this example, it is important to remember that each process
calling the SLUMBER procedure has its own private copies of parameters and
local variables.

```
program ALARMCLOCK;
(* Hoare's (1974) demonstration *)

const
  PMAX = 3;

monitor ALARM;
  export
    SLUMBER, TICK;
  var
    NOW: integer;
    WAKE: condition;

  procedure SLUMBER(N: integer);
  var
    ALARMCALL: integer;
  begin
    ALARMCALL := NOW + N;
    while NOW < ALARMCALL do
    begin
      delay(WAKE);
      resume(WAKE)
    end
  end;    (* SLUMBER *)

  procedure TICK;
  begin
    NOW := NOW + 1;
    resume(WAKE)
  end;    (* TICK *)
```

```
begin     (* body *)
  NOW := 0
end;      (* ALARM *)

monitor SCREEN;
  export
    PRINT;

    procedure PRINT(N: integer);
    begin
      writeln('process ',N:1,' awakes')
    end;      (* PRINT *)

end;      (* SCREEN *)

process DRIVER;
    (* provides the clock 'ticks' *)
begin
  repeat
    sleep(1);
    ALARM.TICK
  forever
end;      (* DRIVER *)

process type SLEEPERTYPE(N: integer);
begin
  repeat
    ALARM.SLUMBER(N);
    SCREEN.PRINT(N)
    (* get up and go to work *)
  forever
end;      (* SLEEPERTYPE *)

var
  SLEEPERS: array[1..PMAX] of SLEEPERTYPE;
  PLOOP: integer;

begin
  cobegin
    DRIVER;
    for PLOOP := 1 to PMAX do
      SLEEPERS[PLOOP](PLOOP)
  coend
end.
```

7.6.6 Simulation of semaphores by monitors

Ever since the introduction of semaphores, researchers proposing new constructs for inter-process communication have wanted to show that their proposal is at least as powerful as semaphores. This is done by showing that the new construct can *simulate* semaphores. This we now do for monitors. The following Pascal-FC program simulates a binary semaphore which, in this case, is used for mutual exclusion. We saw in Chapter 6 that general semaphores can themselves be simulated by binary semaphores together with an integer variable, so that we can be confident that all semaphore algorithms can be replaced by monitor versions (though using a simulation like this may not be the most efficient way of solving the problem). Hence, we can be sure that monitors are no less powerful than semaphores. It is left as an exercise for the reader to show how a monitor's synchronization can be simulated by semaphores.

The program used to illustrate this simulation solves the multiple update problem (as, for example, in the Ornamental Gardens). The reader will realize that, if we have monitors, the most effective way to implement such a program is to declare the shared variable *inside* the monitor, as was done earlier in this chapter. For the purposes of the simulation, the shared variable is global:

```
program SEMMON;
(* simulation of the binary *)
(* semaphore by monitors *)

var
  SHARED: integer;

monitor SEM;
  export
    WAIT, SIGNAL;
  var
    VALUE: integer;
    NOTZERO: condition;

  procedure WAIT;
  begin
    if VALUE = 0 then
      delay(NOTZERO);
    VALUE := 0
  end;    (* WAIT *)

  procedure SIGNAL;
  begin
    VALUE := 1;
    resume(NOTZERO)
  end;    (* SIGNAL *)

begin  (* body *)
  VALUE := 1
end;    (* SEM *)
```

```
process type INC;
var
  LOOP: integer;
begin
  for LOOP := 1 to 20 do
  begin
    SEM.WAIT;
    SHARED := SHARED + 1;
    SEM.SIGNAL
  end
end;     (* INC *)

var
  INC1,INC2: INC;

begin
  SHARED := 0;
  cobegin
    INC1;
    INC2
  coend;
  writeln('Total: ',SHARED:1)
end.
```

7.7 More on the semantics of resume

We have been disciplined in our use of resume: whenever it occurred, it was the last statement in a path through a monitor procedure. Unfortunately, relying on discipline is unsatisfactory; it would be better to enhance resume so that it was impossible for both the calling process and the unblocked one to be active concurrently in the monitor on completion of the operation. We shall here consider in detail the two approaches to this problem that were noted in Section 7.5.2. They are:

(1)   the resume and continue approach;
(2)   a number of methods to implement the immediate resumption approach.

7.7.1 Resume and continue

This approach was adopted in the Mesa language (Mitchell *et al*, 1979). Suppose that a process P releases a process Q by executing resume on a condition. If resume and continue semantics are being used, P may continue to execute arbitrary statements in the monitor, and Q re-enters the monitor (at the earliest) when P leaves it.

The logic behind the use of condition variables is often as follows:

```
(* in the delaying process *)
if not B then
   delay(C)
(* B now assumed to be true *)
   . . .
(* in the resuming process *)
make B true
resume(C)
```

However, if the resumer can execute arbitrary statements after the resume, it could conceivably make B false again. Hence the resumed process is obliged to test the condition again on re-entry. The following code is in fact what is required when resume and continue is in use:

```
while not B do
   delay(C)
(* B certain to be true *)
```

This will remind the reader of the earlier discussion on the release of processes blocked on the event queue of a CCR. Again, the disadvantage is that condition synchronization involves a certain amount of polling.

Resume and continue semantics do, however, have some advantages over the various methods using immediate resumption. We shall return to these in Section 7.7.5.

7.7.2   Forced return: resume and exit

Brinch Hansen (1975), in his Concurrent Pascal, opted for the immediate resumption principle. One of the actions of his continue operation (which was the counterpart of our resume) was to force the calling process to return immediately from the monitor procedure that it had called. As with the other methods embodying the immediate resumption principle, there is no need for the incoming process to re-test the condition: if it was true when the resume was executed, it will still be true (provided it only depends on monitor variables).

7.7.3   Resume and wait

With this method, a process that executes a resume that releases another process must itself immediately block after passing mutual exclusion to the incoming process. It blocks on the monitor boundary queue. However, it must be understood that (if and) when this process eventually executes again, it will continue from the point at which it executed the resume – the act of blocking does not affect the process's program counter.

A possible shortcoming of this approach is that a process that releases another and has to join the boundary queue again may, as a result, now find itself behind other processes that arrived at the monitor boundary after it did: in short, a process can be overtaken. This is not ideal from the point of view of fairness, and the next section considers one possible remedy to this problem.

7.7.4 Resume and urgent wait

Hoare (1974) proposed a somewhat more complex solution to the problem, which is the approach adopted in Pascal-FC and Pascal Plus (Welsh and Bustard, 1979). As well as a boundary queue for each monitor, this approach includes a second queue, which Hoare called 'urgent'. A process that executes a resume that releases another process, having handed mutual exclusion to the incoming process, now becomes blocked on the urgent queue.

The resume operation now becomes:

```
if processes blocked on C then
begin
   unblock the first process waiting on C
   join the urgent queue
end
```

This is executed as an indivisible operation.

Pascal-FC uses this approach, but the term 'chivalry queue' has been adopted in place of Hoare's 'urgent'. The queue is so called because it contains processes that have been chivalrous enough to unblock another process and hand mutually exclusive access of the monitor to it.

The operation of releasing the monitor, which is carried out when a process reaches the end of a monitor procedure or when it executes a delay operation, can now be described as follows:

```
if not empty(ChivalryQueue) then
   UnblockProcess(ChivalryQueue)
else
   if not empty(MonitorBoundaryQueue) then
      UnblockProcess(MonitorBoundaryQueue)
   else
      mark monitor as unoccupied
```

Notice that processes blocked on the chivalry queue are given preference over those waiting at the monitor boundary.

7.7.5 Evaluation of the approaches

A first question is:

> Are these approaches equally powerful?

Andrews (1991) shows that the answer to this is yes: each method can be used to simulate the effects of the others. Moreover, in many (though not all) cases, the safety properties of a given program text are independent of the resume semantics used by the language implementation. The differences between the schemes relate to the following:

- ease of use
- ease of applying proof techniques
- efficiency
- the order in which processes execute.

First consider ease of use. In cases where there are operations to be carried out after a resume, this is easily and obviously coded in all cases, except for resume and exit. When using this approach, a new call must be made to a separate monitor procedure, hence this approach tends to fragment the monitor code into a larger number of procedures. A consequence of this is that the monitor's interface with client software (the **export** list) is complicated. Thus resume and exit can be considered less easy to use than the other approaches.

When efficiency is considered, the resume and wait and resume-and-urgent-wait approaches show their shortcomings, particularly in the many cases in which a resume actually *is* the last statement executed before a return from a monitor procedure. In either of these schemes, a process switch takes place when a resume releases a process queued on a condition, and a further one is required so that the resumer can later re-enter the monitor – only to return from it immediately! Not only is this inefficient from a global system point of view (because process switches are expensive), but it also means that the individual resumer is unnecessarily delayed. Clearly, resume and continue is preferable in this respect. However, there is a price to pay in that a resumed process must re-test its condition, as we saw earlier.

Resume and continue has another attraction: it is natural to include a **broadcast resume**, which can lead to clearer code. A broadcast resume releases *all* processes blocked on a condition (though, of course, they are not allowed concurrently to execute inside the monitor). This is a useful alternative to a cascaded resume (such as we used in the Readers and Writers monitor earlier in this chapter). However, broadcast resume does not fit the immediate resumption model: only *one* process can be immediately resumed. The others would have to re-test their condition on re-entry to the monitor.

Finally, when we consider attempting to prove the correctness of monitors, the resume and wait and the resume and urgent wait semantics introduce difficulties, because it is not easy to know what assertions one can make about the internal state of the monitor at the beginning of the first statement after a resume. It depends on what a resumed process may have done; monitor procedures cannot therefore be proved in isolation from one another. There is no such problem when resume and continue is used because the resumer retains mutual exclusion over the monitor. Again, the price that is paid for this is the need for a resumed process to re-test its condition following a delay.

7.8 Monitor invariants and proofs of monitors

A monitor invariant is useful in proving the correctness of a monitor. The invariant is an assertion involving monitor variables that is true whenever there is no process inside the monitor: it is permitted to be false while a process is executing monitor code. *Whenever there is no process inside the monitor* includes any point at which one process passes exclusive access to another, for example, by executing resume. For analytical purposes, such a switch involves a period during which the monitor is vacant and the invariant must then hold.

As the invariant must hold whenever the monitor is vacant, it must be true:

(1) before the first call is made to any of the monitor's procedures;

(2) whenever a process leaves the monitor.

The code in the monitor body is responsible for establishing (1), while the monitor procedures must be written so that they ensure (2).

It must be borne in mind that processes leave monitors when:

(1) they reach the end of a path through a monitor procedure;

(2) they execute a delay;

(3) they execute a resume that unblocks another process.

The third reason only applies when immediate resumption semantics are in use. A fourth reason in some implementations of monitors is the *nested monitor call*, which is considered in the next section.

As an example of the use of monitor invariants, consider again the code that was given in Section 7.6.1 for the Producer–Consumer problem. The essential safety requirements of this problem are:

PCON1: $\forall e \bullet$ produce$^i \rightarrow$ consume^i
PCON2: $\forall e \bullet$ consume$^i \rightarrow$ produce$^{i\ +\ \text{BUFFSIZE}}$

(where the superscripts indicate the ith execution of the operation concerned). With the code provided in Section 7.6.1, a suitable monitor invariant is:

MI: (COUNT $>=$ 0) and (COUNT $<=$ BUFFSIZE)

(where BUFFSIZE is the number of slots in an empty buffer).

In analysing the monitor, we shall use an approach first introduced by Hoare (1969). We make use of *triples* of the form:

$\{P\}$ S $\{Q\}$

in which P and Q are predicates (expressions that can evaluate to either true or false) and S is a program statement. The interpretation of such a triple is as follows:

If S is begun with P true and S terminates, then Q will be true on completion of S.

P is called the *precondition* of S, and Q is called the *post-condition*.
First, it is easy to show that the code in the monitor body establishes MI as the following holds:

$\{$true$\}$ COUNT := 0 $\{$MI$\}$

(In this case, the precondition is a constant true, which means that the state of the variables before executing S is irrelevant.) Hence the first process to enter the monitor can assume MI. It is now necessary to show that no process can leave the monitor when MI is false.
The PLACE and TAKE procedures in the monitor have a similar structure: each has three points at which a process may 'step outside' the monitor:

- a delay
- a resume
- a simple procedure-call return.

First consider a process that passes through its monitor procedure without either executing a delay or waking another process by way of its resume. The producer's path is then:

```
{(COUNT >= 0) and (COUNT <= BUFFSIZE)}
if . . .    (* condition false *)
{(COUNT >= 0) and (COUNT < BUFFSIZE)}
COUNT := COUNT + 1;
{(COUNT > 0) and (COUNT <= BUFFSIZE)}
resume(NOTEMPTY)    (* null operation *)
{(COUNT > 0) and (COUNT <= BUFFSIZE)}
end;    (* PLACE *)
```

(We have omitted the code manipulating STORE.) The consumer's path is:

```
{(COUNT >= 0) and (COUNT <= BUFFSIZE)}
if . . .    (* condition false *)
{(COUNT > 0) and (COUNT <= BUFFSIZE)}
COUNT := COUNT − 1;
{(COUNT >= 0) and (COUNT < BUFFSIZE)}
resume(NOTFULL)    (* null operation *)
{(COUNT >= 0) and (COUNT < BUFFSIZE)}
end;    (* TAKE *)
```

In both of these cases, MI is maintained, as required.

Suppose, however, that a process *does* wake another by virtue of its resume. Considering first the producer, it begins its resume with the following assertion true:

```
{(COUNT > 0) and (COUNT <= BUFFSIZE)}
```

This becomes the precondition for the consumer, which now executes the path:

```
{(COUNT > 0) and (COUNT <= BUFFSIZE)}
COUNT := COUNT − 1;
{(COUNT >= 0) and (COUNT < BUFFSIZE)}
resume(NOTFULL)
{(COUNT >= 0) and (COUNT < BUFFSIZE)}
end;    (* TAKE *)
```

The producer is not blocked on NOTFULL, so that the resume is a null operation. A similar argument may be used to show that, if the consumer wakes the producer by its resume on NOTFULL, the producer executes the following path:

```
{(COUNT >= 0) and (COUNT < BUFFSIZE)}
COUNT := COUNT + 1;
{(COUNT > 0) and (COUNT <= BUFFSIZE)}
resume(NOTEMPTY)
{(COUNT > 0) and (COUNT <= BUFFSIZE)}
end;    (* PLACE *)
```

Both paths maintain MI.

A process that wakes another by way of a resume becomes blocked on the chivalry queue. There are only two circumstances in which the process may become unblocked:

- when a process executes a return from a monitor procedure;
- when a process executes a delay.

In either case, the process that leaves the chivalry queue re-enters the monitor; it must be able to assume MI. We have just shown that the awakened process eventually leaves the monitor with MI true, but we must now consider what happens when a process becomes blocked by executing its delay on a condition.

This is easily dealt with: a process that enters the monitor and becomes blocked on a condition executes no statements that affect COUNT. Hence the invariant remains true when a process leaves the monitor by this route. The producer's path through PLACE in these circumstances is:

```
{(COUNT >= 0) and (COUNT <= BUFFSIZE)}
if . . .
{(COUNT > 0) and (COUNT = BUFFSIZE)}
delay(NOTFULL);
```

The consumer's path is:

```
{(COUNT >= 0) and (COUNT <= BUFFSIZE)}
if . . .
{(COUNT = 0) and (COUNT <= BUFFSIZE)}
delay(NOTEMPTY);
```

Hence the invariant is maintained in all circumstances.

7.9   The problem of nested monitor calls

One of the potential benefits of monitors is improved software modularity. A large concurrent system could be written as a set of concurrent processes, with the various shared resources implemented as a set of monitors. It is common practice in large systems, such as operating systems, to structure the software as a series of layers so that lower layers provide primitive services for use by higher layers, which in turn provide less primitive services. If monitors are used to implement large systems, it is likely that higher-level monitors will need to call procedures in lower-level monitors. A call from a procedure in one monitor to a procedure of another is called a **nested monitor call**; such calls need to be catered for in the language design because they are a source of potential problems (Lister, 1977).

Suppose that a process running a procedure in a monitor A makes a call to a procedure in monitor B. Should this process retain mutually exclusive hold over A while executing code in B? What should happen if it executes a delay in B? The mutually exclusive hold over B will be released, but what should happen with A?

There are four main approaches to this problem:

(1)   Maintain exclusive hold over A when making a nested call and release only B when executing a delay in B. This means that when the process eventually returns to A it 'knows' that no other process has been active in A since the nested call was made. However, holding a monitor whilst blocked reduces the potential for concurrency and may lead to problems such as deadlock in unfortunate cases.

(2)   Maintain exclusive hold on A when making the nested call, but release both monitors on encountering a delay in B. The potential for deadlock is now removed, but it is necessary to establish the invariant for A before making the nested call, and to remember that such a call makes monitor variables subject to modification by other processes.

(3)   Release A on making the nested call. The potential for concurrency is now maximized, but the disadvantages are the same as in (2).

(4)   Ban nested calls. This means that the language designer does not have to agonize over which of the first three policies to implement, but detracts from the potential for modularity that monitors offer.

Nested monitor calls clearly pose problems for the language designer, and none of the above proposals is entirely satisfactory. Pascal-FC follows approach (1).

SUMMARY

The language features described in this chapter are clearly based on the shared-memory model, but they provide a more structured approach to programming mutual exclusion and condition synchronization than was possible with semaphores. In general, this should promote the production of more reliable software.

Conditional critical regions ensure that shared variables can only be accessed under mutual exclusion, but the applications programmer is still given complete freedom within a CCR to do whatever he or she likes with the data. Moreover, the code that manipulates a particular data structure can be scattered through the program, making the role of the structure more difficult to understand.

Monitors overcome these problems. They provide for the encapsulation of data structures and the procedures that operate on them. This means that the application programmer is forced to use the procedures supplied in the monitor, and has no access to the enclosed data otherwise. The structure and its operators are localized, thus clarifying the purpose of the data structure.

We have not yet finished with the ideas of conditional critical regions and monitors: they have strongly influenced some recent enhancements to the design of the Ada programming language. In the next chapter, we shall introduce these new features (which are also available in Pascal-FC), and discuss the reasons for their inclusion.

FURTHER READING

Andrews G.R. (1991). *Concurrent Programming: Principles and Practice*. Benjamin/Cummings

Brinch Hansen P. (1972). *A Comparison of Two Synchronizing Concepts*. Acta Informatica, **1**, 190–9

Brinch Hansen P. (1975). The Programming Language Concurrent Pascal. *IEEE Transactions on Software Engineering*, **SE–1**(2), 199–207

Dunstan N. (1991). Semaphores for Fair Scheduling Monitor Conditions. *Operating Systems Review*, **25**(3), 27–31

Hoare C.A.R. (1974). Monitors: an Operating System Structuring Concept. *Communications of ACM*, **17**(10), 549–57

Holt R.C. and Cordy J.R. (1988). The Turing Programming Language. Communication of ACM, 31(12), 1410–23

Howard J.H. (1976). Proving Monitors. Communications of ACM, **19**(5), 273–9

Welsh J. and Bustard D.W. (1979). Pascal Plus – Another Language for Modular Multiprogramming. *Software Practice and Experience*, **9**, 947–57

EXERCISES

7.1 Show how conditional critical regions can be used to solve the problem of Readers and Writers. As in the first semaphore solution of Chapter 6, readers should have preference over writers.

7.2 Use conditional critical regions to produce a solution to the Readers and Writers problem in which waiting writers have preference over new readers. (Hint: use two CCRs in the entry protocol for writers.)

7.3 Show how semaphores can be used to simulate the synchronization facilities of conditional critical regions. Follow Brinch Hansen's (1972) proposal that each **shared** variable should have an event queue.

7.4 Show how semaphores can be used to simulate monitors, including condition variables. There should, as in Pascal-FC, be a chivalry queue. (Pretend that the semaphores you are using are FIFO, even though Pascal-FC's are not necessarily FIFO.)

7.5 The program philsem2 in Chapter 6 prevented deadlock by removing the circular wait requirement for the occurrence of deadlock. Another necessary condition is that processes hold resources already allocated to them while waiting for further resources. One way to remove this condition is to insist that a process request all its resources at once: if its request cannot be fulfilled, then *no* resources are allocated and it must wait until it can be satisfied. Use a monitor to solve the problem of the Dining Philosophers using this approach to deadlock prevention. Given that all queues associated with the monitor are FIFO, is it possible for any philosopher to starve in your solution?

7.6 The Smokers' Problem. Consider a system of three cigarette smoker processes and one agent. Each smoker continuously makes a cigarette and then smokes it. Three ingredients are required to make and smoke a cigarette: paper, tobacco and matches. One of the smoker processes has paper, another tobacco and the third matches. The agent has an infinite supply of all three ingredients. The agent places two of the ingredients, chosen at random, on a table. The smoker who has the third ingredient can then make and smoke a cigarette. Once it has finished smoking the cigarette, the smoker signals the agent, who can then choose another two ingredients at random, and so the cycle continues. Provide a solution to this problem in Pascal-FC using a monitor.

7.7 Re-implement the cash dispensing exercises (5.12 and 5.13) using monitors.

7.8 A number of client processes call in on a monitor using the procedure block(n), where n is an integer in the range 1 to 10. All callers are blocked until another client process calls releasing. The blocked processes must then be released (one at a time) in the order dictated by the *n* parameter. When all processes have been released, the releasing process can continue.

7.9 Use a monitor to implement quantity semaphores (see Exercise 6.11).

7.10 The lift control system has been addressed in exercises that require the use of remote invocation (Exercises 5.5 and 5.6) and semaphores (Exercise 6.10); redesign your solutions to these problems so that a monitor (or monitors) is used.

7.11 A collection of eight processes are passed integer keys at initialization such that they form four pairs. Each process must use a monitor with a single exported procedure to exchange data with its partner. Construct the monitor that will facilitate this coupling.

7.12 Consider a producer/consumer structure with an integer buffer of maximum size 16. The consumer reads one integer at a time from the buffer but the producer may need to place up to 16 integers in the buffer in one go (i.e. it is blocked until there is sufficient space available). Using a monitor :w, show how the buffer is implemented.

7.13 Consider the READANDWRITE monitor and assume a language in which all queues associated with monitors (including the chivalry queue) are FIFO. Consider a scenario in which a writer has been active in the protected data structure and in which three readers (A, B and C) have requested permission to operate on the data while it was active. No additional writers are waiting. In what order will the readers *leave* the monitor having completed execution of the OPEN procedure?

7.14 Suppose that a monitor implementation is to use the resume and continue semantics for the resume operation. Write a pseudocode outline of the following monitor operations: (a) resume; (b) broadcast resume; (c) delay; and (d) return from monitor procedure.

8 A Unified Model

In the previous four chapters a number of communication and synchronization models have been described. Given the variety of application needs it is unlikely that a single model will satisfy all user requirements. Nevertheless, it is possible to consider the advantages and disadvantages of the different models and to attempt to define a new model that combines the best features of the earlier primitives. This unified model is presented at the end of this chapter; it follows the arguments that have recently been made for the introduction of protected types in Ada 9X. However, before approaching this model it is worthwhile reviewing semaphores, monitors, synchronous message passing and remote invocation in order to complete their evaluation. This is the first chapter in which this could be done.

8.1 Comparing models

It is usual to compare language features under two criteria:

(1) expressive power
(2) ease of use.

Expressive power is the ability actually to implement a required algorithm; it is an essentially objective criterion. By comparison, ease of use is more subjective and embraces a number of issues:

- how natural it is to use the primitive;
- how easy it is to combine the primitive with other language features;
- how error-prone the primitive is in use.

Often expressive power and ease of use conflict. As an extreme example, assembly language is the most expressive, but is far from easy to use. In our domain of concurrent programming, semaphores represent the low-level primitive with considerable expressive power but poor usability. Monitors represent a higher level of abstraction; they are easy to use for mutual exclusion but are not easily transformed for other requirements, such as those represented in the Readers and Writers problem. In the following section, we consider these issues in more detail.

8.2 Expressive power

As it is the more objective criterion, expressive power is relatively straightforward to evaluate. If the primitives can implement each other then they must have the same expressive power. In Chapter 7 we illustrated how monitors can simulate semaphores. Semaphores can also be used to implement monitors, and this was left as an exercise for the reader. Hence we can deduce that monitors and semaphores are, in terms of expressive power, equivalent. For the message-passing models we shall compare:

- synchronous message passing with symmetric select;
- remote invocation with asymmetric select.

Consider a process that wishes to choose between reading a value and writing a value; in the two language models this would take the following forms:

```
select
  reading ? A;
or
```

```
    writing ! B
  end

  select
    accept reading(Atemp : SomeType) do
      A := Atemp;
  or
    accept writing(var Btemp : SomeType) do
      Btemp := B
  end
```

The remote invocation model removes the need for a symmetric **select** by reversing the communication in the rendezvous.

In general, a remote invocation can involve any number of parameters and embrace a series of computations:

```
accept CALL(A : T1 ; var B : T2 ; var C: T3) do
begin
  (* use A *)
  (* modify B *)
  (* compute C *)
end
```

With synchronous message passing, a number of channels are needed (or A, B and C are made to be components of a single record):

```
chan1 ? A;
chan2 ? B;
  (* use A *)
  (* modify B *)
  (* compute C *)
chan3 ! B;
chan4 ! C
```

A further difference between the two models comes from a single entry being callable by more than one external process:

```
accept CALL(A : SomeType) do
    (* required computations *)
```

Using the simpler model, an array of channels is needed together with a **select** statement:

```
var
  CALL : array [1..N] of SomeChannelType;
  . . .
select
  for i := 1 to N replicate
    CALL [i] ? A;
```

```
        (* required computations *)
  end
```

Note that the channel version needs to know the maximum number of callers; this is not an issue of expressive power, but rather of convenience of use.

These structures show the essential equivalence between the different message-passing models.† To complete the evaluation, semaphores and synchronous message passing will be compared. First we consider a process that acts as a semaphore with an initial value of one. Such a process will need to be called by all client processes wishing to use the semaphore. Arrays of channels are needed as calling is one-to-one with synchronous message passing. An appropriate base type for the channels in this case is synchronous. Assuming that the maximum number of client processes is N, the code is:

```
process semaphore;
  var value, i : integer;
begin
  value := 1;
  repeat
    select
      for i := 1 to N replicate
        signal[i] ? any;
        value := value + 1;
    or
      for i := 1 to N replicate
        when value > 0 =>
        wait[i] ? any;
        value := value − 1;
    or
      terminate
    end
  forever
end;
```

Client process i could use this structure as follows:

```
wait[i] ! any;
  CriticalSection;
signal[i] ! any
```

---

† The equivalence is not maintained if the language contains an abort facility. A single rendezvous may be defined to be atomic with respect to abort (i.e. the rendezvous either completes or does not start). With remote invocation the single rendezvous encompasses the entire interaction; with the synchronous model different rendezvous were needed, hence the abort can catch it in a number of new intermediate stages.

To show equivalence the other way around, we need an example. Consider a channel of integers ch which will be used for input and output in two appropriate processes:

```
ch ? X     (* input *)
ch ! Y     (* output *)
```

This will need to be supported via two procedures: input and output. These procedures will share a boolean variable (first) and a semaphore (second) which is initially zero. The first process that tries to input or output will find the first variable true and will be suspended on the semaphore:

```
program semchan;
var first : boolean;
    MutEx, second : semaphore;
    value : integer;

procedure output(V : integer);
begin
  wait(MutEx);
  value := V;
  if first then
  begin
    first := false;
    signal(MutEx);
    wait(second);
    signal(MutEx)
  end else
  begin
    first := true;
    signal(second)
  end
end;

procedure input(var V : integer);
begin
  wait(MutEx);
  if first then
  begin
    first := false;
    signal(MutEx);
    wait(second);
    V := value;
    signal(MutEx)
  end else
  begin
```

```
            first := true;
            V := value;
            signal(second)
        end
    end;

        process producer;      (* example producer process *)
        var I : integer;
        begin
          for I := 1 to 10 do
            output(I)
        end;

        process consumer;      (* example consumer process *)
        var I,V : integer;
        begin
          for I := 1 to 10 do
          begin
            input(V);
            write(V)
          end
        end;

        begin
          first := true;
          initial(MutEx,1);
          initial(second,0);
          cobegin
            producer;
            consumer
          coend
        end.
```

Note that the shared variables are protected (mutual exclusion) via the semaphore MutEx. If either procedure is executing in the second part (i.e. first = false) then the mutually exclusive hold on the variables is passed to the delayed process, which does a second signal on the semaphore.

The above examples illustrate the essential equivalence between all the language primitives introduced in this book. Although expressive power appears not to be an issue, ease of use is. This is considered below.

8.3   Ease of use

In earlier chapters the lower-level primitives, such as shared variables and semaphores, were criticized as not being sufficiently structured to support reliable use. The motivation for monitors and the rendezvous is to provide direct support for the abstractions needed in concurrent programs.

Mutual exclusion is a key requirement, hence the monitor represents a valuable abstraction. However, to provide the required expressive power it was necessary to introduce a further synchronization primitive: condition variables. Unfortunately these had all the drawbacks of semaphores.

The rendezvous has the advantage of providing a single abstraction for communication and synchronization. Moreover, by making further use of the notion of process, mutual exclusion is no longer a problem as variables cannot be shared. This would appear to imply that message-passing models are easier to use. Many people would support this view, but there are problems that are easier to solve with the monitor model. An essential difference between the two approaches is that:

- monitors use conditional synchronization;
- message models use avoidance synchronization.

To illustrate this difference, consider an example given earlier in the book on resource control. A server process controls access to MAX identical resources. Clients make requests for these resources and may ask for up to M instances at a time ($1 <= M <= MAX$). A request should only be granted if the full set required can be allocated. Our experience with the Dining Philosophers shows that a solution that permits a client to ask for each instance in turn could easily deadlock if all the resources are allocated but no client has sufficient to proceed. The monitor solution is straightforward: if there are not sufficient resources, the caller is suspended. The following code assumes that the semantics for resume follow Hoare's (see Section 7.7): the call to resume will block the caller if a process is woken up – only when the woken process leaves the monitor will the original process continue:

```
monitor CONTROLLER;
export
   ALLOCATE, REPLACE;

var
   wants: condition;
   FREE: integer;

procedure ALLOCATE(N: integer);
begin
   while FREE < N do
   begin
      delay(wants);
      resume(wants)
   end;
   FREE := FREE - N
end;    (* ALLOCATE *)
```

```
procedure REPLACE(N: integer);
begin
  FREE := FREE + N;
  resume(wants)
end;

begin
  FREE := Max
end;    (* CONTROLLER *)
```

If there are insufficient resources when ALLOCATE is called, the caller is blocked on wants. Suppose that three clients are so blocked when REPLACE is called; from the code of REPLACE one of the clients is resumed. It immediately resumes another client, which then resumes the third. At this time three processes are on the chivalry queue: the process that replaced the resources and two of the clients. The third client now executes the loop test and either becomes blocked again or exits the monitor (having removed some of the resources). This is then repeated by the first, and then the second client.† Eventually the replacing process exits.

The 'rendezvous' solution is more problematic. In order to request N instances of the resource, a parameter to the request must hold this value. The server process now has a clear difficulty: to find out how many resources are being requested the calling rendezvous must be accepted, but if the server cannot allocate N the request rendezvous must be terminated without being satisfied. The client then has no choice but to call again. This could easily lead to polling or, at best, an inelegant solution such as that given in Chapter 5. Here clients first call ALLOCATE; if they are unsuccessful, they then block on a call to one of the two RETRYs. This entry is only accepted when resources are freed (REPLACED). Following a release of resources all blocked processes are woken up (one at a time). Those that still cannot be allocated the correct number of resources are required to block on the other RETRY entry. The solution given in Chapter 5 thus has the following outline:

```
process CONTROLLER;
  entry ALLOCATE(N : integer; var OK, queue : boolean);
  entry RETRYA(N : integer; var OK, queue : boolean);
  entry RETRYB(N : integer; var OK, queue : boolean);
  entry REPLACE(N : integer);
  ...
begin
  FREE := MAX;
  repeat
    select
      when FREE > 0 =>
      accept ALLOCATE(N : integer; var OK, queue : boolean) do
        (* allocate resource and reduce FREE *)
```

---

† In the absence of process priorities, the chivalry queue is defined to be LIFO in Pascal-FC.

```
                    (* or tell client to call again on queue *)
          or
            accept REPLACE(N : integer) do
            begin
              FREE := FREE + N;
              (* for each outstanding client *)
              if switch then      (* queue A has clients *)
                accept RETRYA(N : integer; var OK, queue : boolean) do
                    (* allocate resource or tell client to *)
                    (* call again on queue *)
              else     (* queue B has clients *)
                accept RETRYB(N : integer; var OK, queue : boolean) do
                    (* allocate resource or tell client to *)
                    (* call again on queue *)
            end;
              switch := not switch;
          or
            terminate
          end      (* select *)
        forever
      end;      (* CONTROLLER *)
```

If the number of resources is small then some improvements can be made to the above algorithm (clients retry on a specific entry associated with the number of resources requested – this is only accepted when that number is available). In general, however, the ease of use of the rendezvous abstraction must be questioned. Avoidance synchronization can lead to the use of double rendezvous interactions.

One method of improving avoidance synchronization that was discussed in Chapter 5 is to allow a guard to have assess to 'in' parameters to the call:

```
accept ALLOCATE(N : integer) when N <= FREE do
```

This is allowed neither in Pascal-FC nor in Ada, however. The other approach is to *requeue* a request after it has been accepted, but before completion of the rendezvous. Examples of this facility will be given later in this chapter.

8.4   A broadcast example

We conclude this section on comparing the language models with a further example. Here a process wishes periodically to broadcast data to a fixed set of receiver processes. The required behaviour is that all receivers must get the data before the broadcaster can continue. Moreover, the receivers must block if they 'get ahead' of the broadcaster and request the data before it has been produced.

The monitor solution is again straightforward. Each receiver has a condition variable on which it blocks if it calls early. The broadcaster also blocks until all receivers have called in. Hence the last receiver wakes the broadcaster up. In the following, the broadcaster calls WRITING and the receivers call READING:

```
program bcstmon;
(* Program for the broadcasting of integer values *)
(* to three client consumer processes *)

monitor control;
  export WRITING, READING;
  var value, I : integer;
      early : condition;
      OK : boolean;
      available : array[1..3] of boolean;
      suspend : array[1..3] of condition;

  procedure WRITING(V : integer);
    var I : integer;
  begin
    if not OK then
      delay(early);
    value := V;
    OK := false;
    for I := 1 to 3 do
    begin
      available[I] := true;
      resume(suspend[I])
    end
  end;

  procedure READING(Id : integer; var V : integer);
  begin
    if not available[Id] then
      delay(suspend[Id]);
    available[Id] := false;
    V := value;
    if not available[1] and not available[2]
      and not available[3] then
    begin
      OK := true;
      resume(early)
    end
  end;
```

```
begin
  OK := true;
  for I := 1 to 3 do
    available[I] := false
end;    (* monitor control *)

monitor screen;
  export
    PRINT;

    procedure PRINT(ID, N: integer);
    begin
      writeln(ID,N)
    end
end;    (* monitor screen *)

process broadcaster;
  var I : integer;
begin
  I := 1;
  repeat
    control.WRITING(I);
    I := I + 1
  forever
end;

process type consumer(Ident : integer);
  var V : integer;
begin
  repeat
    control.READING(Ident,V);
    screen.PRINT(Ident,V)
  forever
end;

var cons1, cons2, cons3 : consumer;

begin
  cobegin
    broadcaster;
    cons1(1); cons2(2); cons3(3)
  coend
end.
```

The message-passing solution can be structured in a number of ways: the broadcaster can call each consumer or the consumers can call in to the broadcaster. With an asymmetric **select** a process cannot make a non-deterministic choice between alternative entry calls (only **accept** statements are allowed as **select** alternatives). Hence it is easier to structure the solution so that clients call in. The broadcaster must, however, loop around taking one call at a time. In the following example, each consumer calls in on a separate entry; an alternative structure would have a single entry and each caller would pass an identifier (as in the monitor solution):

```
program bcstada;
(* Program for the broadcasting of integer values *)
(* to three client consumer processes *)

process broadcaster;
  entry call1(var I : integer);
  entry call2(var I : integer);
  entry call3(var I : integer);

  var value, count : integer;
      first,second,third : boolean;

begin
  value := 1;
  repeat
    first := true;
    second := true;
    third := true;
    for count := 1 to 3 do
    select
      when first =>
      accept call1(var I : integer) do
        I := value;
        first := false;
    or
      when second =>
      accept call2(var I : integer) do
        I := value;
      second := false;
    or
      when third =>
      accept call3(var I : integer) do
        I := value;
      third := false
    end;      (* select *)
    value := value + 1
  forever
end;

process screen;
  entry PRINT(ID, N: integer);
begin
  repeat
    accept PRINT(ID, N: integer) do
```

```
                writeln(ID,N)
      forever
end;

process cons1;
   var V : integer;
begin
   repeat
      broadcaster.call1(V);
      screen.PRINT(1,V)
   forever
end;

process cons2;
   var V : integer;
begin
   repeat
      broadcaster.call2(V);
      screen.PRINT(2,V)
   forever
end;

process cons3;
   var V : integer;
begin
   repeat
      broadcaster.call3(V);
      screen.PRINT(3,V)
   forever
end;

begin
   cobegin
      broadcaster;
      screen;
      cons1; cons2; cons3
   coend
end.
```

8.5   Evaluation and comparison

We are now in a position to summarize our evaluations of the language features discussed and illustrated in this book.

(1)   *Semaphores and condition variables are too low level for general programming:*
Although semaphores will always have a seminal place in any

discussion of concurrency, they lack the structure required in a general purpose concurrent programming language. They should perhaps be considered to be the *goto* of concurrency.

(2) *Message-passing methods (incorporating the guard facility) represent a more abstract and unified means of programming communication:*
The removal of all shared variables simplifies the language model to one of communicating processes only. Such a model is more natural to use and is amenable to formal analysis.

(3) *Remote invocation is an effective high-level message-passing abstraction:*
Remote invocation has a number of advantages over the simpler synchronous message-passing model. Intermediaries (channels) are not required and the problematic symmetric **select** can be removed. In addition, the language can use an identical syntactic style for procedure calls and remote invocation. This helps to reduce the overall complexity of the language.

(4) *Monitor-like structures are an effective way of encapsulating shared resources:*
This is an important observation, and one that is, in some ways, at variance with the view that a pure process model gives the best abstraction.

In Chapter 3 it was noted that, in general, a program consists of active and passive objects. Active objects must be implemented by processes, but how should passive objects be encapsulated? The pure message-passing model also requires passive objects to be represented as processes. Although this has the advantage of simplicity, it has two significant drawbacks:

- it is not the abstraction users have;
- it leads to inefficient implementations.

The distinction between active and passive objects seems to be a fundamental one. Many users of, for example, Ada and occam complain that it is unnatural to have to use an active entity for a passive resource just to enforce a required synchronization on its usage. Issues of efficiency are, however, the key ones in the sometimes heated debate about this aspect of language design.

Efficiency of implementation is not normally a key issue when discussing concurrency, and we have not previously paid much attention to it in this book. Nevertheless, a language primitive that appears to be intrinsically inefficient is clearly inappropriate. Moreover, as we observed in Chapter 1, one of the main application areas for concurrency is in embedded real-time systems where efficiency, although not the overriding issue, is necessarily significant.

Implementing a passive resource as a process forces the program to experience an excessive number of context switches. Consider the resource control example given earlier in this chapter; the double rendezvous must involve at least five context switches. The broadcast example is also illustrative: the broadcaster process must run between each receiver; this does not occur with the monitor solution.

It is not clear whether a primitive that causes more context switches is intrinsically inefficient. One could argue that we are merely waiting for hardware techniques to catch up with the language models. However, in the debate over the Ada language those that support the pure process model have had to agree that certain active objects can be implemented as passive ones in order to achieve the required efficiency. Thus monitor-like processes can actually be implemented as monitors (by automatic 'optimization' techniques), but at the source program level they still look like processes.

Within the Ada debate, the above view has lost out. Users do not wish to rely on compiler tricks to get efficiency and they are happy to see the passive object as a distinct abstraction. One of the most vocal requirements for Ada 9X is for the language definition to support directly a lower-level, more efficient, synchronization primitive. The language redesigners have devised a high-level abstraction for a passive object. We shall present an equivalent model in the next section.

8.6   The unified model

In this unified model a program consists of **processes**, **resources** and **data**. Processes can encapsulate data and may interact with each other using remote invocation. Resources embody shared entities (in particular data) and protect access; they do not, however, have a thread of control. Thus processes model active objects while resources implement passive objects. Data is neutral.

Resources provide (by definition) mutually exclusive access and support avoidance synchronization by the use of guards. The ease of use of these guards is improved by including a requeue facility (see Section 8.6.1). In structure, a resource is a combination of a monitor and a conditional critical region (see Section 7.3). The declaration of a resource follows the Pascal-FC monitor style:

```
resource_declaration ::=

resource identifier;
        export_list
        resource_declaration_part
    [resource_body]
    end;
```

The declarations may include constants, types, variables, procedures and functions, but not processes, monitors or other resources. Only procedure identifiers may appear in the **export** list.

A resource module thus exports procedures just as a monitor does, but it does not use condition variables. Rather, the condition for the execution of an exported procedure is expressed as a guard. For reasons that will be made clear later, processes should not, while they have exclusive hold of a resource, use any means of blocking other than these guards.

Some examples may help to clarify the semantics of resources. First consider a simple shared integer variable (SHARED) that only requires mutual exclusion to inhibit multiple updates:

```
program UPDATING;

(* safe updating of a shared variable with resources *)

resource COUNTER;
  export
    UPDATE, EXAMINE;
  var
    COUNT: integer;

    procedure UPDATE(INCREMENT: integer);
    begin
      COUNT := COUNT + INCREMENT
    end;    (* UPDATE *)

    procedure EXAMINE(var RESULT: integer);
    begin
      RESULT := COUNT
    end;    (* EXAMINE *)

begin    (* body *)
    COUNT := 0
end;    (* COUNTER *)

process type ADDER;
begin
  repeat
    COUNTER.UPDATE(1)
  forever
end;    (* ADDER *)

process type LOOKER;
var
    LOCAL: integer;
begin
  repeat
```

```
          COUNTER.EXAMINE(LOCAL);
          (* use value in LOCAL *)
      forever
    end;    (* LOOKER *)

(* declarations of process objects *)

begin
  cobegin
    . . .
  coend
end.
```

The variable is embedded in the resource, which exports two procedures: one to read its value, the other to update it. As this example only requires mutual exclusion (not condition synchronization), it is similar to a monitor solution to the same problem.

The following program illustrates the use of guards and avoidance synchronization; it implements the now familiar bounded buffer producer–consumer algorithm:

```
program PCRES;

(* Producer-Consumer example with resources. *)

resource buffer;
  export
    PLACE, TAKE;
  const
    MAX = 5;
    inxmax = 4;
  var
    store: array[0..inxmax] of char;
    nextin, nextout, NUMBER: integer;

  guarded procedure PLACE(ch: char) when NUMBER < MAX;
  begin
    store[nextin] := ch;
    nextin := (nextin + 1) mod MAX;
    NUMBER := NUMBER + 1
  end;    (* PLACE *)

  guarded procedure TAKE(var ch: char) when NUMBER <> 0;
  begin
    ch := store[nextout];
    nextout := (nextout + 1) mod MAX;
    NUMBER := NUMBER − 1
  end;    (* TAKE *)
```

```
begin      (* body *)
  nextin := 0;
  nextout := 0;
  NUMBER := 0
end;      (* buffer *)

process producer;
var
  ch: char;
begin
  for ch := 'a' to 'z' do
    buffer.PLACE(ch)
end;      (* producer *)

process consumer;
var
  local: char;
begin
  repeat
    buffer.TAKE(local);
    write(local)
  until local = 'z';
  writeln
end;      (* consumer *)

begin
  cobegin
    producer;
    consumer
  coend
end.
```

The semantics for a resource (with guards) are as follows:

- if a call is made on a guarded procedure then the guard is evaluated;
- the guard is evaluated under mutual exclusion;†
- if the guard is true, the procedure is executed;
- if the guard is false, the caller is suspended (on that guard) and the mutually exclusive hold on the resource is released;
- whenever the execution of a resource procedure is completed, all guards that have at least one outstanding caller are evaluated;
- if there is at least one caller that can now proceed, then exactly one

---

† All code inside a resource, including guard evaluation, is executed under mutual exclusion of all other code *inside the same resource*. In general, the guards should only involve variables also declared inside the resource, because there is nothing to prevent any global variables being concurrently modified by a process executing outside this resource.

caller is chosen and the mutually exclusive hold on the resource is passed to this caller;

- the decision about which caller to choose is non-deterministic.

The reader should now not be surprised by the non-deterministic character of the choice.

The above points can be animated by considering a generalized version of the buffer example in which there may be multiple producers and/or consumers. Assume that the buffer is initially empty and that a call to TAKE is made. The guard (NUMBER > 0) is evaluated and found to be false: hence the caller is suspended and the mutually exclusive hold on the resource is released. Now suppose that another consumer calls TAKE: the above action will be repeated with the result that a further process will be suspended on that guard. Next let a producer call PLACE. The guard for this procedure (NUMBER < MAX) evaluates true and so the procedure is executed, which has the effect of incrementing NUMBER. When the producer has completed the procedure, the guards are re-evaluated; the guard (NUMBER > 0) is now true and hence one of the suspended processes will now take over the mutually exclusive hold on the resource. When it has completed its execution, the (NUMBER > 0) guard will be evaluated again (because there is a process waiting), but it is now false so no suspended process can proceed. The mutually exclusive hold on the resource is thus released and any process waiting outside could gain access.

Nested calls to exported procedures of other resources are allowed. This is akin to the nested monitor call and, as was the case with Pascal-FC monitors, mutually exclusive hold on the current resource is retained when such a call is made. No restriction is actually enforced in Pascal-FC, though it would be contrary to the spirit of resources to have a blocking operation (such as sleep) within such a procedure. The reason for this will become clear in Section 8.7.1.

As the above examples show, the resource has two kinds of procedure: one ordinary, one guarded. The execution of an ordinary procedure can always take place once a mutual exclusion lock on the resource has been obtained. Guarded procedures can, however, lead to suspension if the conditions are not appropriate for continuation. Pascal-FC uses the reserved word **guarded** to emphasize the distinction between the two kinds of procedure. The recommended style of use of these procedures is that (apart from the requirement to obtain mutual exclusion on entry to the resource) only a guarded procedure should allow any possibility of blocking the calling process.

If the semantics for a resource are compared with those of monitors and condition variables, then it can be seen that they are somewhat more straightforward. With a monitor, a procedure could call a resume at any time. Thus the language design must ensure that the unblocked process and the resumer are not concurrently active in the monitor. A **resource** cannot have two processes active, as each guard is only re-evaluated when the current caller is exiting.

The model may seem somewhat inefficient (when compared with a monitor) as all guards need to be re-evaluated on exit (rather than the programmer explicitly waking up the next caller using a condition). However, an implementation can make a number of simplifications. For example:

- guards are only re-evaluated if there are outstanding callers on that procedure;
- guards are only re-evaluated if variables they use have been changed.

A consequence of these valid simplifications is that the programmer cannot rely on how many times a guard will be evaluated. A guard should therefore not have side-effects (which would be poor programming anyway).

The following example of the use of resources and remote invocation illustrates the programming of a mode change operation. Many embedded systems are designed to execute in a number of distinct modes. The programming of mode changes can, however, be problematic as they are usually asynchronous activities. In the following program, processes input, control and output represent a control data flow through an embedded system from sensor reading to actuator setting. The three processes are synchronized and thus pass data via remote invocation (rendezvous).

The control system is deemed to have two modes of operation – fast and slow. In the fast mode the control process will produce an adequate control value in as short a time as possible. When operating in the slow mode a more precise control value will be produced – but will take more time. As the mode change is an asynchronous event, the control process does not wish to rendezvous with a further process to decide if a mode change event has occurred. Rather, it accesses a resource (change) that has the current mode status defined. On each iteration of the control loop, control reads the mode status from the resource. The process responsible for changing mode (changer) calls the resource when a mode change is required. In a real-time system this changer would be given a high priority so that the mode change is registered as soon as possible.

```
program moderes;

resource change;
  export writing, reading;
  var fast : boolean;
  procedure writing(ft : boolean);
  begin
    fast := ft
  end;
  procedure reading(var ft : boolean);
```

```
    begin
      ft := fast
    end;
begin
  fast := false
end;


process changer;
begin
  sleep(5);
  change.writing(true);
  sleep(1);
  change.writing(false)
end;


process output;       (* notional output to actuator *)
  entry PUT(value : integer);
begin
  repeat
    select
      accept PUT(value : integer) do
        writeln(value);
    or
      terminate
    end
  forever
end;


process control;
  entry PUT(value : integer);
var variable : integer;
    fast : boolean;
begin
  repeat
    change.reading(fast);
    select
      accept PUT(value : integer) do
        variable := value;
    or
      terminate
    end;
    if fast then
      variable := variable + 100
    else
    begin
      variable := variable + 1000;
      sleep(2)
    end;
    output.PUT(variable)
  forever
end;
```

```
process input;      (* notional input from sensor *)
var I : integer;
begin
  for I := 1 to 25 do
    control.PUT(I)
end;

begin
  cobegin
    input;
    output;
    control;
    changer
  coend
end.
```

In the above program the slow mode of control is simulated by a greater increase in the control variable plus a sleep operation. The changer process undertakes a couple of mode changes during the program's execution. An example output from the program is:

```
Program modres  ...  execution begins  ...
  1001
  1002
  1003
  1004
   105
   106
   107
   108
   109
   110
   111
   112
   113
   114
   115
   116
   117
   118
  1019
  1020
  1021
  1022
  1023
  1024
  1025

Program terminated normally
```

One of the things to note about the above program is that it uses a resource to obtain an asynchronous relationship between two processes. Rather than support an explicit asynchronous message primitive, the resource abstraction adequately fulfills the need for loose coupling between processes. Thus the unified model has synchronous message passing and a means of programming asynchronous behaviour.

The motivation for the unified model of processes, resources and data comes from the assessment, presented earlier in this chapter, of the other features found in concurrent programming languages. Remote invocation is supported for direct interaction between active objects. Where passive objects are used to communicate data, the resource abstraction directly supports the required encapsulations. Neither semaphores nor condition variables are needed; the guard is considered to be a more appropriate method of supporting condition synchronization.

The expressive power of the model is easily illustrated by showing how it can implement semaphores:

```
program SEMRES;

(* simulation of binary semaphore by resources *)

var
   COUNT: integer;

resource BINSEM;
  export
    WAIT, SIGNAL;
  var
    VALUE: integer;

  guarded procedure WAIT when VALUE > 0;
  begin
    VALUE := 0
  end;     (* WAIT *)

  procedure SIGNAL;
  begin
    VALUE := 1
  end;     (* SIGNAL *)

begin     (* body *)
  VALUE := 1
end;     (* BINSEM *)

process type INC;
var
   I: integer;
```

```
begin
  for I := 1 to 20 do
    begin
    BINSEM.WAIT;
    COUNT := COUNT + 1;
    BINSEM.SIGNAL
    end
end;    (* INC *)

var
  TURNSTILE1, TURNSTILE2: INC;

begin
  COUNT := 0;
  cobegin
    TURNSTILE1;
    TURNSTILE2
  coend;
  writeln('Final total; ',COUNT:1)
end.
```

We conclude this section by giving a version of the broadcast problem using resources. In this version each of the three consumers must call in on a separate guarded procedure. They each block until the broadcaster process has written a value into the resource. The guard OK prevents the broadcaster calling again before the earlier value has been read. When the broadcaster has written a value, each consumer is released. They then close their guards (for their next call), read the value in the resource and proceed. The last consumer opens the OK guard again:

```
program bcstres;

(* Program for the broadcasting of integer values *)
(* to three client consumer processes *)

resource control;
  export WRITING, READING1, READING2, READING3;
  var value, I : integer;
      OK : boolean;
      available : array[1..3] of boolean;

  guarded procedure WRITING(V : integer) when OK;
    var I : integer;
  begin
    value := V;
    OK := false;
    for I := 1 to 3 do
      available[I] := true
  end;
```

```
    guarded procedure READING1(var V : integer) when available[1];
    begin
      available[1] := false;
      V := value;
      if not available[1] and not available[2]
        and not available[3] then
        OK := true
    end;

    guarded procedure READING2(var V : integer) when available[2];
    begin
      available[2] := false;
      V := value;
      if not available[1] and not available[2]
        and not available[3] then
        OK := true
    end;

    guarded procedure READING3(var V : integer) when available[3];
    begin
      available[3] := false;
      V := value;
      if not available[1] and not available[2]
        and not available[3] then
        OK := true
    end;

begin
  OK := true;
  for I := 1 to 3 do
    available[I] := false
end;     (* resource control *)

resource screen;
  export
    PRINT;

  procedure PRINT(ID, N: integer);
  begin
    writeln(ID,N)
  end;
end;     (* resource screen *)

process broadcaster;
  var I : integer;
begin
  I := 1;
```

```
        repeat
          control.WRITING(I);
          I := I + 1
        forever
    end;

    process type consumer(Ident : integer);
      var V : integer;
    begin
      repeat
        case Ident of
          1: control.READING1(V);
          2: control.READING2(V);
          3: control.READING3(V)
        end;
          screen.PRINT(Ident,V)
      forever
    end;

    var cons1, cons2, cons3 : consumer;

    begin
      cobegin
        broadcaster;
        cons1(1); cons2(2); cons3(3)
      coend
    end.
```

The above structure has the disadvantage that it does not easily scale up, as each consumer must call its own procedure. To obtain a more succinct version, however, requires the use of requeue.

8.6.1   Ease of use and requeue

In the assessment presented earlier in this chapter (and in Chapter 5) it was noted that avoidance synchronization (in the **select** statement) was not as easy to use, in all circumstances, as the condition synchronization provided by semaphores or condition variables. This assessment is equally valid for the form of avoidance synchronization used with resources. Such poor usability was illustrated by the resource control problem in which an unknown number of resource instances are requested at one time.

The unified model presented in this chapter increases the usability of the guard by adding a **requeue** facility. This will allow the execution of a guarded procedure to be abandoned, with the caller being transferred to a different guarded resource procedure. To give a simple illustration of **requeue**, consider the following stylized program in which a single caller process (with the calling boolean variable KEY) is blocked until the value of KEY is equal to a local variable LOCK:

```
resource example;
  export request, change;

  var LOCK : boolean;
      changed : boolean;

  guarded procedure await(KEY : boolean) when changed;
  begin
    null
  end;

  procedure change;
  begin
    LOCK := not LOCK;
    changed := true
  end;

  guarded procedure request(KEY : boolean) when true;
  begin
    if KEY <> LOCK then
    begin
      changed := false;
      requeue await(KEY)
    end
  end;

begin
  LOCK := true
end;    (* resource *)
```

Note that the procedure request is guarded even though its guard is ineffective (i.e. always true). This is because Pascal-FC enforces the rule that a **requeue** statement can only be placed in a guarded procedure. As we pointed out earlier, the call of an ordinary resource procedure should not block, except to gain entry to the resource.

When the client process calls request it obtains a mutually exclusive hold over the internal variables LOCK and changed. If KEY is not equal to LOCK then the caller must be blocked. This is achieved by requeuing the call onto await – having first closed the guard on await. Subsequently a call to change will assign true to the guard variable (also called *lowering the barrier*): this will cause the original caller to proceed.

The use of requeue helps construct a more general version of the broadcast program given above. Now all consumers call READING and are subsequently requeued on READ. The barrier on READ is lowered by the broadcaster when it calls WRITING. The broadcaster itself is requeued on WRIT so that it can lower the barrier once the consumers have left the resource:

```
program bcstres;
(* Program for the broadcasting of integer values *)
(* to three client consumer processes *)

resource control;
  export WRITING, READING;
  var value : integer;
      OK, OK2, barrier : boolean;
      available : array[1..3] of boolean;
      I : integer;

  guarded procedure WRIT when OK2;
  begin
    barrier := false
  end;

  guarded procedure WRITING(V : integer) when OK;
    var I : integer;
  begin
    value := V;
    OK := false;
    barrier := true;
    OK2 := false;
    requeue WRIT
  end;

  guarded procedure READ(Id : integer; var V : integer)
    when barrier;
  begin
    V := value;
    available[Id] := true;
    if available[1] and available[2] and available[3] then
      OK2 := true
  end;

  guarded procedure READING(Id : integer; var V : integer)
    when true;
  begin
    available[Id] := false;
    if not available[1] and not available[2]
      and not available[3] then
      OK := true;
    requeue READ(Id,V)
  end;

begin
  OK := false;
  barrier := false;
  for I := 1 to 3 do
    available[I] := false
end;     (* resource control *)
```

```
resource screen;
  export
    PRINT;

  procedure PRINT(ID, N: integer);
  begin
    writeln(ID,N)
  end
end;     (* resource screen *)

process broadcaster;
  var I : integer;
begin
  I := 1;
  repeat
    control.WRITING(I);
    I := I + 1
  forever
end;

process type consumer(Ident : integer);
  var V : integer;
begin
  repeat
    control.READING(Ident,V);
    screen.PRINT(Ident,V)
  forever
end;

var cons1, cons2, cons3 : consumer;

begin
  cobegin
    broadcaster;
    cons1(1); cons2(2); cons3(3)
  coend
end.
```

The **requeue** gives all the flexibility of condition variables but in a much more structured way. The reader should now be able to see how the resource control problem can be coded. This, and other standard problems, are left as exercises. It is important to understand that a requeue is not a standard procedure call. If procedure P calls procedure Q, after Q has completed control passes back to P, which then continues. By contrast, when P requeues on Q, the execution of P terminates; when Q has completed, control is passed back to the caller of P.

We now conclude with a further example of the use of requeue. In the previous chapter (Section 7.6.3) we illustrated how a monitor could be used to implement a simple alarm clock. A set of SLEEPER processes call

SLUMBER when they wish to delay for a number of ticks of the alarm. The algorithm requires each sleeper to wake up on each tick and then either to leave the alarm or return to sleep. We can now code this using a resource and requeue. However, the solution is not as straightforward as the monitor one was. As a resume operation on a condition variable can occur at any time (in a monitor), the blocked processes can perform a cascaded wake-up (see Section 7.6.3). A requeue is the last operation of a guarded procedure, so it follows that a woken process (if it cannot proceed) must become blocked on a different guarded procedure. The program below uses two extra guarded procedures, SLUMBER1 and SLUMBER2. On every tick all blocked processes move from one guarded procedure to the other (unless their alarm goes off, in which case they exit). Because there is mutual requeuing between SLUMBER1 and SLUMBER2, a forward declaration is needed:

```
program ALARMCLOCK;

const
  PMAX = 3;

resource ALARM;
  export
    SLUMBER, TICK;
  var
    NOW: integer;
    queue : integer;      (* takes values 1 or 2 *)
    freed1, freed2 : boolean;

  guarded procedure SLUMBER2(AL: integer) when true; forward;

  guarded procedure SLUMBER1(AL: integer) when freed1;
  begin
    if NOW < AL then
        requeue SLUMBER2(AL)
  end;    (* SLUMBER *)

  guarded procedure SLUMBER2;
  begin
    if NOW < AL then
        requeue SLUMBER1(AL)
  end;    (* SLUMBER *)

  guarded procedure SLUMBER(N: integer) when true;
  var
    ALARMCALL: integer;
  begin
    ALARMCALL := NOW + N;
    if NOW < ALARMCALL then
```

```
        if queue = 1 then
            requeue SLUMBER1(ALARMCALL)
        else
            requeue SLUMBER2(ALARMCALL)
    end;      (* SLUMBER *)

    procedure TICK;
    begin
      NOW := NOW + 1;
      if queue = 1 then
      begin
        queue := 2;
        freed1 := true;
        freed2 := false
      end else
      begin
        queue := 1;
        freed1 := false;
        freed2 := true
      end
    end;      (* TICK *)

begin     (* body *)
  NOW := 0;
  queue := 1;
  freed1 := false
end;     (* ALARM *)

resource SCREEN;
  export
    PRINT;

  procedure PRINT(N: integer);
  begin
    writeln('process ',N:1,' awakes')
  end      (* PRINT *)
end;     (* SCREEN *)

processDRIVER;
    (* provides the clock "ticks" *)
begin
  repeat
    sleep(1);
    ALARM.TICK
  forever
end;     (* DRIVER *)

process type SLEEPERTYPE(N: integer);
begin
  repeat
```

```
            ALARM.SLUMBER(N);
            SCREEN.PRINT(N)
            (* get up and go to work *)
        forever
    end;      (* SLEEPERTYPE *)

var
    SLEEPERS: array[1..PMAX] of SLEEPERTYPE;
    PLOOP: integer;

begin
    cobegin
        DRIVER;
        for PLOOP := 1 to PMAX do
            SLEEPERS[PLOOP](PLOOP)
    coend
end.
```

8.7　The Ada 9X language

It was noted earlier that in the debate about the Ada programming language, considerable support was given to the introduction of a language primitive similar to the resources notion described above. Ada uses a **protected record** as the easiest way of introducing the concept to an existing language was to see the data to be encapsulated as a special form of record. Because guards are associated with entries in Ada 83, the language redesigners decided to make a clear distinction between a procedure that does not have a guard (i.e. can always be executed) and one that is guarded. The latter (the **guarded procedure** in Pascal-FC) retains the Ada 83 term **entry**. Hence the specification of the 'semaphore' protected type has the form:

```
protected semaphore is
    procedure signal;
    entry wait;
private record
    sem : integer:= 1;-- for example
end record;

protected body semaphore is
    procedure signal is
    begin
        sem := sem + 1;
    end;
```

```
   entry wait when sem > 0 is
   begin
      sem := sem − 1;
   end;
end;
```

It is proposed that protected records are full types; hence the programmer can (for example) declare arrays of such records. The Pascal-FC **resource**, like the monitor, does not have this (useful) refinement.

8.7.1 Implementing resources and protected records

In the previous section, the Ada 9X protected type construct was introduced and compared with the **resource** abstraction in Pascal-FC. Unlike Pascal-FC, Ada is designed to support real-time applications. Consequently, it is important that it allows protected records to be implemented in an efficient and temporally predictable way. In this section we consider an implementation strategy that is recommended for single processor Ada systems.

First it should be noted that Ada uses priority to control the non-determinancy evident in concurrent systems. Each task (remember that Ada uses the term *task* rather than *process*) is given a unique (if possible) priority. Whenever two tasks are competing, either for the processor or on an entry queue, the one with the highest priority will be chosen. If all tasks execute independently of each other then the allocation of unique priorities will allow the temporal behaviour of each task to be predicted – as was discussed in Chapter 2.

When tasks interact, a phenomenon called **priority inversion** can occur. To illustrate this, consider three periodic tasks T1, T2 and T3. Let the priorities be assigned such that:

$$priority(T1) > priority(T2) > priority(T3)$$

Assume further that T1 and T3 share a resource R (i.e. both tasks access R, and R must be accessed under mutual exclusion). With this formulation, the following behaviour is possible: T3 becomes runnable (while T1 and T2 are sleeping) and gains access to the resource R. While T3 is using R, T2 becomes runnable and pre-empts T3 as it has a higher priority. T1 then wakes from its delay and pre-empts T2; it continues to execute until it needs R. Now it must wait until T3 has finished with R. But T3 will not execute again until T2 has finished. The result of this behaviour (which is perfectly legal within the priority model) is that the highest priority task T1 is prevented from executing by:

- the time T2 is executing, plus
- the time T3 is executing with R.

The latter time period is inevitable and is the consequence of giving mutual exclusion over R. It can be kept short by bounding the time for which T3 has access to R (hence the undesirability of any blocking while executing in a resource that was noted earlier). The delay imposed by T2, however, is unacceptable as it completely undermines the priority model.

A number of methods are used to remove the pessimistic priority inversion illustrated above. Within the context of protected types (resources) there is one technique that delivers three important properties:

(1)   prevents pessimistic priority inversion

(2)   provides mutual exclusion over resources

(3)   prevents deadlock occurring as a result of resource usage.

Note that these properties are only true for single processor implementations.

The technique is known as **immediate priority ceiling inheritance**. In a program that consists of processes and resources, both are assigned priorities. A resource has a *ceiling priority* which is defined to be the maximum priority of all the processes that access it. The *immediate* part comes from the run-time behaviour: whenever a process accesses a resource, its priority is immediately raised to the ceiling value. When it exits the resource, its priority is lowered to the level it had before entering.

Mutual exclusion is supplied because, while process P (say) is accessing the resource, no other process that may wish to access the resource can execute: P has a higher priority than any possible competing process. (The reader should now understand why the above semantics are not sufficient for multiprocessor systems.)†

The lack of pessimistic priority inversion can best be described by returning to the example of the three tasks T1, T2 and T3, and the resource R. With immediate ceiling priority inheritance, R will have a ceiling priority equal to the priority of T1. Hence, whenever T3 has the resource it will run in preference to T2. Indeed, while it has the resource it will run in preference to T1. As a result, T1 may be delayed at the start of its execution by the time that T3 has R. As was noted earlier, this time interval is unavoidable but can usually be made acceptably small. T1 is never blocked by T2.

The lack of deadlock is more difficult to illustrate. Indeed, the formal proof of this property is quite complex (see the Further Reading list). In Chapter 3 it was noted that one of the four necessary and sufficient conditions for deadlock must be broken if deadlock is to be prevented. One of these was the need for a circular relationship between processes and

---

† In order for the model to be absolutely correct, it is necessary for a process holding the ceiling to run in preference to any other process with that priority. This is because one of the resource users has a priority equal to the ceiling. An alternative formulation of the model defines the ceiling priority to be one greater than the maximum priorities of its users. There is then no possible competition.

resources. The immediate ceiling priority inheritance model prohibits this by not allowing resources to be allocated that could lead to this circular relationship. If you consider T1, then it is prohibited from starting until all the resources it might need are released. (This is because any process using such resources must have at least T1's priority while doing so.) It then runs through its resource usages without interference. As long as a process does not delay (sleep) while holding a resource, then the scheme is deadlock-free. Note, however, that in the unified model presented in this chapter, processes can still communicate directly using remote invocation and that the misuse of this primitive can still lead to deadlock.

The above implementation mechanism is recommended by Ada 9X. In addition, when a task completes its execution of a protected type procedure or entry and causes a suspended task to run (because the associated guard is now true), the code for the awakened task is executed on its behalf by the original task that woke it. This reduces the number of context switches and makes other aspects of the full language model more straightforward.

SUMMARY

This chapter concludes the analysis presented in earlier chapters with respect to the main communication and synchronization primitives found in concurrent programming languages. The main conclusions of this analysis are that, in terms of expressive power, there is nothing to choose between the models. However, when considering usability, guarded communication was found to be the most appropriate abstraction, although for some algorithms it led to inelegant solutions.

One of the clear distinguishing features between the language models presented in Chapters 4 and 5, and those of Chapters 6 and 7, is the representation of passive entities. Should they be encapsulated in processes or in some special protected module? There is no simple answer to this question. If you believe in a pure message-passing language model, then the occam and Ada 83 models are recommended. However, if you feel that passive entities should be represented by an appropriate distinctive abstraction, then the unified model described in this chapter is perhaps the best formulation yet devised as it does not need to make use of low-level primities such as condition variables.

In the unified model (which gets its inspiration from that proposed in Ada 9X) passive entities are encapsulated in resources. Resources enforce mutual exclusion and provide avoidance synchronization by the use of guarded procedures. Only when an associated guard is true can a called procedure actually be executed. As there are some situations in which avoidance synchronization is not as usable as the lower-level provisions of condition variables or semaphores, a requeue facility is provided in the unified model.

When a process (while executing a resource procedure) executes a requeue on to another resource procedure, the guard associated with the new procedure may prevent further progress. This gives equivalent usability to any lower-level primitive. The reader is encouraged to use the unified model in the exercises that follow.

FURTHER READING

Baker T.P. (1990). Protected Records, Time Management and Distribution. *Ada Letters*, **X**(9), 17–28

Baker T.P. (1990). A Stack-Based Resource Allocation Policy for Realtime Processes. In *Proceedings of the 11th IEEE Real-Time Systems Symposium 1990*

Baker T.P. (1991). Stack-Based Scheduling of Realtime Processes. *Journal of Real Time Systems*, **3**(1)

Pilling M., Burns A. and Raymond K. (1990). Formal Specification and Proofs of Inheritance Protocols for Real-Time Scheduling. *Software Engineering Journal*, **5**(5), 263–79

Sha L. and Goodenough J.B. (1990). Real-Time Scheduling Theory and Ada. *IEEE Computer*

EXERCISES

8.1 Program the Ornamental Gardens problem using resources.

8.2 Program the Readers and Writers problem using a resource (see Exercise 4.3).

8.3 Show how the resource control problem can be solved using a resource and requeue.

8.4 Reprogram Exercise 5.4 using a resource to represent the buffer.

8.5 The final version of the broadcast program given in this chapter used **requeue** to enable all consumers to call in on the same (guarded) procedure. Modify this program so that only those consumers that have called in since the last broadcast are released (i.e. the broadcaster and the other consumers are not delayed by a tardy consumer).

8.6 Consider a producer–consumer structure with an integer buffer of maximum size 16. The consumer reads one integer at a time from the buffer but the producer may need to place up to 16 integers in the buffer in one go (i.e. it is blocked until there is sufficient space available). Using **requeue**, show how the buffer is implemented.

8.7   Two processes start by each holding an array of integers. As the program executes, the processes swap integers (via a resource). The objective is to bring the average of the sets of integers held by the two processes as close together as possible. Write the program that implements these processes and the resource.

8.8   Consider a program that consists of two processes and a resource. The resource contains an arbitrary set of green and red balls. One process calls in for a single ball; if it is green it throws it away, but if it is red it replaces it. The other process extracts two balls (in one go). If they are both green it replaces one of them; if they are both red it throws them away and returns a new green ball; if they are mixed the red one is returned and the green one is thrown away. Implement this program. What is the final state of the resource? Could this behaviour have been predicted?

8.9   One method of finding the maximum of a set of integers is to hold the set in a resource and have a number of processes call in on the resource. Each time a process calls, it extracts two integers and returns the larger. Program this algorithm using five worker processes. When the final value is returned, this should invoke a write action.

8.10   The Smokers' Problem (see Exercise 7.6) can be solved (using a resource) by allowing the three smoker processes to call in on difference procedures. However, it can also be solved by using just a single procedure and **requeue**. Program both of these solutions and compare the resulting programs.

8.11   Two processes interact via a buffer (a resource). A producer process writes either one, two or three integers into the buffer. The consumer process must block unless there are seven integers available; it then reads all seven integers in one go (using an array). Write a program that simulates this behaviour. Give the buffer a maximum size of 16 integers and have the producer process block if there is not sufficient room for the input.

8.12   A distributed application contains a number of clocks which are programmed as resources:

```
resource clock;
  export time, settime;
  . . .
end;
```

As clocks drift, it is necessary periodically to resynchronize them. Write a process that will do this. Note that clocks must never be moved backwards.

8.13   If Pascal-FC did not contain a 'sleep' (delay) primitive it would be possible to program one using a resource. Construct such a resource.

8.14   In Section 3.8.2, four necessary and sufficient conditions were given for deadlock to occur. Consider how the resource abstraction introduced in this chapter can lead to one or more of these conditions being prevented.

Advanced exercises

8.15 An earlier exercise considered a lift (elevator) control system. Now consider a two-lift system. There are five floors in the building. On each floor there is a single 'request lift' button. In each lift there are buttons for each floor. The behaviour of the passengers should be implemented by a single process that makes arbitrary calls on the five floors (and when the lift arrives requests any other floor). Your program should work in real-time by simulating the time it takes to open and close doors and move the lift between floors.

8.16 Suppose there are *n* passenger processes waiting for a train. The train moves round a circular track which has four stations. The train has a capacity of *m* (*m* < *n*). When a passenger calls in on a particular station, it specifies which station it wishes to travel to (it can specify the same station if it wants a round trip). Each passenger (and the train) should be represented by a process; each passenger process should be suspended when it makes its call and only execute again when it has reached its destination. Write a program that simulates this behaviour.

8.17 A data-flow architecture is characterized by the use of simple processes that are released by the arrival of data. These processes then either produce data for the environment or for other processes. The figure below illustrates a small data-flow program. Four data items are input; the output represents the value of (MAX(A,B) − C)*(D − C). Note that, for example, the MAX node is only **fired** (released) when both input data items have arrived. Each node is fired each time the appropriate data is available. A node is unable to pass on new data to another node until the last item has been read. Write a program that implements this data-flow diagram.

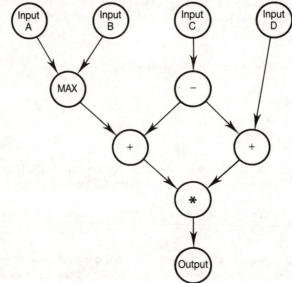

Figure 8.1 Write a program that implements the above data-flow diagram.

8.18 In a LINDA programming environment, processes interact via a tuple space. Processes extract data from the tuple space and are also responsible for generating data for the tuple space. If a process wishes to read an item of data that is not yet available, it must remain blocked until the data has been produced (by some other process). Write a program that contains an array of integers (to represent the tuple space – strictly a LINDA tuple space is unordered) and a group of processes that are responsible for creating the data in the array. For example, the tuple space could consist of nine elements; six processes interact with the tuple space in the following way:

> Process A reads items 1 and 3 and writes item 5
> Process B reads items 3, 5 and 7 and writes items 2, 6 and 8
> Process C writes item 4
> Process D reads item 4 and writes items 7 and 9
> Process E reads item 4 and writes item 1
> Process F reads item 9 and writes item 3

The program should contain an additional single client process that requests a specific item of data from the array. Write the program so that this client makes a 'random' choice as to which data item it requires. Once an item of data is placed in the tuple space it remains unaltered for the rest of the program's execution.

8.19 Compare the structure of your solutions to Exercises 8.17 and 8.18. What is the relationship between the data in the system and the processes? What conditions are necessary for a process to execute in the two models?

8.20 One method of constructing a concurrent program, which is particularly effective in a multiprocessor environment, is to deploy a pool of worker processes. Each worker process calls into the pool and is either blocked or is given a job to do; when this job is complete, it returns to the pool. Write a program that uses this structure. One possible problem to address is finding the maximum value in an array. A worker process will respond to a request by splitting the problem it is given into two and resubmitting these jobs to the pool. Each worker process will thus split the problem until it becomes trivial (i.e. only two values need sorting). Your program should either assume an infinite number of workers (this is equivalent to having dynamic processes) or a finite number (in which case an empty pool indicates that the worker must do all the work itself).

8.21 Assume an infinite number of workers in the previous exercise. How does the structure of this program compare with the use of recursion in a sequential programming context?

9 Concurrency Architectures

9.1 Introduction	9.4 Data flow models and networks
9.2 Embedded systems architecture	9.5 LINDA-type architectures
9.3 Discrete event simulation	9.6 Process farms

The previous six chapters focused on communication and synchronization models. In this chapter we return to a consideration of the notion of process and how to structure programs so that they can exploit concurrency. Consideration is given to embedded systems, simulation, data flow models, LINDA-type structures and process farms. These represent the main concurrency architectures. The term 'architecture' is used here to imply program structure – not implementation strategy or hardware platform. It is not possible to give a detailed description of all the above architectures. To do so would require a more detailed knowledge of the application domains in which they are used. Rather, a brief description followed by a programmed example (using the unified language of the previous chapter) is given. The examples used are the 'advanced exercises' at the end of the previous chapter. Readers may wish to undertake these exercises (if they have not already done so) before proceeding with this chapter.

9.1 Introduction

Throughout the book attention has been limited to concurrent programs and languages in which the concurrency is explicit; some visible notion of process is evident. Before continuing in this vein it is perhaps worth paying some attention to other abstractions.

As indicated earlier, one of the motivations for concurrency comes from the need to exploit parallel hardware. However, the application of processes is not the only approach.

One of the most successful parallel machines is the vector (or array) processor. Here parallelism comes from exploiting **concurrent operators**. For example, if A, B and C are all objects of some large array type, then the assignment:

A := B + C

could be implemented in a number of ways. On a single (non-vectored) processor the associated compiler would generate a loop (or set of loops) that dealt with each element of A (and hence B and C) in turn. However, on a vectored machine, each element of A could be assigned in parallel. Both of these implementations are valid if the '+' operator is interpreted as being concurrent. As with all concurrency abstractions, a sequential or parallel implementation is acceptable.

The need to exploit vectored processors is typically found in numerical analysis, where FORTRAN is still predominant. A number of versions of FORTRAN support explicit concurrency operators.

Both concurrent processes and concurrent operators have the potential for parallel execution expressed in the application programs. With imperative programming languages (such as FORTRAN, COBOL, C, Pascal, Modula and Ada) it has been found to be very difficult to exploit parallel hardware without some guidance being given in the program (via some concurrency construct or abstraction). This difficulty is a result of the fundamental sequential nature of imperative programming languages. Whether a sequence of statements can be broken up, so that parts can be executed in parallel, can depend on quite subtle semantics of the program. It is difficult for a software tool to recognize these properties.

To give an example of the need to express concurrency (so that parallel hardware can be beneficial), consider a pipeline of transputers as shown in Figure 9.1. The transputer is a processor that can easily link up to other transputers and has the property that it can communicate with other

Figure 9.1 Pipeline of transputers.

transputers at the same time as executing internal code. On a transputer pipeline, each processor can be viewed as executing the following abstract code:

```
repeat
   input(A);
   B := F(A);
   output(B)
forever
```

The input and output activities are actions on the links to adjacent transputers. The function F represents the actions of this particular transputer, that is, it is some computationally expensive transformation of A into B.

An inspection of the above code shows it to be sequential. There does not seem to be any potential for exploiting the transputer's properties. However, the above code can be rewritten as:

```
input(A);
repeat
   B := F(A);
   output(B);
   input(A)
forever
```

Now the input and output actions can be undertaken in parallel:

```
input(A);
repeat
   B := F(A);
   cobegin
      output(B);
      input(A)
   coend
forever
```

The transformation to the code of this skeleton program is only valid if F has no side-effects that cause A to change. In general it is not possible for a compiler to undertake the transformations automatically (although some research work is addressing this issue).

If we move away from imperative programming languages, then the potential for exploiting parallelism increases. Both functional and logic programming (i.e. declarative) languages require a run-time engine to implement their programs. If this engine (which may itself be written in an imperative language) has a concurrent structure, then faster executions on parallel hardware are possible. For example, the inference engine of

PROLOG tries to find ways of satisfying the input clause. A number of possible solutions exist, which could be searched for in parallel (although it is not quite as simple as it sounds).

One of the advantages claimed for declarative styles of language is that concurrency does not have to be addressed by the programmer: it can be left to the implementation. These concurrent implementations are, however, not yet common! For the rest of this chapter we return to imperative programming languages. Here the notion of process both aids parallel execution and is an important abstraction in its own right.

9.2 Embedded systems architecture

With this type of application the structure of the concurrent program is dictated by the structure of the program's environment, that is, the system in which the program is embedded. Most of the programs given in this book are influenced by this model. Real-time systems and monitoring and control systems usually employ designs that reflect the larger system in which the digital computer is interfaced.

For example, in a railway signalling control system, each train may be represented by an active object. Points and lights are resources; sections of track are also resources and require mutually exclusive access. In a computer's operating system each device and interactive user is allocated a process. Indeed, each job that a user performs may be implemented as a distinct process.

If the application domain is very dynamic (e.g. an unbounded number of user jobs being allowed), then a dynamic process model is needed. Alternatively, if the system is static (as is usual in embedded systems), then a static model is adequate.

Most design methods aimed at embedded systems allocate processes to real-world entities. Typically, most input and output activities are assigned processes (if they are active) or resources (if they are passive). The necessary processing between input and output is allocated to internal processes and resources. If processing activity only takes place when input is forced into the system (i.e. by some form of interrupt), then the system is said to be **reactive**. However, most embedded systems are a mixture of reactive elements and polling activities. The polling of input devices usually takes place at a fixed periodic rate. The period itself is determined by the rate of change of the environmental variable being monitored.

Gomaa (1984) has identified six criteria for deciding if some processing activity should be implemented as a process:

(1) Input/output dependences – as an activity linked to an I/O device must run at a speed determined by the device.

(2) Time-critical functions – to meet a deadline a high priority may have to be attached to this activity.

(3) Computationally intensive functions – so that the activity can be assigned a low priority and not interfere with time-critical functions.

(4) Functional cohesion – to reduce excessive inter-process communication.

(5) Temporal cohesion – to group together all activities that should happen together.

(6) Periodic execution – a special case of (5) in which the activities are repeated regularly.

A number of examples of embedded systems have already been given in this book. The design of embedded systems is primarily concerned with the top-level structure of processes and resources. The internal code for each element is usually less problematic.

EXAMPLE 9.1 _____

Consider a two-lift (elevator) control system. There are five floors in the building being served. On each floor there is a single 'request lift' button. In each lift there are buttons for each floor. The behaviour of the passengers should be implemented by a single process that makes arbitrary calls on the five floors (and, when the lift arrives, requests any other floor). The program should work in real-time by simulating the time it takes to open and close doors and move the lifts between floors.

Solution We shall develop a simple lift control system in which the lifts move continuously between the floors. Refinements to this model will then be left to the reader as exercises.

A necessary part of any embedded program is the input and output routines that actually control the equipment of the larger system. These cannot, of course, be given for our simple example and so the following routines will be called by the control software:

```
procedure OpenDoors(L : integer);
begin
    (* open door for lift L *)
    sleep(2)
end;

procedure CloseDoors(L : integer);
begin
    (* close door for lift L *)
    sleep(2)
end;
```

```
procedure MoveLift(L : integer; UP : boolean);
begin
    (* move lift L one floor *)
  sleep(5)
end;
procedure StopLift(L : integer);
begin
    (* stop lift at next floor *)
  sleep(1)
end;
procedure lights(F : integer; ON : boolean);
begin
    (* turn floor button light on or off *)
end;
```

The sleep routine is called to model the time that would be consumed by these routines (e.g. 2 seconds to open the doors).

Our simple model only has one 'request' button on each floor. If the lift that stops is going in the wrong direction then the user must press the button again to re-register his or her request. All outstanding (i.e. currently unsatisfied) requests are held in a resource. A resource must be used as the lift controllers and the users (passengers) will make concurrent calls on the information it contains. The interface to this requests resource will need three routines: add for the users, and cancel and enquire for the lift controllers. The outstanding calls can be held in an array of booleans, hence:

```
resource requests;
    (* This resource holds outstanding requests from all floors *)
  export add, cancel, enquire;
  var I : integer;
  calls : array[1..floors] of boolean;
  procedure add(F : integer);
  begin
    calls[F] := true;
    lights(F,true)
  end;
  procedure cancel(F : integer);
  begin
    calls[F] := false;
    lights(F,false)
  end;
  procedure enquire(F : integer; var waiting : boolean);
  begin
    waiting := calls[F]
  end;
begin
  for I := 1 to floors do
```

```
      begin
        calls[I] := false;
        lights(I,false)
      end
end;      (* requests *)
```

As we cannot implement a complete lift system, we must simulate the behaviour of the user:

```
process passengers;
      (* This process simulates calls to the floor buttons *)
var F : integer;
begin
    repeat
      F := random(floors −1) + 1;
      requests.add(F);
      sleep(1)
    forever
end;
```

There are two lifts and hence a process type is required. The interface to this type defines a unique identifier num and an initial floor on which the lift should start. Two lift objects are required and, together with the passenger process, they represent the only threads in the system:

```
process type lifts(num, start : integer);
      (* Each lift starts on floor 'start' *)
    . . .

var lift1, lift2 : lifts;

begin
    cobegin
      lift1(1,1);
      lift2(2,floors);
      passengers
    coend
end.
```

As the lift moves continuously (apart from stopping at requested floors) a pseudocode description of its repeated behaviour is as follows:

```
repeat
    calculate next floor and direction
    move to next floor
    if internal or external request for this floor then
    begin
        stop lift
        cancel internal button
        open doors
```

```
        if external request then
          begin
          simulate up to 6 people boarding
          each of above presses an internal button
          cancel external request
          end
        wait for 2 seconds to allow people off
        close doors
      end
```

Note that both internal and external buttons can be cancelled even if at the time they are not pressed. This removes a possible race condition that could occur if both lifts stop at the same floor; both will cancel the request.

The actual code for the lifts is given below as part of the complete program for this embedded example:

```
program LiftControl;

const floors = 5;
(* First a collection of low level control procedures *)
procedure OpenDoors(L : integer);
begin
    (* open door for lift L *)
  sleep(2)
end;
procedure CloseDoors(L : integer);
begin
    (* close door for lift L *)
  sleep(2)
end;
procedure MoveLift(L : integer; UP : boolean);
begin
    (* move lift L one floor *)
  sleep(5)
end;
procedure StopLift(L : integer);
begin
    (* stop lift at next floor *)
  sleep(1)
end;
procedure lights(F : integer; ON : boolean);
begin
    (* turn floor button light on or off *)
end;

resource requests;
    (* This resource holds outstanding requests from all floors *)
  export add, cancel, enquire;
  var I : integer;
```

```
        calls : array[1..floors] of boolean;
        procedure add(F : integer);
        begin
          calls[F] := true;
          lights(F,true)
        end;
        procedure cancel(F : integer);
        begin
          calls[F] := false;
          lights(F,false)
        end;
        procedure enquire(F : integer; var waiting : boolean);
        begin
          waiting := calls[F]
        end;
      begin
        for I := 1 to floors do
        begin
          calls[I] := false;
          lights(I,false)
        end
      end;     (* requests *)


      process passengers;
      (* This process simulates calls to the floor buttons *)
      var F : integer;
      begin
        repeat
          F := random(floors −1) + 1;
          requests.add(F);
          sleep(1)
        forever
      end;


      process type lifts(num, start : integer);
      (* Each lift starts on floor 'start' *)
      var buttons : array[1..floors] of boolean;     (* floors requested *)
          dirUP : boolean;     (* true if lift going up *)
          people, but, P, I : integer;
          next : integer;
          pressed : boolean;
      begin
        next := start;
        if start > 1 then dirUP := false
                    else dirUP := true;
        for I := 1 to floors do
        buttons[I] := false;
        repeat
          if dirUP then
            if next < floors then
```

```
                    next := next + 1
                else
                begin
                    next := floors −1;
                    dirUP := false
                end
            else
                if next > 1 then
                    next := next − 1
                else
                begin
                    next := 2;
                    dirUP := true
                end;
            MoveLift(num,dirUP);
            requests.enquire(next,pressed);
            if pressed or buttons[next] then
            begin
                StopLift(num);
                buttons[next] := false;
                OpenDoors(num);
                requests.enquire(next,pressed);
                if pressed then
                begin
                    (* assume up to 6 passengers get on *)
                    people := random(5) + 1;
                    for P := 1 to people do
                    begin
                        repeat
                            but := random(floors−1) + 1
                        until but <> next;
                        buttons[but] := true
                    end;
                    requests.cancel(next)
                end;
                sleep(2);
                CloseDoors(num)
            end
        forever
    end;     (* lifts *)

    var lift1, lift2 : lifts;

begin
    cobegin
        lift1(1,1);
        lift2(2,floors);
        passengers
    coend
end.
```

Using this simple structure the reader can now expand the program to make it more realistic.

EXERCISES

9.1 Replace the single floor button by two buttons, one for UP and the other for DOWN. A lift should only stop when travelling in the requested direction.

9.2 Modify the program so that the lift will stop (with its doors open) if no internal buttons are pressed and there are no outstanding external requests.

9.3 Modify the program so that there are now *N* lifts. When all lifts are stationary (i.e. no internal or external calls) then they should move to different floors (e.g. with two lifts, one should be at the top of the building and the other at the bottom).

9.4 Extend your solution to Exercise 9.3 so that only the closest lift moves to a new request.

9.5 For any of the above solutions, add an internal alarm fire button. If this is pressed a new process should be released (from a new resource). It will cause fire bells to sound, stop all lifts at the next floor they will pass (using direct calls to the lift mechanism's control I/O), and cancel and disable all external button presses.

9.3 Discrete event simulation

Whereas embedded systems typically have to control some engineering activity (and hence operate in the time of the application), concurrent programs may be used merely to simulate the behaviour of some (usually) large discrete system. Here every active entity in the system is modelled as a process. These processes use resources and progress through a well defined life-cycle. Often many instances of the same process type are used: for example, the simulation of a traffic system may assign a process to each vehicle in the system. Each vehicle, although of the same type, may be parameterized to give it a specific speed or destination.

Because simulations often make use of a very large number of entities, they are not often implemented in a concurrent programming language. This is because of the inefficiency usually associated with a large number of processes in a single program. The problem is thus one of performance and not expressive power: concurrency remains an important abstraction in discrete event simulation.

EXAMPLE 9.2

Suppose there are n passenger processes waiting for a train. The train moves round a circular track which has four stations. The train has a capacity of $m(m < n)$. When passengers call in on a particular station, they specify the station they wish to travel to (they can specify the same station if they want a round trip). Each passenger (and the train) should be represented by a process; each passenger process should be suspended when it makes its call and only executes again when it has reached its destination.

Solution As this is a simulation, each passenger is represented by a process:

```
process type passenger;
   var home, away : integer;
begin
  repeat
    home := random(3) + 1;
    away := random(3) + 1;
    case home of
      1 : st1arrive.arrive(away);
      2 : st2arrive.arrive(away);
      3 : st3arrive.arrive(away);
      4 : st4arrive.arrive(away)
    end
  forever
end;
```

Thus each passenger randomly decides which station to go to and, from there, where to travel to. It then calls the appropriate resource to simulate arriving at the station (stlarrive, for example). A resource is used as each passenger will be blocked until the train arrives at its 'home' station; it will then be requeued and further blocked until the train subsequently arrives at the 'away' destination.

Ideally each station should be represented by a single resource. However, mutual requeuing in Pascal-FC is not possible, so two resources are used (e.g. st2arrive and st2depart). Passengers call st2arrive and are then requeued onto st2depart.

The resource st2depart deals with the activities of people leaving the train (and hence the station). The train process calls, for example, the following:

```
st2depart.stopping(volume);
st2depart.alloff(volume)
```

where volume holds the current number of people on the train. The procedure stopping opens the train doors to let the appropriate passengers off; alloff returns the changed value of volume. Note that the call of alloff will only be accepted once all passengers wishing to alight at that station have done so. The resource is thus:

```
resource st2depart;
    export alight, stopping, alloff;
    var OnTrain : integer;
        trainstopping : boolean;
    guarded procedure alight(source : integer) when trainstopping;
    begin
      OnTrain := OnTrain − 1;
      writeln('Arrived at station2 from',source)
    end;
    procedure stopping(passengers : integer);
    begin
      OnTrain := passengers;
      trainstopping := true
    end;
    procedure alloff(var passengers : integer);
    begin
      trainstopping := false;
      passengers := OnTrain
    end;
    begin     (* station2 *)
    trainstopping := false
    end;
```

The train process uses st2arrive in a similar way:

```
st2arrive.boarding(volume);
st2arrive.closedoors(volume)
```

The resource is as follows:

```
resource st2arrive;
    export arrive, boarding, closedoors;
    var OnTrain : integer;
        trainboarding : boolean;
    guarded procedure arrive(destination : integer)
      when trainboarding and (OnTrain < capacity);
    begin
      OnTrain := OnTrain + 1;
      case destination of
        1 : requeue st1depart.alight(2);
        2 : requeue st2depart.alight(2);
        3 : requeue st3depart.alight(2);
        4 : requeue st4depart.alight(2)
      end
```

```
    end;
    procedure boarding(passengers : integer);
    begin
      OnTrain := passengers;
      trainboarding := true
    end;
    procedure closedoors(var passengers : integer);
    begin
      trainboarding := false;
      passengers := OnTrain
    end;
  begin      (* station2 *)
    trainboarding := false
  end;
```

Note that the guard now stops too many passengers getting onto the train. The train process itself simply loops around the stations.

The full program can now be given:

```
  program trains;

    const capacity = 10;      (* very small train *)

    resource st1depart;
      export alight, stopping, alloff;
      var OnTrain : integer;
          trainstopping : boolean;
      guarded procedure alight(source : integer) when trainstopping;
      begin
        OnTrain := OnTrain − 1;
        writeln('Arrived at station1 from',source)
      end;
      procedure stopping(passengers : integer);
      begin
        OnTrain := passengers;
        trainstopping := true
      end;
      procedure alloff(var passengers : integer);
      begin
        trainstopping := false;
        passengers := OnTrain
      end;
    begin      (* st1depart *)
      trainstopping := false
    end;

    resource st2depart;
      export alight, stopping, alloff;
      var OnTrain : integer;
```

```
    trainstopping : boolean;
  guarded procedure alight(source : integer) when trainstopping;
  begin
    OnTrain := OnTrain − 1;
    writeln('Arrived at station2 from',source)
  end;
  procedure stopping(passengers : integer);
  begin
    OnTrain := passengers;
    trainstopping := true
  end;
  procedure alloff(var passengers : integer);
  begin
    trainstopping := false;
    passengers := OnTrain
  end;
begin     (* st2depart *)
  trainstopping := false
end;


resource st3depart;
  export alight, stopping, alloff;
  var OnTrain : integer;
      trainstopping : boolean;
  guarded procedure alight(source : integer) when trainstopping;
  begin
    OnTrain := OnTrain − 1;
    writeln('Arrived at station3 from',source)
  end;
  procedure stopping(passengers : integer);
  begin
    OnTrain := passengers;
    trainstopping := true
  end;
  procedure alloff(var passengers : integer);
  begin
    trainstopping := false;
    passengers := OnTrain
  end;
begin     (* st3depart *)
  trainstopping := false
end;


resource st4depart;
  export alight, stopping, alloff;
  var OnTrain : integer;
      trainstopping : boolean;
  guarded procedure alight(source : integer) when trainstopping;
  begin
    OnTrain := OnTrain − 1;
```

```
              writeln('Arrived at station4 from',source)
          end;
          procedure stopping(passengers : integer);
          begin
            OnTrain := passengers;
            trainstopping := true
          end;
          procedure alloff(var passengers : integer);
          begin
            trainstopping := false;
            passengers := OnTrain
          end;
        begin      (* st4depart *)
          trainstopping := false
        end;


        resource st1arrive;
          export arrive, boarding, closedoors;
          var OnTrain : integer;
              trainboarding : boolean;
          guarded procedure arrive(destination : integer)
            when trainboarding and (OnTrain < capacity);
          begin
            OnTrain := OnTrain + 1;
            case destination of
              1 : requeue st1depart.alight(1);
              2 : requeue st2depart.alight(1);
              3 : requeue st3depart.alight(1);
              4 : requeue st4depart.alight(1)
            end
          end;
          procedure boarding(passengers : integer);
          begin
            OnTrain := passengers;
            trainboarding := true
          end;
          procedure closedoors(var passengers : integer);
          begin
            trainboarding := false;
            passengers := OnTrain
          end;
        begin      (* st1arrive *)
          trainboarding := false
        end;


        resource st2arrive;
          export arrive, boarding, closedoors;
          var OnTrain : integer;
              trainboarding : boolean;
          guarded procedure arrive(destination : integer)
```

```
    when trainboarding and (OnTrain < capacity);
  begin
    OnTrain := OnTrain + 1;
    case destination of
      1 : requeue st1depart.alight(2);
      2 : requeue st2depart.alight(2);
      3 : requeue st3depart.alight(2);
      4 : requeue st4depart.alight(2)
    end
  end;
  procedure boarding(passengers : integer);
  begin
    OnTrain := passengers;
    trainboarding := true
  end;
  procedure closedoors(var passengers : integer);
  begin
    trainboarding := false;
    passengers := OnTrain
  end;
begin     (* st2arrive *)
  trainboarding := false
end;


resource st3arrive;
  export arrive, boarding, closedoors;
  var OnTrain : integer;
      trainboarding : boolean;
  guarded procedure arrive(destination : integer)
    when trainboarding and (OnTrain < capacity);
  begin
    OnTrain := OnTrain + 1;
    case destination of
      1 : requeue st1depart.alight(3);
      2 : requeue st2depart.alight(3);
      3 : requeue st3depart.alight(3);
      4 : requeue st4depart.alight(3)
    end
  end;
  procedure boarding(passengers : integer);
  begin
    OnTrain := passengers;
    trainboarding := true
  end;
  procedure closedoors(var passengers : integer);
  begin
    trainboarding := false;
    passengers := OnTrain
  end;
begin     (* st3arrive *)
```

```
                    trainboarding := false
                end;

                resource st4arrive;
                    export arrive, boarding, closedoors;
                    var OnTrain : integer;
                        trainboarding : boolean;
                    guarded procedure arrive(destination : integer)
                        when trainboarding and (OnTrain < capacity);
                    begin
                        OnTrain := OnTrain + 1;
                        case destination of
                            1 : requeue st1depart.alight(4);
                            2 : requeue st2depart.alight(4);
                            3 : requeue st3depart.alight(4);
                            4 : requeue st4depart.alight(4)
                        end
                    end;
                    procedure boarding(passengers : integer);
                    begin
                        OnTrain := passengers;
                        trainboarding := true
                    end;
                    procedure closedoors(var passengers : integer);
                    begin
                        trainboarding := false;
                        passengers := OnTrain
                    end;
                begin     (* st4arrive *)
                    trainboarding := false
                end;

        process type passenger;
            var home, away : integer;
        begin
            repeat
                home := random(3) + 1;
                away := random(3) + 1;
                case home of
                    1 : st1arrive.arrive(away);
                    2 : st2arrive.arrive(away);
                    3 : st3arrive.arrive(away);
                    4 : st4arrive.arrive(away)
                end
            forever
        end;

        process train;
            var volume : integer;
        begin
```

```
        volume := 0;
        repeat
          st1depart.stopping(volume);
          st1depart.alloff(volume);
          st1arrive.boarding(volume);
          st1arrive.closedoors(volume);
          writeln('on board',volume);

          st2depart.stopping(volume);
          st2depart.alloff(volume);
          st2arrive.boarding(volume);
          st2arrive.closedoors(volume);
          writeln('on board',volume);

          st3depart.stopping(volume);
          st3depart.alloff(volume);
          st3arrive.boarding(volume);
          st3arrive.closedoors(volume);
          writeln('on board',volume);

          st4depart.stopping(volume);
          st4depart.alloff(volume);
          st4arrive.boarding(volume);
          st4arrive.closedoors(volume);
          writeln('on board',volume)
        forever
      end;

      var crowd : array[1..15] of passenger;
          P : integer;

      begin
        cobegin
          for P := 1 to 15 do
            crowd[P];
          train
        coend
      end.
```

EXERCISES

9.6 How would resource types help in programming this example?

9.7 Simulation programs often have to calculate the average time for various activities to take place. Modify the program so that a virtual clock is included. As the train moves between stations 'time' should progress. Passengers should note how long each journey takes. Note that this is not a real-time program but a simulation program that simulates the passage of time, but runs as quickly as possible.

9.8 Modify the program so that there are two trains moving in opposite directions. Passengers should travel by the train taking the shortest route.

9.4 Data flow models and networks

A distinctive characteristic of embedded systems is that the processes involved are usually significant programs in their own right. They may embody complex control algorithms and hence contain non-trivial amounts of code. Indeed, it would usually be the case that the process contains internal modular decomposition in order to manage its structure.

A different perspective on concurrent programs is possible if the process is viewed as a simple entity lacking an internal structure. A program will then consist of a large number of simple processes with the complexity of the application being reflected in the way the data flows through these simple entities.

With this architecture, the concurrent program is best described as a data flow network in which the connections represent simple transformations to data. In a pure data flow model, each process is restricted to have a simple model. It has a fixed number N of input channels. When data is present on all its N input channels, the process is said to 'fire': all the N input values are read, internal computation takes place and data becomes available on some or all of the process's output channels. The process then remains dormant until data again becomes available on its input channels (i.e. all of them).

A data flow network is defined by linking a process's output (and input) to the input (or output) of other processes.

As processes are simple, a sizable application would give rise to a very large number of processes. As with the simulation models, this large number prohibits effective implementations. Hence there is a tendency to make the processes not quite as simple (and not as numerous). It is recognized that to implement data flow models properly requires different hardware primitives. Considerable experimentation is currently being undertaken into data flow machines.

The idea of simple processor units but extensive inter-process connections is also at the heart of the development of neural nets. These attempt to mimic the behaviour of the brain by having tens of thousands of simple processing units with extensive connections. However, rather than program such hardware, practitioners train them!

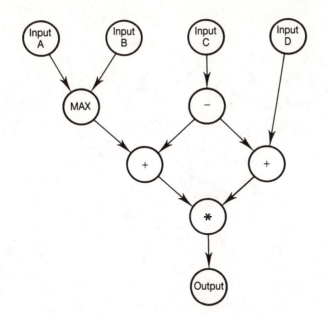

Figure 9.2 Data flow diagram for Example 9.3.

EXAMPLE 9.3 _____

Figure 9.2 illustrates a small data flow program. Four data items are input; the output represents the value of: (MAX(A,B) − C)*(D − C). Implement this data flow.

Solution Each node must clearly be represented by a process. As data is not buffered, it is appropriate for these processes to pass information directly between themselves. Hence each process must wait until it has all its input data and then produce its output data. Let the nodes be numbered as shown in Figure 9.3.

```
process node4;
    (* Adds tokens and passes on to node 5 *)
    entry LeftToken(V : integer);
    entry RightToken(V : integer);
  var T, T1,T2 : integer;
      I : integer;
      open1, open2 : boolean;
  begin
    open1 := true;
    open2 := true;
    repeat
      for I := 1 to 2 do
      select
        when open1 =>
```

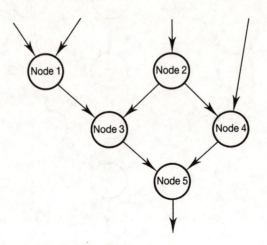

Figure 9.3 Node numbering.

```
      accept LeftToken(V : integer) do
      begin
        T1 := V;
        open1 := false
      end;
    or
      when open2 =>
      accept RightToken(V : integer) do
      begin
        T2 := V;
        open2 := false
      end
    end;
    open1 := true;
    open2 := true;
    T := T1 + T2;
    node5.RightToken(T)
  forever
end;    (* Node 4 *)
```

A **select** statement is used so that the order in which input is taken is arbitrary. The input processes are coded simply as:

```
process inputA;
  var A : integer;
  begin
    repeat
```

```
        write('A?');
        read(A);
        node1.LeftToken(A)
    forever
end;
```

Node 5 will produce the required output directly. The following is therefore the complete program for the example. Note that the code must be given 'in reverse order' as each node calls the one below it.

```
program dataflow;

    process node5;
        (* Mutiplies tokens and writes result *)
        entry LeftToken(V : integer);
        entry RightToken(V : integer);
    var T, T1,T2 : integer;
        I : integer;
        open1, open2 : boolean;
    begin
      open1 := true;
      open2 := true;
      repeat
        for I := 1 to 2 do
        select
          when open1 =>
          accept LeftToken(V : integer) do
          begin
            T1 := V;
            open1 := false
          end;
        or
          when open2 =>
          accept RightToken(V : integer) do
          begin
            T2 := V;
            open2 := false
          end
        end;
        open1 := true;
        open2 := true;
        T := T1 * T2;
        writeln(T)
      forever
    end;    (* Node 5 *)

    process node4;
        (* Adds tokens and passes on to node 5 *)
        entry LeftToken(V : integer);
```

```
        entry RightToken(V : integer);
var T, T1,T2 : integer;
    I : integer;
    open1, open2 : boolean;
begin
  open1 := true;
  open2 := true;
  repeat
    for I := 1 to 2 do
    select
      when open1 =>
      accept LeftToken(V : integer) do
      begin
        T1 := V;
        open1 := false
      end;
    or
      when open2 =>
      accept RightToken(V : integer) do
      begin
        T2 := V;
        open2 := false
      end
    end;
    open1 := true;
    open2 := true;
    T := T1 + T2;
    node5.RightToken(T)
  forever
end;     (* Node 4 *)


process node3;
    (* Adds tokens and passes on to node 5 *)
  entry LeftToken(V : integer);
  entry RightToken(V : integer);
var T, T1,T2 : integer;
    I : integer;
    open1, open2 : boolean;
begin
  open1 := true;
  open2 := true;
  repeat
    for I := 1 to 2 do
    select
      when open1 =>
      accept LeftToken(V : integer) do
      begin
        T1 := V;
        open1 := false
      end;
```

```
      or
        when open2 =>
        accept RightToken(V : integer) do
        begin
          T2 := V;
          open2 := false
        end
      end;
      open1 := true;
      open2 := true;
      T := T1 + T2;
      node5.LeftToken(T)
    forever
end;     (* Node 3 *)


process node2;
      (* Produces negative of token and passes on to nodes 3 and 4 *)
    entry Token(V : integer);
var T : integer;
begin
  repeat
    accept Token(V : integer) do
      T := V;
    node3.RightToken(-T);
    node4.LeftToken(-T)
  forever
end;     (* Node 2 *)


process node1;
      (* Finds maximum of tokens and passes on to node 3 *)
    entry LeftToken(V : integer);
    entry RightToken(V : integer);
var T, T1,T2 : integer;
    I : integer;
    open1, open2 : boolean;
begin
  open1 := true;
  open2 := true;
  repeat
    for I := 1 to 2 do
    select
      when open1 =>
      accept LeftToken(V : integer) do
      begin
        T1 := V;
        open1 := false
      end;
    or
      when open2 =>
      accept RightToken(V : integer) do
```

```
              begin
                T2 := V;
                open2 := false
              end
           end;
           open1 := true;
           open2 := true;
           if T1 > T2 then T := T1 else T := T2;
           node3.LeftToken(T)
        forever
      end;    (* Node 1 *)
         (* The following four processes drive input into the nodes *)
      process inputA;
      var A : integer;
      begin
        repeat
          read(A);
          node1.LeftToken(A)
        forever
      end;
      process inputB;
      var B : integer;
      begin
        repeat
          read(B);
          node1.RightToken(B)
        forever
      end;
      process inputC;
      var C : integer;
      begin
        repeat
          read(C);
          node2.Token(C)
        forever
      end;
      process inputD;
      var D : integer;
      begin
        repeat
          read(D);
          node4.RightToken(D)
        forever
      end;

   begin
```

```
    cobegin
      node1; node2; node3;
      node4; node5;
      inputA; inputB; inputC; inputD
    coend
  end.
```

EXERCISES

9.9 Write a data flow program that will evaluate the following expression:
$(A - B + C) + (A + B - C)$.

9.10 Write a data flow program to solve quadratic equations.

9.11 In the example given above, the structure of each node process is essentially the same. Consider what language features would need to be added to Pascal-FC (a) to allow all node processes with the same number of inputs and outputs to be generated from the same process type; (b) to allow processes with different numbers of inputs and output to be generated from the same type.

9.5   LINDA-type architectures

In the LINDA programming environment, processes interact via a **tuple space**. This is a common (unordered) data area into which processes can read and write. An interesting feature of this tuple space is that a process will block until the process that is responsible for creating the required data does so. Indeed, processes can be constructed so that their termination is commensurate with data being written into the tuple space. Thus a process wishing to read some data will either obtain the data immediately, if it is there, or will block waiting for some other process to terminate and thus furnish the tuple space with the required data. As processes can only interact via the tuple space, the design of the concurrent program is essentially concerned with the design of the tuple space.

A further refinement of the above structure allows a 'lazy' process model to be defined in which all processes in the system are responsible for creating data in the tuple space. A process will, however, only start its execution if the data it supplies has been requested. A system is therefore initialized with an empty tuple space and a set of uninitialized processes. An external agent then attempts to read some data item. As this item is not present, it causes some process to become active and work towards producing the data. If, in order to do this, some other data is needed from the tuple space then other processes will be activated. This structure can be considered 'lazy' (in the functional programming sense) as processes only execute when they are needed.

It is interesting to compare this lazy LINDA-type architecture with the data flow model. In one sense the systems are similar as they both involve processes that execute only when their input/output conditions require it. However, from an architectural viewpoint the models are really opposites. With data flow the system is driven by input flowing into the program; output will appear if the program's semantics define an output action to be a consequence of the particular input pattern. With the LINDA model, the system is output-driven. A request for the system to produce a particular effect will force internal computations to take place, which may in turn dictate input actions.

EXAMPLE 9.4 _____

Write a program that contains an array of integers (to represent the tuple space – strictly a LINDA tuple space is unordered) and a group of processes that are responsible for creating the data in the array. For example, the tuple space could consist of nine elements; six processes interact with the tuple space in the following way:

        Process A reads items 1 and 3 and writes item 5
        Process B reads items 3, 5 and 7 and writes items 2, 6 and 8
        Process C writes item 4
        Process D reads item 4 and writes items 7 and 9
        Process E reads item 4 and writes item 1
        Process F reads item 9 and writes item 3

The program should contain an additional single client process that requests a specific piece of data from the array. Write the program so that this client makes a 'random' choice as to which data item it requires. Once an item of data is placed in the tuple space it remains unaltered for the rest of the program's execution.

Solution As the tuple space is passive, but must prevent calls to get (read) being completed before calls to put (write), we implement it as a resource:

```
resource TupleSpace;
        (* A single resource implements the tuple space *)
        (* Client processes call get and put *)
        (* A call to get is blocked if the tuple is absent *)
        export get,put;
        var space : array[1..9] of integer;
            available : array[1..9] of boolean;
```

```
      ADD : integer;
   ...
begin     (* Tuple Space *)
   for ADD := 1 to 9 do
      available[ADD] := false
end;
```

A call to put simply assigns the appropriate tuple value and then marks is as available:

```
procedure put(adds : integer; V : integer);
begin
   space[adds] := V;
   available[adds] := true
end;
```

A call to get must return the appropriate value if the tuple is available, otherwise it must requeue the call so that it is blocked until the tuple does become available:

```
guarded procedure wait1(adds : integer; var V : integer)
         when available[1];
begin
   V := space[1]
end;

guarded procedure get(adds : integer; var V : integer) when true;
begin
   if available[adds] then
      V := space[adds]
   else
   case adds of
      1 : requeue wait1(adds,V);
      ...
   end
end;
```

Unfortunately, as there are no procedure types in Pascal-FC, each tuple value must have its own procedure. This would make it extremely tedious to program a large tuple space in Pascal-FC. In Ada, for example, it would be possible to program the above effectively as an entry family.

The producers for this tuple space simply call the correct put and get routines. For example, process C is simply:

```
process C;
begin
   TupleSpace.put(4,26)
end;
```

The more complex process B is equally straightforward:

```
process B;
   var te1, te2, te3 : integer;
begin
   TupleSpace.get(3,te1);
   TupleSpace.get(5,te2);
   TupleSpace.get(7,te3);
   TupleSpace.put(2,te1+te2);
   TupleSpace.put(6,te1+te3);
   TupleSpace.put(8,te1+te2+te3)
end;
```

All these processes are coded to have a simple relationship between input and output. The client process has a simple structure, which is included in the following complete program:

```
program Linda;

resource TupleSpace;
     (* A single resource implements the tuple space *)
     (* Client processes call get and put *)
     (* A call to get is blocked if the tuple is absent *)
   export get,put;
   var space : array[1..9] of integer;
       available : array[1..9] of boolean;
       ADD : integer;
   guarded procedure wait1(adds : integer; var V : integer)
            when available[1];
   begin
     V := space[1]
   end;
   guarded procedure wait2(adds : integer; var V : integer)
            when available[2];
   begin
     V := space[2]
   end;
   guarded procedure wait3(adds : integer; var V : integer)
            when available[3];
   begin
     V := space[3]
   end;
   guarded procedure wait4(adds : integer; var V : integer)
            when available[4];
   begin
     V := space[4]
   end;
```

```
    guarded procedure wait5(adds : integer; var V : integer)
          when available[5];
begin
  V := space[5]
end;
    guarded procedure wait6(adds : integer; var V : integer)
          when available[6];
begin
  V := space[6]
end;
    guarded procedure wait7(adds : integer; var V : integer)
          when available[7];
begin
  V := space[7]
end;
    guarded procedure wait8(adds : integer; var V : integer)
          when available[8];
begin
  V := space[8]
end;
    guarded procedure wait9(adds : integer; var V : integer)
          when available[9];
begin
  V := space[9]
end;

    guarded procedure get(adds : integer; var V : integer) when true;
    begin
      if available[adds] then
        V := space[adds]
      else
      case adds of
        1 : requeue wait1(adds,V);
        2 : requeue wait2(adds,V);
        3 : requeue wait3(adds,V);
        4 : requeue wait4(adds,V);
        5 : requeue wait5(adds,V);
        6 : requeue wait6(adds,V);
        7 : requeue wait7(adds,V);
        8 : requeue wait8(adds,V);
        9 : requeue wait9(adds,V)
      end
    end;
    procedure put(adds : integer; V : integer);
    begin
      space[adds] := V;
      available[adds] := true
    end;
begin    (* Tuple Space *)
  for ADD := 1 to 9 do
```

```
        available[ADD] := false
end;

process A;
  var te1, te2 : integer;
begin
  TupleSpace.get(1,te1);
  TupleSpace.get(3,te2);
  TupleSpace.put(5,te1+te2)
end;

process B;
  var te1, te2, te3 : integer;
begin
  TupleSpace.get(3,te1);
  TupleSpace.get(5,te2);
  TupleSpace.get(7,te3);
  TupleSpace.put(2,te1+te2);
  TupleSpace.put(6,te1+te3);
  TupleSpace.put(8,te1+te2+te3)
end;

process C;
begin
  TupleSpace.put(4,26)
end;

process D;
  var te1 : integer;
begin
  TupleSpace.get(4,te1);
  TupleSpace.put(7,te1+5);
  TupleSpace.put(9,2*te1)
end;

process E;
  var te1 : integer;
begin
  TupleSpace.get(4,te1);
  TupleSpace.put(1,te1+10)
end;

process F;
  var te1 : integer;
begin
  TupleSpace.get(9,te1);
  TupleSpace.put(3,te1+1)
end;
```

```
      process client;
         var temp, place, I : integer;
      begin
        for I := 1 to 20 do
        begin
          place := random(8) + 1;
          TupleSpace.get(place,temp);
          writeln(place,temp)
        end
      end;

  begin
    cobegin
      A; B; C; D; E; F;
      client
    coend
  end.
```

EXERCISES

9.12 Change process C so that it now gets from tuple 8 before putting into 4. How could the resulting deadlock have been predicted?

9.13 Modify the given program so that it implements lazy semantics. As Pascal-FC does not allow dynamic process creation, each put process must block until the values it is responsible for are requested.

9.14 Implement the data flow examples using a tuple space.

9.15 Implement the tuple space example using a data flow architecture.

9.6 Process farms

Our final architecture involves a collection of worker processes that attempt to contribute to the 'job in hand'. The concurrent program consists of a pool of worker processes which may be finite or, logically, infinite. When a worker process has completed the job it had, it terminates if the pool is infinite, or attempts to find (or is given) further work to do.

The benefit of this architecture is that it deals well with dynamic problems. If a problem is statically allocated to a fixed set of processes, then it may be the case that one process is given a more difficult section of the problem space (more difficult in that it will take more computation time). On a single processor system this will not matter, but on a multiprocessor implementation there will be times when all but one of the processors are idle. To remove the potential bottleneck that occurs because of static allocation, the completed processes should be able to remove some of the work from the overloaded process. **Process farms** enable this to be done.

To implement a process farm there must be a means of dynamically allocating work to worker processes. Two methods are possible:

- workers remain idle until given work to do
- workers actively search for work.

In the former case when a worker process is given a job to do, it will decide (either initially or as it progresses) if the job is too big. If it is, the worker then looks in the pool of workers to see if there are any free. A sub-job can be allocated to any free worker. If the pool is empty then, in a dynamic system, a new worker can be created and the sub-job allocated. If the pool is finite and empty, the original process must proceed with the full job 'as best it can'. It may occasionally re-examine the pool to see if a worker is now free.

With the second alternative, some common area must contain the outstanding work. Once a process has finished its current task it looks into this work area and extracts a new job. If the job is too large it will split it up and return sub-jobs to the work area. Note that there are some similarities between this use of a work area and the tuple space discussed above.

EXAMPLE 9.5 ————————————————————————

Write a program that finds the largest element in an array of integers using *N* worker processes. A client process inputs a request. Each worker process will split the problem it receives until it becomes trivial (i.e. only two values need analysing).

Solution Of the two possible architectures discussed above, the following solution uses a passive form, that is, each worker process (called farmer in the following) waits until it is given a job to do. The fact that the farmer is free is registered in a resource called pool. This pool exports two procedures: one that each farmer calls when it is free (return) and an extract routine for obtaining information on free farmers. As only a finite set of farmers is available, a call to request must return a boolean flag to indicate whether the request was successful. The resource pool is thus as follows:

```
resource pool;
  export extract, return;
  var free : array[1..poolsize] of boolean;
      P : integer;
  procedure extract(var OK : boolean; var worker : integer);
  var P : integer;
```

```
    begin
      P := 1;
      OK := false;
      repeat
        if free[P] then
        begin
          OK := true;
          free[P] := false;
          worker := P
        end;
        P := P + 1
      until OK or (P > poolsize)
    end;
    procedure return(worker : integer);
    begin
      free[worker] := true
    end;
  begin      (* pool *)
    for P:=1 to poolsize do
      free[P] := true
  end;
```

Each worker (farmer) has the following skeleton structure:

```
process type farmer(me : integer) provides
  entry job(. . .);
end;

var farmers : array[1..poolsize] of farmer;

process type farmer(me : integer);
  entry job(. . .);
  var . . .
    worker1, worker2 : integer;
  . . .

begin
  repeat
    accept job(. . .) do
    begin
      . . .
    end;
    if job too big then
    begin
        (* get more workers *)
      pool.extract(OK1, worker1);
      pool.extract(OK2, worker2);
        (* use the two workers if available *)
    end
    (* produce result *)
```

```
              pool.return(me)
          forever
      end;      (* farmer *)
```

The above architecture is application independent. To solve the specific problem requires a further resource that holds intermediate results:

```
resource results;
    export set, newvalue, best, active, inactive;
    var numactive : integer;
        bestvalue : integer;
    procedure set;
    begin
        bestvalue := −maxint
    end;
    procedure newvalue(newone : integer);
    begin
        if bestvalue < newone then bestvalue := newone
    end;
    guarded procedure best(var result : integer) when numactive=0;
    begin
        result := bestvalue
    end;
    procedure active(num : integer);
    begin
        numactive := numactive + num
    end;
    procedure inactive;
    begin
        numactive := numactive − 1
    end;
    begin      (* results *)
        numactive := 0
    end;
```

The client calls set to start the solution activity. The farmer processes call newvalue with the local maxima that they find. To get the final best (i.e the maximum) result the client calls best. However, there is now a potential problem. The value returned by best should not be the best result so far, but the final maximum. To achieve this the following method is used:

- the results resource keeps a track of how many farmer processes are active in producing the result;
- as a farmer is assigned part of the job, it is registered as active on the problem;
- when a farmer has completed its work, it calls inactive to 'resign' from the problem;

- the client process, when it calls best, is blocked until no more active farmers are working on the problem.

To solve the specific problem, each farmer gets a portion of the array to analyse. The array itself, although small in this example, could be very large and so is stored in a shared (global) data area. If the job is too big for the farmer, it attempts to find two other farmers and gives them each half the problem. It has then completed its work. If it is unable to obtain one, or both, helpers then it must do the work itself (using a shared search procedure):

```
procedure search(F,L : integer; var MAX : integer);
  var I : integer;
begin
  MAX := vector[F];
  for I := F to L do
  if MAX < vector[I] then MAX := vector[I]
end;

process type farmer(me : integer);
  entry job(F,L : integer);
  var first, last, middle, MAX : integer;
      OK1, OK2 : boolean;
      worker1, worker2 : integer;
begin
  repeat
    accept job(F,L : integer) do
    begin
      first := F;
      last := L
    end;
    if last − first > 2 then
    begin
      middle := (first+last) div 2;
      pool.extract(OK1, worker1);
      pool.extract(OK2, worker2);
      if OK2 and not OK1 then
      begin       (* unusual race condition *)
        OK1 := true;
        OK2 := false;
        worker1 := worker2
      end;
      if OK1 and OK2 then      (* two workers available *)
      begin
        results.active(2);
        farmers[worker1].job(first,middle);
        farmers[worker2].job(middle+1,last)
      end else
```

```
        if OK1 and not OK2 then     (* only one worker available *)
        begin
          results.active(1);
          farmers[worker1].job(first,middle);
          search(middle+1,last,MAX);
          results.newvalue(MAX)
        end else
        begin      (* no other workers available *)
          search(first,last,MAX);
          results.newvalue(MAX)
        end
      end else
      begin
        search(first,last,MAX);
        results.newvalue(MAX)
      end;
      results.inactive;
      pool.return(me)
    forever
end;     (* farmer *)
```

Only one part of this code should need further explanation. If there is only one farmer available then it would normally be the first request that is successful (and the second not). However, it is possible for the first extract request to fail but for the second to be successful as an interleaving has enabled a farmer to return itself to the pool between the two calls. If this does occur, the workers are simply interchanged.

The full code for the program can now be given:

```
program ProcessFarm;
  const size = 15;
  const poolsize = 6;
  var vector : array[1..size] of integer;
      I : integer;

  resource results;
    export set, newvalue, best, active, inactive;
    var numactive : integer;
        bestvalue : integer;
    procedure set;
    begin
      bestvalue :=-maxint
    end;
    procedure newvalue(newone : integer);
    begin
      if bestvalue < newone then bestvalue := newone
    end;
    guarded procedure best(var result : integer) when numactive=0;
    begin
```

```
        result := bestvalue
    end;
    procedure active(num : integer);
    begin
      numactive := numactive + num
    end;
    procedure inactive;
    begin
      numactive := numactive − 1
    end;
  begin     (* results *)
    numactive := 0
  end;


resource pool;
export extract, return;
var free : array[1..poolsize] of boolean;
    P : integer;
procedure extract(var OK : boolean; var worker : integer);
var P : integer;
begin
  P := 1;
  OK := false;
  repeat
    if free[P] then
    begin
      OK := true;
      free[P] := false;
      worker := P
    end;
    P := P + 1
  until OK or (P > poolsize)
end;
procedure return(worker : integer);
begin
  free[worker] := true
end;
begin     (* pool *)
  for P:=1 to poolsize do
    free[P] := true
end;


process type farmer(me : integer) provides
  entry job(F,L : integer);
end;


var farmers : array[1..poolsize] of farmer;


procedure search(F,L : integer; var MAX : integer);
  var I : integer;
```

```
begin
  MAX := vector[F];
  for I := F to L do
  if MAX < vector[I] then MAX := vector[I]
end;

process type farmer(me : integer);
  entry job(F,L : integer);
  var first, last, middle, MAX : integer;
      OK1, OK2 : boolean;
      worker1, worker2 : integer;
begin
  repeat
    accept job(F,L : integer) do
    begin
      first := F;
      last := L
    end;
    if last − first > 2 then
    begin
      middle := (first+last) div 2;
      pool.extract(OK1, worker1);
      pool.extract(OK2, worker2);
      if OK2 and not OK1 then
      begin     (* unusual race condition *)
        OK1 := true;
        OK2 := false;
        worker1 := worker2
      end;
      if OK1 and OK2 then      (* two workers available *)
      begin
        results.active(2);
        farmers[worker1].job(first,middle);
        farmers[worker2].job(middle+1,last)
      end else
        if OK1 and not OK2 then      (* only one worker available *)
        begin
          results.active(1);
          farmers[worker1].job(first,middle);
          search(middle+1,last,MAX);
          results.newvalue(MAX)
        end else
        begin      (* no other workers available *)
          search(first,last,MAX);
          results.newvalue(MAX)
        end
    end else
    begin
      search(first,last,MAX);
      results.newvalue(MAX)
```

```
          end;
        results.inactive;
        pool.return(me)
      forever
  end;      (* farmer *)

  process client;
  var V : integer;
        worker : integer;
        OK : boolean;
  begin
    (* arbitrary values are given to the vector array *)
    vector[1] := 36; vector[2] := 4;
    vector[3] := 34; vector[4] := 0;
    vector[5] := −12; vector[6] := 15;
    vector[7] := 31; vector[8] := 9;
    vector[9] := 10; vector[10] :=−13;
    vector[11] := 8; vector[12] := 23;
    vector[13] := 9; vector[14] := 2;
    vector[15] := 7;
    results.set;
    pool.extract(OK,worker);
    results.active(1);
    farmers[worker].job(1,size);
    results.best(V);
    writeln(V)
  end;

  begin
    cobegin
      client;
      for I := 1 to poolsize do
        farmers[I](I)
    coend
  end.
```

EXERCISES

9.16 Modify the above program so that two (or more) problems can be solved simultaneously (i.e. farmers are told which array to work on).

9.17 Restructure the program so that workers call in for jobs.

9.18 Change the program so that the sum of the elements in the array is output.

9.19 Change the program so that a particular value is searched for (in the array). Once the value is found, the search should be abandoned.

9.20 How could the process farm architecture be used for sorting an array?

SUMMARY

This chapter has addressed the issue of designing concurrent programs by considering a number of possible architectures for concurrent programs. Although a top down development path requires an application to be designed before it is programmed, designers must be aware of (and use) the abstractions available at the programming level. That is why this book has focused more on programming than design. Before a detailed design can be derived, an architecture must be chosen. This is as true for a program as it is for a building.

Any concurrency architecture is inevitably influenced by the synchronization and communication primitives of the implementation language. The unified model of the previous chapter has both synchronous message passing (remote invocation) and shared objects (resources), and has therefore been able to express example programs that adhere to these architectural models.

The architectures described in this chapter have been selected because of their relevance to a number of application areas. However, it has not been possible to give details of each of these areas. Rather, by discussing in detail the design of a (simple) example, it is hoped that the essential properties of each model have come through.

FURTHER READING

Carriero N. and Gelernter D. (1989). Linda in Context. *Communications of ACM*, **32**(4), 444–58

Carriero N. and Gelernter D. (1989). How to Write Parallel Programs: A Guide to the Perplexed. *ACM Computer Surveys*, **21**(3), 323–58

Gomaa H. (1984). A Software Design Method for Real-Time Systems. *Communications of ACM*, **27**(9), 938–49

Schiper A. (1989). *Concurrent Programming*. North Oxford Publishers

10 Postscript

In this chapter, we take one final glance at the material presented and anticipate further explorations which the reader might undertake.

Concurrency is a key abstraction in many areas of computing and hence it is unlikely that a single set of primitives will cater for all needs, either today or in the future. All of the constructs introduced in Chapters 4 to 7 have their place and uses. Although a single unified model was presented in Chapter 8, this does not imply that the other models are now redundant. It is, however, appropriate here to repeat the key observations made in Chapter 8:

(1) semaphores and condition variables are too low level for general programming;

(2) message-passing methods (incorporating the guard facility) represent a more abstract and unified means of programming communication;

(3) remote invocation is an effective high-level message-passing abstraction;

(4) monitor-like structures are an effective way of encapsulating shared resources.

The emphasis in the book has been on the programming of concurrent systems, that is, on the production of programs in which concurrency is explicit. As indicated in the previous chapter, one of the motivations for making use of concurrency is to exploit parallel hardware, but the introduction of the notion of process is not the only way of achieving this. Vector and array processing hardware is best exploited by the use of data-oriented concurrent operators. Other forms of parallel hardware, such as data flow architectures, lend themselves to a more declarative style of programming. Here concurrency is introduced during the translation of the source program, not in the source program itself. Notwithstanding these approaches, concurrent programming remains one of the key methods of gaining access to parallel execution.

One of the important application areas of concurrent programming is in embedded real-time systems. Here the natural parallelism of the system's environment inevitably affects the system design. Concurrency represents the enabling abstraction for dealing with this application area. Although the additional needs of real-time systems have not been addressed in any detail in this book, it is perhaps interesting to relate how a course on real-time system engineering can make use of the Pascal-FC approach to concurrency.

The need for practical experience in real-time and embedded programming is as important as it is for concurrent programming. Once all the issues of concurrency are covered, the addition of further facilities enables real experiments to be attempted. In the real-time laboratory at Bradford University, a version of Pascal-FC is available that generates code for a 68000 processor, which is linked via memory-mapped I/O to a number of external devices. Such devices include switches, lights, heaters, cooling fans and motors. Students write concurrent programs in Pascal-FC to control sets of experiments. All concurrency models can be used.

In addition to the concurrency constructs, a number of other facilities are needed:

- access to a real clock;
- a 'delay' statement to enable periodic processes to be programmed;
- control over data mapping so that memory-mapped registers can be accessed;
- process priorities to guarantee timing requirements;
- interrupt handling.

A clock is available via a function call, and the 'delay' statement is facilitated by the sleep procedure. Both of these are available in all implementations of Pascal-FC (and were briefly introduced in Section 2.7), but in most cases only very approximate timing is provided by them. With the 68000 real-time version, the parameter to the sleep routine is given a precise time meaning. Data mapping follows the model of Modula-1. Priorities are assigned via a simple mechanism (the priority procedure). All these facilities are illustrated in an example given below.

Interrupt handling presents a more interesting issue. One way of considering an interrupt is as a synchronization call from an external 'hardware' process to an internal 'software' process. It is therefore possible to model interrupt handling via the synchronization primitives of the concurrency model. As Pascal-FC provides a number of synchronization primitives, it would be appropriate for each to be potentially associated with an interrupt. The current real-time version does not bring monitors or resources into the interrupt-handling scheme, but an interrupt can be modelled as one of the following:

- a 'signal' on a semaphore – the interrupt-handler process executes a wait on the semaphore, which is initially set to a zero value;
- a 'write' to a channel – the interrupt-handler process performs a read on the channel;
- a remote invocation 'call' on a defined entry – the interrupt-handler process executes an **accept** on the entry.

In all of these cases, the hardware 'process' *implicitly* executes an action which would, if the communication were between two software processes, be explicit. The Pascal-FC compiler system is able to 'connect' the interrupt source to the communication primitive provided the programmer supplies information about the source of the interrupt (this is the relevant interrupt vector for the 68000 version). For example, the following outline shows how a process can be written to handle interrupts from vector 64 using the occam model:

```
const
  IntVec = 64;
  IntPriority = ...;      (* hardware interrupt priority *)
var
  Int at IntVec: channel of synchronous;
  ...

process handler;
begin
  priority(IntPriority);
  repeat
    Int ? any;
    (* handle interrupt *)
  forever
end;
```

The **at** construction in the declaration of Int provides the method of connecting the interrupt source to the synchronization primitive. Note also that the handler process must, in general, run at the hardware priority of the interrupting device. This is one application of Pascal-FC's priority procedure. More generally, it can be used to indicate the relative priorities of different processes.

The **at** construction is also used to map entries onto a source of interrupts. An outline handler using this style is given below:

```
process handler;
  entry Int at IntVec;
begin
  priority(IntPriority);
```

```
        repeat
          accept Int do
            . . .;
          (* handle interrupt *)
        forever
      end;
```

A semaphore version is given later.

Monitors could be brought into the interrupt-handling scheme by allowing the **at** construction to be applied to an exported procedure. This procedure would then be executed when an interrupt was received from the associated source. The following outlines the approach:

```
      monitor InterruptHandler;
      export interrupt, handler;
      var
        barrier : boolean;
        ready : condition;

      procedure interrupt at IntVec;
      begin
        barrier := false;
        resume(ready)
      end;

      procedure handler;
      begin
        if barrier then
          delay(ready);
        barrier := true
      end;

      begin
        barrier := true
      end;
```

The interrupt procedure in this case performs the minimum action required to log the occurrence of the interrupt: a process needing to coordinate its actions with the interrupt source calls the procedure handler.

Note that condition variables are not themselves mapped onto sources of interrupts in this scheme. This is because condition variables do not 'remember' resume operations: an interrupt that arrived before the handling process had become blocked on the condition would therefore leave no trace of its occurrence and the handler process would needlessly block. This is also what would happen if the above monitor had not introduced an additional boolean variable.

The resource model may be brought into this scheme for handling interrupts in a similar way. The following example illustrates the approach:

```
resource InterruptHandler;
export interrupt, handler;
var
  barrier : boolean;

procedure interrupt at IntVec;
begin
  barrier:= false
end;

guarded procedure handler when not barrier;
begin
  barrier:= true
end;

begin
  barrier:= true
end;
```

The similarity with the monitor version is evident, but the programmer's intentions are probably made clearer by the use of the guarded procedure.

For illustrative purposes only, the following example of real-time Pascal-FC is given. It uses most of the features discussed above. The code implements a cyclic process that inputs a reading from a simple analogue-to-digital converter by setting particular bits in a memory-mapped control/status register (csr), waiting for an interrupt (which in this example is mapped onto a semaphore) and then reading the input value from a second (data) register. It compares this value with a threshold (safety) level and alerts another process (by means of the semaphore alarm) if it is too high. The following data declarations are made:

```
const
  IntVec = 64;
  IntPriority = 4;
  AdcAddress = ... ;      (* hardware address *)
  SamplePeriod = .. ;     (* suitable integer value *)
  Threshold = .. ;      (* alarm threshold *)
type
  adctype =
    record
      csr: integer;      (* control/status register *)
      data: integer
    end;
var
  interrupt at IntVec: semaphore;     (* initially 0 *)
  adc at AdcAddress: adctype;
  alarm: semaphore;      (* initially 0 *)
```

The converter is conveniently represented as a record. This variable is then mapped, using the **at** construction, to the actual hardware address of the device. A suitable interrupt-handler process is as follows:

```
process handler;
var
   NewReading: integer;
   CycleStart: integer;
begin
   priority(IntPriority);
   repeat
     CycleStart := clock;
     adc.csr := 1;      (* go ! *)
     wait(interrupt);
     adc.csr := 0;      (* turn off interrupt *)
     NewReading := adc.data;
     if NewReading > Threshold then
        signal(alarm);
     sleep(SamplePeriod - (clock - CycleStart))
   forever
end;
```

Although real-time embedded systems are an important application of concurrency, they are far from being the only motivation for studying the subject. Concurrency is a significant abstraction in its own right. All computer scientists, software engineers and other engineering disciplines have an obligation to understand the many issues involved in exploiting concurrency. This book has attempted to initiate this understanding.

As indicated in the Preface, the use of a single language notation (Pascal-FC) and the availability of that language for undertaking practical work has proved to be a valuable tool for teaching concurrent programming. As well as extending the language to facilitate real-time programming, issues of distributed programming and fault-tolerant programming will also be addressed in future versions of the language (Pascal-DP and Pascal-FT). For distribution, the issues are: unit of distribution, configuration, allocation and communication (e.g. asynchronous messages or remote procedure calls). Again it is possible to construct a number of language models and to experiment with their interactions. Similarly, for fault tolerance there are comparative issues of reconfiguration, recovery blocks, exception handling and replication. All are valid subjects for study and experimentation.

In this book we have attempted to give an informal and practical introduction to concurrency. Some rigorous analysis was introduced on occasions but the reader may now wish to study in detail a formal approach to concurrency. A number of formal theories are covered in the Further Reading section below. Once the notion of concurrency is understood these mathematical treatments become tractable.

FURTHER READING

Baeten J.C.M. and Weijland W.P. (1990). *Process Algebra*. Cambridge University Press

Best E. (1988). *Nonsequential Processes* (EATCS Monograph on TCS). Springer-Verlag

Hoare C.A.R. (1985). *Communicating Sequential Processes*. Prentice-Hall

Milner R. (1989). *Communication and Concurrency*. Prentice-Hall

Ostrof J. (1989). *Temporal Logic for Real-Time Systems*. John Wiley

Rydeheard D.E. and Burstall R.M. (1988). *Computational Category Theory*. Prentice-Hall

Appendix A

Language Reference Manual for Pascal-FC

A.1 Introduction

This appendix provides a brief Language Reference Manual for the features of Pascal-FC that are used in this book. We have used a similar approach for our description to the one adopted in the Ada Language Reference Manual (ANSI, 1983). Specifically, the syntax is described in a variant of Backus–Naur Form (BNF), supplemented with ordinary English. Semantics are described in ordinary English.

The following conventions are adopted for the BNF notation:

- Each rule is introduced by the name of a syntactic category followed by '::='.

- Lower case words, some of which contain underscore characters, are used to denote syntactic categories. For example:

  identifier
  select_statement

- Bold face words are used to denote reserved words. For example:

  begin
  process

- Square brackets enclose optional items, except when enclosed in double quotes, when they stand for themselves. For example:

  if_statement ::=
  if *boolean*_expression **then**
      statement
  [**else**
      statement]

```
array_index ::=
    "["expression{,expression}"]"
```

The optional part is either absent, or *one* such part is permitted.

- Braces enclose repeated items, except when enclosed in double quotes, when they stand for themselves. For example:

```
identifier ::=
    letter{letter | digit}
comment ::=
    comment_start {character} comment_end
comment_start ::=
    "{" | (*
comment_end ::=
    "}" | *)
```

When braces enclose a repeated item, the item may be repeated zero or more times.

- Alternatives are separated by the '|' character, as in the above examples.

- Italics are used to convey some semantic information. For example:

    *boolean*_expression

Such information is provided as a hint to the reader: a context-free grammar is, of course, not capable of representing the difference between, for example, a boolean expression and an integer expression.

As Pascal-FC is based on the familiar sequential Pascal (henceforward 'Pascal'), we do not attempt a full description here. In particular, we shall not describe those features that are the same as in sequential Pascal.

A.2 Program structure

The only compilation unit in Pascal-FC is the *program*. This section describes the overall form of a program and some of its components: later sections provide detail for the specialized components.

A.2.1 Program

A program is defined a follows:

```
program ::=

    program_header
        global_declaration_part
    begin
```

```
        main_statement_part
    end

program_header ::=
    program identifier;

identifier ::=
    letter{letter | digit}
```

Here, letter signifies the normal upper and lower case alphabetical characters and digit denotes the decimal digits.

Certain forms of declaration are only permitted in a global declaration part: these include monitor, resource and process declarations. The following syntax lists the possible forms of declaration:

```
global_declaration_part ::=

    {
      constant_declaration
    | type_declaration
    | variable_declaration
    | monitor_declaration
    | resource_declaration
    | procedure_declaration
    | function_declaration
    | process_type_declaration
    | process_object_declaration
    }
```

The main statement part is the only place where a concurrent statement may be placed, and there may be one of these at most. The allowable forms of the main statement part are:

```
main_statement_part ::=
    statement_sequence
    [;concurrent_statement
    [;statement_sequence]]
    | concurrent _statement
    [;statement_sequence]

statement_sequence ::=
    statement
      {;statement}
```

A concurrent statement has the form:

```
concurrent_statement ::=
    cobegin
```

```
    statement_sequence
    coend
```

Although arbitrary statements may be placed in a concurrent statement, only *processes* (see Section A.3) are executed concurrently.

A.2.2 Declarations

Monitor, resource and process declarations are ignored here as they are covered in later sections. The remaining forms are, for the most part, like those of Pascal, but with some additional restrictions. One such restriction is that constant declarations cannot be made for strings. Hence:

```
constant_declaration ::=
    const
     identifier = constant;
    {identifier = constant;}
```

where:

```
constant ::=
      constant_identifier
    | integer_literal
    | real_literal
    | character_literal
```

Real and character literals have the same form as in Pascal. Integer literals can be expressed as in Pascal, but there is also a form allowing expression in bases other than 10. This facility is intended for use in implementations for real-time programming and has not been used in this book.

As in Pascal, a type declaration has the form:

```
type_declaration ::=
    type
       identifier = type;
      {identifier = type;}
```

The allowable forms for a type are slightly different: Pascal-FC does not have subrange, set or pointer types, but it does introduce an additional channel type:

```
type ::=
      type_identifier
    | enumeration_type
    | array_type
    | record_type
```

```
| channel_type
```

Enumeration and array types are as in Pascal: record types in Pascal-FC differ from Pascal only in that variant records are not allowed. A channel type is defined as follows:

```
channel_type ::=
    channel of type
```

Variable declarations are similar to Pascal.

```
variable_declaration ::=
    var
    identifier_list : type;
    {identifier_list : type;}

identifier_list ::=
    identifier{,identifier}
```

Procedure and function declarations are largely as in Pascal. Forward declarations are supported. However, there are no conformant array parameters, or parameters that are themselves subprograms.

A.2.3 Statements

The allowable statements in Pascal-FC are described by the following syntax:

```
statement ::=

        assignment_statement
    | procedure_call
    | for_statement
    | repeat_statement
    | while_statement
    | if_statement
    | case_statement
    | compound_statement
    | empty_statement
    | concurrent_statement
    | process_activation
    | monitor_call
    | channel_operation
    | select_statement
    | entry_call
    | accept_statement
    | resource_call
    | requeue_statement
```

```
| null_statement
```

Assignment statements, procedure calls, the empty statement, the compound statement and if and case statements have the same form as in Pascal. The loops are also similar, except that the for statement has no 'downto' variant, and the repeat statement is augmented to be:

```
repeat_statement ::=
  repeat
    statement_sequence
  repeat_limit

repeat_limit ::=
    until boolean_expression
  | forever
```

The null statement has the form:

```
null_statement ::=
  null
```

The concurrent statement was described earlier. The remaining forms of statement are considered in appropriate sections below.

A.3 Processes

Process declarations may *only* be made in a global declaration part and processes may only be activated within a concurrent statement. Process declarations are either process object declarations or process type declarations.

A.3.1 Process type declarations

```
process_type_declaration ::=
  [process_type_provides_declaration]
  process_type_body_declaration

process_type_provides_declaration ::=
  process type identifier[formal_part] provides
    entry_declaration
    {entry_declaration}
  end;

process_type_body_declaration ::=
  process type identifier[formal_part];
```

```
    {entry_declaration}
    [declaration_part]
begin
    statement_sequence
end;
```

Where the optional 'provides' declaration is used, the following points should be noted:

- there must be a corresponding body declared later in the same declaration part;
- these two components may be separated by other declarations;
- the two parts must correspond exactly in their formal parts;
- the number of entries, their identifiers and the formal parts of the entries, must match exactly;
- the order of declaration of the entries is not constrained to be the same.

The declaration of a process type does not bring into existence any objects of that type, but instead introduces a type identifier which may be used in type and variable declarations. Process types can be elements of arrays, but not of records.

The formal parameters of a process have the same form as the formal parameters of procedures and functions:

```
formal_part ::=
    ([var] identifier_list : type_identifier
    {;[var] identifier_list : type_identifier})
```

There are certain restrictions on the types of formal parameters. Process type identifiers are not permitted and identifiers of types containing semaphores, conditions or channels must be **var** parameters.

A.3.2 Process object declarations

A process object declaration brings into existence an executable instance of a process type (anonymous or named). It introduces an identifier which may then be used in a process activation (see Section A.3.3):

```
process_object_declaration ::=
    anonymous_process_type_declaration
  | process_variable_declaration

anonymous_process_type_declaration ::=
    [provides_declaration]
```

> process_body_declaration

The forms of the 'provides' and 'body' declarations are the same as those described in the previous section, except that **type** is omitted. Restrictions are also the same.

A process variable declaration may only appear in a **var** declaration in a global declaration part. It has the following form:

> process_variable_declaration ::=
>   identifier_list : *process*_type;

> *process*_type ::=
>   *process*_identifier
> | *process*_array_type

A.3.3 Process activation

A process object declaration brings into existence an instance of a process type, but it does not automatically make it executable. A process activation is required:

> process_activation ::=
>   *process_object*_identifier[array_index][actual_parameters]

Process activations may *only* be done in a concurrent statement. Within the concurrent statement, any particular process may only be activated once. The language prescribes no particular scheduling policy for processes. The concurrent statement cannot terminate until all activated processes have terminated. If any process encounters a fatal error during its execution, the entire program is aborted.

A.4 Semaphores

A standard type, semaphore, is included. Semaphores may be declared singly or as components in arrays or records (types or variables). Semaphores, or objects containing them, may only be declared in a global declaration part. Moreover, such objects may be passed as parameters to subprograms, but the corresponding formal parameters must be **var** parameters. Semaphores are guaranteed to have no processes blocked on them initially, but the value is undefined until the semaphore has been passed to the initial procedure.

The allowable operations on semaphores are restricted to:

- the wait and signal procedures

- the initial procedure
- the write(ln) procedure.

Each of wait and signal takes a single parameter, which must be a semaphore. A call to the initial procedure has the form:

    initial(s,v)

where s is a semaphore and v is an integer expression. An implementation must not permit the execution of initial when v is less than zero. Only the main program thread must be allowed to execute this procedure. Such a call can appear in the main statement part or in the statement part of a subprogram called by the main program. (The implementation must not permit a *process* to execute initial by calling such a subprogram.)

The language does not prescribe any particular queueing discipline on semaphores: if a signal is carried out on a semaphore on which several processes are currently 'blocked', *one* of them will be allowed to proceed, but the decision as to which is arbitrary. Nor does the language specify whether semaphore 'blocking' should be implemented by busy-waiting or by rendering the process concerned unexecutable.

A.5 Monitors

A.5.1 Declaration

A monitor is one of the forms of declaration that can only be permitted in a global declaration part. It has the following form:

    monitor_declaration ::=
      monitor identifier;
        export_list
        {
        constant_declaration
        | type_declaration
        | variable_declaration
        | procedure_declaration
        | function_declaration
        }
      [monitor_body]
      end;

    export_list ::=
      export procedure_identifier_list;
      {export procedure_identifier_list;}

```
monitor_body ::=
      begin
          statement_sequence
```

Certain instances of type and variable declaration are not permitted in a monitor: specifically, those involving processes, semaphores and channels (types or variables).

The only declarations in a monitor that are visible from outside that monitor are procedures for which identifiers appear in the export list (these are called 'exported procedures'). It is an error for such an identifier not to have a corresponding procedure declared in the monitor. Moreover, exported procedures may not be nested within subprogram declarations.

The body of a monitor, if present, is executed once before the first statement of the main statement part. If several monitors are declared in a program, the order in which their bodies are executed is not defined by the language.

Code within a monitor is guaranteed to be executed under mutual exclusion. A **boundary queue** is used to block processes wishing to gain access to a monitor already occupied by a process. The queue is defined to be a **priority queue**: a FIFO discipline is used within a given priority value. The queuing scheme hence degenerates to plain FIFO in an implementation in which process priorities are not discriminated.

A.5.2 Calls to monitors

A monitor call is a call to an exported procedure of a monitor. In general, it takes the form:

*monitor*_identifier.*exported_procedure*_identifier[actual_parameters]

If the called procedure is declared within the same monitor as the call, a shorter form may be used as an alternative:

*exported_procedure*_identifier[actual_parameters]

This is semantically equivalent to the longer form. In particular, there is no attempt in either case to gain mutually exclusive access, since the calling process must already have such access.

Nested monitor calls are permitted: in this case, mutual exclusion on the monitor from which the call is made is retained.

A.5.3 Condition variables

The standard type condition is provided. Condition variables may be declared, but there are no constants of this type. Conditions may be declared as simple variables or as components of arrays or records (types or variables). Condition types must be declared either in the global declaration part or in the declaration part of a monitor. Condition variables may only be declared in the declaration part of a monitor. Conditions declared as formal parameters to subprograms must be **var** parameters.

The operations on conditions are restricted to:

- the delay and resume procedures
- the empty function.

Each of these subprograms takes a single parameter, which must be a condition variable.

Conditions are defined to be priority queues. Within a given priority value, a FIFO discipline is used. Hence conditions degenerate to FIFO queues in implementations that do not discriminate process priority. Conditions are guaranteed to be initialized to the empty queue on declaration.

If a resume operation unblocks a process, the calling process immediately relinquishes its mutual exclusion on the enclosing monitor and joins a **chivalry queue** associated with that monitor. The chivalry queue is again defined to be a priority queue. Processes blocked on a chivalry queue have preference over any waiting on the same monitor's boundary queue when mutual exclusion of that monitor is released by another process.

A.6 Rendezvous by channel

A.6.1 Channel declarations

Channels are strongly typed; channel types and objects may only be declared in a global declaration part. Channels may be components in arrays or records. Any type may be specified as the 'base' type of a channel, but the effects of sending and receiving channels, conditions, semaphores and processes along channels are not defined. Channels may be formal parameters of subprograms, but they must be declared as **var** parameters.

A.6.2 Operations on channels

Two operations are defined for channels:

```
channel_operation ::=
    send | receive

send ::=
    channel_variable ! expression
```

```
receive ::=
    channel_variable ? variable
```

In both cases, the type of the right hand operand must be equivalent to the base type declared for that channel.

Channel operations implement a synchronous communication, which takes place when one sender and one receiver are ready to communicate along a specific channel. The party that arrives first at the point where the communication would take place is blocked until the other party is ready to participate in the communication.

Channels are for point-to-point communication between a single sender and a single receiver: it is an error for more than one sender or more than one receiver simultaneously to attempt to communicate along the same channel.

A.6.3   The type synchronous

The predefined type synchronous is provided. Variables and types may be declared, but there are no constants of this type. Objects of type synchronous are contentless and their intended role is for use in synchronization-only communication by channel. Variables of this type may appear on the right hand side of a channel operation, but the language specifies that such an operation has no effect on the synchronous variable itself. A predefined variable any of this type is automatically declared in the global declaration part of every Pascal-FC program.

A.7   Ada-style rendezvous

A.7.1   Process entry declarations

An entry declaration takes the following form:

```
entry_declaration ::=
    entry identifier[formal_part];
```

In cases where a provides_declaration (see Sections A.1 and A.2) has been used, the entry declarations must all be repeated exactly in the corresponding process body declaration. Specifically, the number of entries, their names and their formal parameters must match exactly. The *order* in which the various entries are declared in the two places need not match, however.

A.7.2 Entry calls

An entry call has the form:

> entry_call ::=
>   *process*_variable.*entry*_identifier[actual_parameters]

The actual parameters must match the profile defined in the formal part of the entry declaration.

A.7.3 The accept statement

An accept statement has the form:

> accept_statement ::=
>   **accept** *entry*_identifier[formal_part] **do**
>   statement

The formal part must exactly match the formal part in the corresponding entry declaration. The formal parameters are in scope for the statement following **do** unless hidden by formal parameters of a nested accept statement.

An accept statement may only be placed in the statement part of a process body (not in a subprogram nested within a process, for example).

An extended rendezvous takes place when a caller and an acceptor arrive respectively at an entry call and an accept statement for a given entry. The party that arrives first at the point where the communication takes place becomes blocked. The entry caller in any case remains blocked for the execution of the statement following **do** in the accept statement. Any **var** parameters to which assignments are made in the accept statement will return these values on completion of the rendezvous.

It is permitted for more than one entry caller to be simultaneously blocked on a given entry: the language prescribes a priority queue on entries.

A.8 Selective waiting

The selective waiting construct is intended for use with either the Ada-style rendezvous or rendezvous by channel. Its syntax is as follows:

> select_statement ::=
>   **[pri] select**
>   select_alternative
>   {**;or** select_alternative}
>   [else_part]
>   **end**

```
select_alternative ::=
    channel_alternative
  | replicate_alternative
  | accept_alternative
  | timeout_alternative
  | terminate

channel_alternative ::=
  [guard]
   channel_operation
  [;statement_sequence]

guard ::=
  when boolean_expression =>

replicate_alternative ::=
  for variable := expression to expression replicate
     channel_alternative

accept_alternative ::=
  [guard]
   accept_statement
  [;statement_sequence]

timeout_alternative ::=
  [guard]
   timeout integer_expression
  [;statement_sequence]

else_part ::=
  else statement_sequence
```

The timeout alternative, terminate alternative and else part are mutually exclusive.

Alternatives for which the guards evaluate to true, or which have no guards (including all terminate alternatives), are said to be 'open' for that execution of the select statement. It is an error for a select statement to have no open alternatives, unless there is an else part.

If, on a given execution of the select statement, more than one open-guarded alternative has a pending rendezvous, the decision as to which to take is not defined by the language unless the **pri select** form is being executed. In the latter case, the open alternatives are tested for a pending call in their textual order and the first such call is taken.

If, on some execution, there are no alternatives with pending calls, the else part is immediately executed (if there is one). If there is no else part, the process executing the select becomes blocked on all open alternatives. The alternative with the first call becomes effective, unless a timeout alternative expires or the terminate alternative becomes effective.

More than one timeout alternative is allowed, but only the one with the smallest timeout value will ever become effective. If more than one alternative has this value, the language does not define which of them becomes effective. A timeout of zero becomes immediately effective and thus has a similar effect to an else part. A negative value is equivalent to zero.

A terminate alternative becomes effective if there are no other extant processes or all such processes are themselves blocked on terminate alternatives.

A.9 Resources

A.9.1 Declaration

The rules concerning the place of declaration of resources are the same as those for monitors: in particular, a resource may only be declared in a global declaration part. The syntax of a resource declaration is as follows:

```
resource_declaration ::=
    resource identifier;
      export_list
      resource_declaration_part
    [resource_body]
    end;

resource_declaration_part ::=
      {constant_declaration
    | type_declaration
    | variable_declaration
    | procedure_declaration
    | function_declaration
    | guarded_procedure_declaration}

guarded_procedure_declaration ::=
      full_guarded_procedure_declaration
    | deferred_guarded_procedure_declaration

full_guarded_procedure_declaration ::=
    guarded procedure identifier[formal_part]
      when boolean_expression;
      [declaration_part]
    begin
      statement_sequence
    end
```

```
deferred_guarded_procedure_declaration ::=
   forward_guarded_procedure_header
   guarded_procedure_body

forward_guarded_procedure_header ::=
   guarded procedure identifier[formal_part]
     when boolean_expression;forward;

guarded_procedure_body ::=
   guarded procedure identifier;
     [declaration_part]
   begin
     statement_sequence
   end;

resource_body ::=
   begin
     statement_sequence
```

Note the following:

- resources may only be declared in a global declaration part;
- only identifiers that appear in the export list are in scope from outside the resource;
- the identifiers in the export list must be the names of procedures or guarded procedures declared inside the resource;
- exported procedures must not be nested within other subprograms declared in the resource;
- guarded procedures, whether exported or not, must not be nested inside other subprograms;
- the formal parameters of a guarded procedure are not in scope until *after* the guard expression;
- type and variable declarations involving semaphores, channels and processes are not permitted anywhere in a resource;
- where a deferred guarded procedure declaration is used, the header and the body may be separated by other declarations.

A.9.2 Calls to resources

A call to a resource is a call to an exported procedure (guarded or otherwise) of that resource. It has the form:

```
resource_call ::=
   resource_identifier.
     exported_procedure_identifier[(actual_parameters)]
```

As with monitors, if the procedure concerned is declared within the current resource, a shortened notation (consisting simply of the procedure identifier and the actual parameters) is permitted. This is semantically equivalent to the longer version given above.

If a guarded procedure is called for which the guard evaluates to false, the calling process becomes blocked and leaves the resource. Any process leaving a resource must attempt to find a candidate that will inherit mutual exclusion on the resource. The candidate will be selected from among those blocked on guards which now evaluate to true. No particular queueing discipline is specified for guards and the choice among the procedures with open guards is arbitrary. Processes leave resources when they complete an execution path through an exported procedure or when they become blocked on a guard in that resource.

Nested calls are permitted from one resource to an exported procedure of another. In such a case, mutual exclusion on the current resource is retained.

A.9.3 The requeue statement

A **requeue** statement may only be used in the statement part of a **guarded procedure** (i.e. not within a subprogram nested within such a procedure). Its effect is to abandon the current procedure and transfer the call to another, either within the current resource or within another. Its syntax is:

```
requeue_statement ::=
    requeue [resource_identifier.]
        guarded_procedure_identifier[(actual_parameters)]
```

The optional identifier, if present, must be the name of a resource. If it is the name of the resource enclosing the **requeue** statement, it has no effect. The second identifier in the above syntax must be the name of a **guarded procedure**. If the associated guard is open, the procedure is executed as normal. If the guard is closed, the calling process must become blocked (and leave the resource), but it must attempt to find a candidate for awakening.

Control does *not* eventually return to the statement following a **requeue** statement: its execution causes the *abandonment* of the current guarded procedure. An ordinary procedure call from within a resource to a guarded procedure is not permitted.

A.10 Reserved words

The following are the reserved words of Pascal-FC:

accept	and	array
at	begin	case
channel	cobegin	coend
const	div	do
else	end	entry
export	for	forever
forward	function	guarded
if	in	mod
monitor	not	null
of	offset	or
pri	procedure	process
program	provides	record
repeat	replicate	requeue
resource	select	terminate
then	timeout	to
type	until	var
when	while	

A.11 Predefined identifiers

A.11.1 Features included from standard Pascal

The following are predefined identifiers in standard Pascal which have been retained in Pascal-FC:

abs	arctan	boolean
char	chr	cos
eof	eoln	exp
false	integer	ln
maxint	odd	ord
pred	read	readln
real	round	sin
sqr	sqrt	succ
true	trunc	write
writeln		

A.11.2 Introduced standard types

The following standard types have been introduced into Pascal-FC:

bitset
condition

semaphore
synchronous

The type bitset is introduced for real-time versions of the language and has not been used in this book.

A.11.3   Introduced subprograms

The following subprograms have been provided:

bits
clock
delay
empty
initial
int
priority
random
resume
signal
sleep
wait

The bits and int functions are for type transfers between bitsets and integers and have not been used in this book.

A.11.4   Predefined variable

A predefined variable any is declared automatically in the global declaration part of any Pascal-FC program. It has the type synchronous.

Appendix B

Implementation Notes

B.1   Introduction

This appendix outlines the implementation of the Pascal-FC system for computers, such as the IBM PC, which has been produced at the University of Bradford. It is not intended to suggest that this represents the only (or even the best) method of implementation: the purpose of the description is to provide interested readers with more insight into how concurrent programming languages can be implemented.

B.2   Overview of the compilation process

A compiler takes as its input a source program written in one language and produces as its output an equivalent program written in a different language (the machine code of the target system, for example). Often the compiler runs on the same class of machine used to execute the compiled program: this is called a **native compiler**. In other cases, the compiler runs on one type of machine, but the compiled program runs on a totally different type: this is called a **cross-compiler**.

When a new language, such as Pascal-FC, is designed, the availability of a suitable compiler on a variety of machine architectures is important. However, no-one wants to write a completely different compiler for every type of machine, and the key to portability is modularity of the compiler system. In particular, we must separate those components of the compilation process that are independent of the target machine from those that are not. It turns out that a large proportion of a compiler can be made to be machine independent. This aids portability, because only a small proportion needs to be rewritten when implementation on a new target is required.

A common strategy is to write a machine-independent compiler **front end** in a portable and widely available language such as C. All that we need to do to run this front end on a variety of different types of machine is to compile it using the C compiler for each machine type. But what is the *output* of this front end? Clearly, if the front end really is machine independent, it should not be the machine code of some particular target.

B.2.1 Intermediate code

A common approach to this issue is to write a compiler front end that produces **intermediate code**. This can be construed as the assembly language, not of any real machine, but of some imaginary or **virtual** machine. The intermediate code could, for example, be output from the front end in the form of a file for further processing by other programs in the compiler system. The front end is then not committed to any particular real machine architecture. Given that we have now produced code for a non-existent machine, how do we execute our program?

Two strategies are commonly used for making the intermediate code executable:

- the virtual machine is simulated by writing a program (called an **interpreter**) in a language such as C;
- a **back end** is written that translates the intermediate code into the machine language of some specific target.

The first method has the advantage that porting the system to a new architecture simply requires recompilation of the interpreter. By contrast, the second method necessitates the writing of a new back end by someone with an intimate knowledge of the new architecture. The second method, however, scores heavily when efficiency comparisons are made: interpreters, in general, result in much slower execution of the program.

Pascal-FC was designed for teaching purposes and the Bradford implementations were not built for speed. Hence the interpreter method is the one that will be described here. Moreover, we shall concentrate on the interpreter rather than on the compiler front end. We shall refer to the intermediate code produced by the compiler front end as **P-code**.

B.3 Outline of an interpreter for a sequential Pascal

This section presents only the briefest introduction to an interpreter for sequential Pascal. Berry (1982) provides a more detailed description, including a listing of a complete compiler and interpreter for Pascal-S.

B.3.1 Execution of P-machine instructions

In principle, an interpreter for a sequential language is very simple. It executes a fetch–execute cycle in which the next instruction is fetched and then executed. It continues to do this until the current instruction indicates the end of the program or until some fatal error condition (such as an attempt to divide by zero) is encountered. The following code outlines the action of an interpreter:

```
repeat
  fetch code[pc];
  pc := pc + 1;
  execute instruction
until status <> run
```

Here code is an array of P-code instructions generated by the compiler. The global variable status can be considered an enumeration type, the value of which is affected by some of the instructions. For example, the code for the stop instruction (generated at the final **end** of a Pascal program) might be simply:

```
status := finished
```

The intermediate code produced by the Bradford Pascal-FC compiler has a simple format: it consists of an **op-code** and zero, one or two **arguments**. The following record definition describes this:

```
type
  order =
    record
      OpCode: ... ;      (* an enumeration type for mnemonics *)
      ArgX: ... ;
      ArgY: ...
    end;
```

Not all of the instructions in the P-machine instruction set use both arguments: some do not use either.

The interpreter's data structure for the compiler-generated code may now be understood:

```
const
  MaxCodes = ... ;      (* some suitable value *)
var
  code: array[0..MaxCodes] of order;
```

The actual execution of instructions is implemented by writing a piece of code for each P-code in the instruction set of the P-machine. A **case** statement can be used for this, as follows:

```
case OpCode of
  stop: status := finished;
  ...
end
```

B.3.2   Run-time stacks

The virtual machine for which the P-code is the assembly language is a stack machine. This means that arithmetic and logical operations required during the evaluation of expressions are not carried out in CPU registers, but rather on a stack. A simplified structure for a stack is as follows:

```
const
  MaxStack = ...;    (* some suitable value *)
var
  stack: array[1..MaxStack] of integer;
```

To illustrate the use of the stack, consider the following assignment statement:

```
x := y + 1
```

We shall suppose that x and y have both been declared as integers. The Pascal-FC compiler produces the following five P-code instructions for the above statement:†

```
ldadr    x    ; push the address of x
ldval    y    ; push the value of y
ldcon    1    ; push the constant value, 1
add           ; replace the two items on top of the
              ; stack with their sum
store         ; move the value from the top of the
              ; stack to the address stored just below it
```

The ldadr instruction is in outline as follows:

```
sp := sp + 1;
if sp > MaxStack then
  set error status
else
  stack[sp] := ...    (* the address of a variable *)
                      (* calculated from parameters *)
```

The ldval instruction is similar, but it is a *value* which is pushed onto the stack rather than an address.

---

† The use of the arguments has been deliberately abstracted: in reality the addresses of variables have two components, as in the Pascal-S systems described by Berry (1982) and Ben Ari (1982).

The Idcon instruction has the following outline:

```
sp := sp + 1;
if sp > MaxStack then
    set error status
else
    stack[sp] := yArgument
```

where yArgument is the y argument of the P-code.

The add instruction has the following outline:

```
sp := sp − 1; stack[sp] := stack[sp+1] + stack[sp]
```

Finally, the store instruction has the following outline:

```
stack[stack[sp−1]] := stack[sp];
sp := sp − 2
```

Of course, a running Pascal program does not only need to evaluate expressions of type integer. Consequently, the P-machine has a stack that can accommodate all the data types available in Pascal: even arbitrary structured types can be placed on it when required.

B.3.3 Allocation of storage to variables

The use of the run-time stack for holding the partial results developed during expression evaluation was illustrated in the above section. However, the stack is not used solely for this purpose: all variables declared in the source program are also allocated a space on the stack. Global variables are assigned to locations that are 'permanent' in the sense that they are allocated for the duration of the execution of the program. Local variables and parameters in subprograms are part of an **activation record** that is created on top of the stack when the subprogram is invoked and destroyed when it is exited. Details of the addressing of program variables and the use of activation records will not be given here. The interested reader is referred to Berry (1982) or to the Appendix of Ben Ari (1982).

B.4 Implementation of concurrency

In order to implement concurrency, three things must be added to our outline interpreter.

- Each process needs its own private program counter and stack pointer. A process descriptor is assigned to each process. This has fields for the Program Counter (PC) and the Stack Pointer (SP) for the process, amongst other pieces of information. One possible implementation of process descriptors is as follows:

```
type
  procptr = ↑pdtype;
  pdtype =
  record
    pc: integer;
    sp: integer;
    status: (...);      (* suitable enumeration type *)
      ...
    nextpd: procptr
  end;
```

- As expressions are evaluated on a stack, rather than in CPU registers, each process must have its own private stack.

- A process scheduler is introduced to switch a process out of the P-machine's processor and to find another (if there is one) to switch in. The scheduler must be called whenever a process terminates or becomes blocked. Also, in the case of the fair scheduler, it is invoked when a process has used its current 'ration' of P-machine instructions (as determined by a random number generated when it was last put into the processor).

  A concurrent fetch–execute cycle may be expressed as follows:

```
repeat
  fetch code[curpr↑.pc];
  curpr↑.pc := curpr↑.pc + 1;
  execute instruction;
  stepcount := stepcount − 1;
  if status = run then
    if stepcount = 0 then
      call scheduler
until status <> run
```

Here curpr is of type procptr (a pointer to a process descriptor). An outline of the scheduler is as follows:

```
attempt to find an executable process;
if no executable process then
  check for deadlock
else
begin
  curpr := ChosenProcess;
  stepcount := RandomNumber
end
```

The random number is a positive integer. As the purpose of the fair scheduler is to exercise a variety of legal execution orders, it is usually chosen to be a small integer (for example, in the range from 1 to 8) so that process switches are frequent.

For every process declared in a program (including every element of an array of processes), the compiler implicitly declares a variable. During the processing that takes place in the **cobegin/coend** structure, the process variable associated with each activated process is set to point to the relevant process descriptor. The variable belonging to any process that was declared, but is not activated in the **cobegin/coend**, will retain its initial null value. Process variables are important in handling the Ada-style rendezvous, as will be seen in Section B.7.4.

B.4.1 Implementing atomic operations

The implementation of inter-process synchronization and communication primitives requires that certain actions be carried out atomically. This is a simple matter at the level of the intermediate code, because any P-code is an atomic instruction in the scheme outlined above: process switches may only take place *between* P-codes and not *during* them.

B.5 Semaphores

B.5.1 Data structures

In the version of Pascal-FC described here, a semaphore object can be considered as a two-field record, as follows:

```
type
  semframe =
    record
      value: 0..maxint;
      blocked: procptr
    end;
```

The blocked field is a pointer to a list of process descriptors, which represent the processes currently blocked on this semaphore. Initially it is automatically given the null value. The value field initially has an undefined value.

B.5.2 P-machine instructions for semaphores

Three special P-codes have been introduced for semaphore operations:

```
swait   (semaphore wait)
```

```
signl   (semaphore signal)
sinit   (semaphore initialization)
```

Each will be outlined below.

Semaphore initialization

Given the statement:

```
initial(s,1)
```

where s is a semaphore, the compiler generates the following P-codes:

```
ldadr    s     ; push address of s
ldcon    1     ; push constant 1
lobnd    0     ; perform range check
sinit          ; initialize semaphore
```

The range check in this case ensures that the value on top of the stack does not fall below the value specified as an argument. The initial procedure always generates zero for this argument, regardless of the initial value being given to the semaphore. The program status will be affected if the value fails the test, leading to program termination.

The sinit operation has the following form:

```
if curpr <> MainProgram then
   status := SemaphoreInitializationError
else
begin
   pop value;
   pop address of s;
   stack[address] := value
end
```

Semaphore wait

Given the statement:

```
wait(s)
```

the compiler will generate the following code:

```
ldadr    s     ; push address of s
swait
```

The swait operation itself closely follows the definition of the semaphore wait given in Chapter 6, and may be summarized as follows:

```
    pop address of s;
    if s.value > 0 then
      s.value := s.value − 1
    else
    begin
      join the queue on s;
      call the scheduler
    end
```

Semaphore signal

Given the source statement:

```
    signal(s)
```

the compiler again generates two instructions, as follows:

```
    ldadr    s    ; push address of s
    signl
```

The signl operation may be described as follows:

```
    if the queue on s is empty then
      s.value := s.value + 1
    else
    begin
      select a process and wake it;
      call the scheduler
    end
```

'Waking' a process involves moving its process descriptor from the queue on s to the 'ready' queue. Pascal-FC does not attempt to define which process should be awoken in the event that there is more than one. However, the version being described here uses a random number to decide: the order in which the original waits were executed is not taken into account, for example.

B.6   Monitors

B.6.1   Data structures

The data structure that appears on the stack to represent a monitor may be described as a record:

```
type
  monframe =
    record
      occupier: procptr;
      boundary: procptr;
      chivalry: procptr
    end;
```

The occupier field is either a null pointer or it points to the process currently holding mutual exclusion on the monitor. The other two fields are pointers to queues. All three fields are automatically initialized to the null value.

A second data structure is associated with monitors and underlies the implementation of condition variables. Each condition is simply a pointer of type procptr. The compiler automatically initializes all such pointers to the null value.

B.6.2 P-machine instructions associated with monitors

Including operations on condition variables, there are seven instructions associated with monitors. They are:

```
mexec   (execute monitor body code)
mretn   (return from monitor body)
enmon   (enter a monitor procedure)
exmon   (return from monitor procedure)
delay   (condition delay)
resum   (condition resume)
empty   (empty function)
```

Monitor body execution

The mexec and mretn codes implement the execution of a monitor body. One mexec is generated by the compiler for each monitor declared in the program: these are all placed before the first P-code for the statement part of the main program, so that monitor bodies are guaranteed to have been executed before the main body begins. A mexec instruction has a parameter, which is the start address of the body code for the monitor. This instruction is a 'lightweight' procedure call in which the only context that needs to be stacked is the return address. Hence mexec is described as follows:

```
push curpr↑.pc;
branch to monitor body
```

The final P-code produced by the statements of a monitor body is followed by the mretn instruction: it is a 'lightweight' procedure return, which may be described as follows:

```
pop return address;
curpr↑.pc := return address
```

Calling exported monitor procedures

The sequence for calling an exported monitor procedure relies heavily on the normal procedure call sequence (which has not been described in this Appendix). However, the normal sequence is bracketed by the enmon/exmon pair of P-codes, as follows:

```
ldadr    m      ; push address of monitor
enmon
  ..
                 ; normal procedure call sequence
  ..
exmon
```

The enmon operation may be described as follows:

```
pop address of new monitor;
push curpr↑.curmon;
curpr↑curmon := new monitor address;
if monitor.occupier = null value then
   monitor.occupier := curpr
else
begin
   join monitor.boundary;
   call scheduler
end
```

The curmon field of the process descriptor has not been mentioned previously: it has the null value unless the process has requested access to a monitor. Stacking the old value at the beginning of enmon permits nesting of monitor calls.

The exmon operation is:

```
release current monitor;
pop value for curpr↑.curmon
```

Releasing the monitor is as follows:

```
if non-empty chivalry queue then
begin
   wake a process;
   mark it as the occupier;
   call scheduler
end else
   if non-empty boundary queue then
   begin
```

```
            wake a process;
            mark it as occupier;
            call scheduler
        end
    else
        occupier := null value
```

Operations on condition variables

Given the source code:

```
    delay(c)
```

the following P-codes would be generated:

```
    ldadr    c    ; push address of c
    delay
```

The delay operation is as follows:

```
    pop address of c;
    join the queue on c;
    release the monitor;
    if no process was awakened then
        call scheduler
```

The action of releasing the monitor was outlined when considering the exmon operation.

The source code:

```
    resume(c)
```

would generate the instructions:

```
    ldadr    c    ; push address of c
    resum
```

The resum operation is as follows:

```
    pop address of c;
    if non-empty queue on c then
    begin
        wake a process;
        mark awakened process as occupier;
        join chivalry queue for curpr↑.curmon;
        call scheduler
    end
```

The final operation that can be carried out on a condition is the empty function. This is a trivial operation to implement and will not be described here.

B.7 Rendezvous

This Appendix deals only with the implementation of Pascal-FC on uniprocessor systems. On such architectures it is possible for all processes to be given access to the memory space (stack segments) of other processes. This makes possible an implementation of message passing that is based on the use of shared data structures to represent channels or entries, and pointers for source and destination addresses.

This section is concerned with the occam-style and the Ada-style rendezvous, excluding selective waiting. A common data structure (the link) underlies both forms of rendezvous, but different instructions are involved in the two cases.

B.7.1 Data structures

For every channel or entry declared in a program, the compiler implicitly declares a link, which can be thought of as a record with the following structure:

```
type
link =
  record
    data:      (* stack address of source/destination *)
    waiting: procptr;
    reader: boolean
  end;
```

The use of this structure differs somewhat between the occam- and Ada-style rendezvous: these differences are brought out below.

B.7.2 Occam-style rendezvous

This section describes the code that is generated by a channel read or write operation *outside* a **select** statement: different codes are generated when channel operations are alternatives in a **select**. They will be described later.

Two P-codes have been introduced to implement the basic occam-style rendezvous:

```
chanrd     (channel receive)
chanwr     (channel send)
```

Suppose that the following source statement is encountered by the compiler (chan has been declared as a channel of integer):

```
chan ! 22
```

The following sequence of P-codes would be generated by the compiler:

```
ldadr    chan ; push address of chan
ldcon    22   ; push constant value 22
chanwr
```

In outline, the chanwr operation is as follows:

```
pop data;
pop pointer to link;
if first at rendezvous then
begin
  link.data := address of source data;
  link.reader := false;
  link.waiting := curpr;
  call scheduler
end else
  if not link.reader then
    status := channel error
  else
  begin
    copy data from source to destination;
    wake sleeping process;
    link.waiting := null value
  end
end
```

The waiting field of the link permits a process executing chanwr to know whether it is the first to arrive at the rendezvous. If it is, this pointer will have the null value and it is necessary for the process to become blocked on the link. This is done by placing a pointer to the current process in link.waiting and changing the status of the current process to blocked. Before exiting via the scheduler, the calling process must also assign a value to the reader field and place a pointer to the source data in the data field: the actual data transfer is always carried out by the process that arrives *second* at the rendezvous (whether this be a reader or a writer).

Given that the corresponding channel read is represented by the following source code:

```
chan ? local
```

where local is an integer variable, the following P-codes would be generated by the compiler:

```
ldadr     chan ; push address of chan
ldadr     local ; push address of local
chanrd
```

The chanrd operation is as follows:

```
pop address of destination;
pop address of link;
if first at rendezvous then
begin
  link.data := address of destination data;
  link.reader := true;
  link.waiting := curpr;
  call scheduler
end else
  if link.reader then
    status := channel error
  else
  begin
    copy data from source to destination;
    wake sleeping process;
    link.waiting := null value
  end
```

The symmetry of the channel reading and writing operations is clear from the above descriptions.

B.7.3 Ada-style rendezvous

Though the link data structure described above is also used with the Ada style of rendezvous, there are some differences in its application. In the occam style, each channel declaration causes the implicit declaration of a link (including a separate link for every component of an array or record of channels). As channels are declared in the main program declaration part, such links are allocated space on the stack segment of the main program. Entries are declared in process declarations and the links are allocated space on the stack segment of the process concerned. Additionally, space is added to a link to cater for the entry parameters: sufficient space is allocated for copies of all value parameters and for the addresses of **var** parameters.

Three P-codes have been provided to implement the basic Ada rendezvous: one of these (ecall) is for the entry call and the other two for the **accept** statement. The codes are:

```
ecall     (execute entry call)
acpt1     (accept leading code)
acpt2     (accept trailing code)
```

The following skeleton program will be used to illustrate the simple Ada-style rendezvous:

```
program simple;

process p;
   entry e(n: integer);
begin
   accept e(n: integer) do
       (* statements *)
end;     (* p *)

process q;

begin
   p.e(27)
end;   (* q *)

begin
   cobegin
      p;
      q
   coend
end.
```

B.7.4   Entry call

First, consider the compiler's actions on processing an entry call, such as the one in process q above. The following codes are generated:

```
ldadr    p          ; push address of 'accepting' process
ldcon    offset     ; push an offset
   . . .
                     ; push parameters

   . . .
ecall    psize
```

The first instruction pushes the address of the process variable for the process that owns the entry being called. This ultimately allows the ecall instruction to do two things:

- to ascertain whether the intended acceptor process is active;
- to locate the run-time stack for the acceptor process (if it is active).

As it is an error to attempt to rendezvous with a process that was never activated, or has terminated for some reason, the first action will result in program termination if the intended acceptor is not active. The second action is important when the entry caller is the second to arrive at the rendezvous. In this case, the caller is responsible for transferring the parameters, which it does by directly copying them to the acceptor's stack.

The 'offset' pushed by the second of the above instructions is the offset of the particular entry from the bottom of the acceptor's stack. This is again used by an entry caller that arrives second at a rendezvous; it permits the link and the parameter locations to be determined.

Following the pushing of the process variable address and the entry offset, an arbitrary number of parameters is pushed (a series of push operations is generally generated). For correct processing, the interpreter needs to know how much parameter information has been pushed: this is known at compile-time and is therefore passed as a parameter of the ecall instruction (psize in the example).

In essence, the ecall instruction is as follows:

```
retrieve the address of the acceptor;
retrieve the entry offset;
if acceptor not active then
   set error
else
begin
   if acceptor is waiting then
   transfer parameters to acceptor;
   join the queue on link;
   link.reader := true
end
```

It must be remembered that in the Ada-style rendezvous provision must be made for an arbitrary number of entry callers to be blocked on an entry at any time. The waiting field of the link is in this case interpreted as a pointer to a (possibly empty) queue of entry callers. The first such caller will have set the reader field to false (entry callers are considered as 'writers' at this low level, but see the remarks made in Chapter 5 about the confusing nature of such terms as 'sender' and 'receiver' in the context of the Ada rendezvous).

Use of the waiting and reader fields enables a calling process to know what to do. If waiting is the null value, then the owner of the entry is not yet ready for a rendezvous, but no other entry callers are blocked. If waiting has a non-null value then at least one other process is already blocked on this entry. This could be either another entry caller or the process that owns the entry (we shall describe below the action of the acpt1 instruction). In this case, the value of the reader field determines what action is taken.

B.7.5 Accept statement

The following P-codes are generated for a typical accept statement:

```
ldadr    entry     ; push address of entry
```

```
        acpt1
          . . .
                            ; instructions generated by the accept body
          . . .
        ldadr     entry     ; push address of entry
        acpt2
```

The outline of acpt1 is:

```
        pop entry address;
        if no pending call then
        begin
            join 'queue' on entry;
            entry.reader := true
        end else
            transfer parameters
```

The semantics of the Ada-style rendezvous are such that once a process has become blocked on an entry by executing acpt1 no further processes will join that 'queue' until an ecall has been carried out.

The acpt2 instruction is responsible for bringing a rendezvous to end. It has the following outline:

```
        pop entry address;
        awake blocked caller;
        call scheduler
```

B.8   Selective waiting

The selective waiting construct, as might be expected, is the most complex of the inter-process communication facilities, and a fairly large number of instructions is generated by the compiler for a typical **select** statement. The implementation of selective waiting in the existing Pascal-FC systems is the same whether channel alternatives or **accept** alternatives are involved.

Perhaps the best way to approach the implementation of selective waiting is to consider the overall strategy used by the interpreter in executing a **select** statement. It falls into two parts:

- push a set of 'select frames' – one for each open alternative;
- process the frames.

The second of these phases is accomplished by a single P-code instruction selec. The action of this P-code is considered below, after the select frame has been introduced.

B.8.1   Select frames

One select frame will be pushed for every channel, **accept** or **timeout** alternative that is open at the time that the **select** is executed (a **terminate** alternative is not represented by a select frame). A select frame can be viewed as a record with the following structure:

```
type
   SelectFrame =
      record
         LinkPtr: .. ;      (* the address of a link *)
         data: .. ;      (* pointer to source/destination *)
         TransactionType: (ChanRead,ChanWrite,Ada);
         TransactionSize: 0..maxint;
         NewPC: 0..maxint;
         ReplicateIndex: ..
      end;
```

LinkPtr points to the link that underlies the channel or entry concerned with this alternative. This pointer must be followed by selec to determine whether or not there is a pending call on that link. The data field points to the data to be transferred. This is used only in the occam-style rendezvous. TransactionType indicates whether the operation required by this alternative is a channel read, a channel write or an **accept**. The other type of alternative that generates a select frame is **timeout**. Such an alternative is indicated by a null value in the LinkPtr. TransactionSize is used only with a channel alternative; it represents the size of the data object to be transferred along the channel. NewPc indicates the value that the process's program counter should have if this alternative is taken. It is the address of the first instruction of the **accept** body in the case of an **accept** alternative or of the first instruction following the channel operation for an occam-style alternative. Following any such code, there is an unconditional jump to the first P-code following the **select** statement. The ReplicateIndex is only used in the case of a **replicate** alternative (using the occam-style rendezvous). It represents the value that the **replicate** 'loop index' variable must have if this is the chosen alternative. Note that the **replicate** alternative is processed in such a way that a separate select frame is pushed for every open alternative.

B.8.2   Pushing the select frames

During the first phase of the processing of the **select** statement, the interpreter will push an arbitrary number of select frames (possibly none). The selec P-code must be able to determine how many there are. This is done by first pushing a special marker value, which can then be detected. Following this, the compiler must generate code that pushes select frames as appropriate. Which frames to push depends on run-time evaluation of boolean expressions in the case of guarded alternatives. The compiler makes use of conditional and unconditional jump P-codes to 'thread through' the alternatives of the **select**, unconditionally pushing a select frame if there is no guard, and inserting code to evaluate the guard expression on any alternative that has a guard. The final alternative is followed by an unconditional jump to the selec P-code for that **select** statement.

B.8.3 The selec instruction

This is a large and complex instruction, so only a brief outline is given here. In outline, the action of this P-code is as follows:

```
count select frames;
if no select frames then
  if terminate then
    set terminate status
  else
  begin
    if no else part then
      set error status
  end
else
begin      (* links to check *)
  check for calls;
  if no calls then
  begin
    if no else part then
    begin
      sleep on all links;
      exit via scheduler
    end
  end else
  begin
    take a call;
    pc := chosen select arm
  end
end
```

Both the *x* and *y* parameters of a P-code are used by selec to indicate the following:

- whether this is a **pri select** or an ordinary one;
- whether or not there is a **terminate** alternative;
- whether or not there is an **else** part.

The first thing that the selec code must do is to determine how many select frames there are on the stack. If there are none, further processing depends on whether there is an **else** part or a **terminate** alternative. (This can be determined from the parameters.) If there is neither, the program status is set to indicate a 'closed guards' error. Otherwise, if there is an else part, then it is taken. The first code of the **else** part always immediately follows the selec code, so this transfer of control requires no special action.

If there are select frames on the stack, an attempt is made to find a rendezvous. This attempt begins from the first select frame if the parameters indicate that this is a **pri select**: otherwise a random number is generated to determine which select frame is the first to be investigated. In either case, the search continues until either a frame is checked that points to a link on which there is a pending call or until all the select frames have been checked without finding such a call. (As the selec code is executed as an atomic operation, the status of the links involved cannot change during the execution of this code.) If a pending call is found, then the rendezvous proceeds as appropriate and the other process (which must have been blocked) is unblocked.

In the event that no link has a pending call, the process executing selec must block on all links represented by the select frames. This will involve joining queues on those links and marking the associated reader fields as appropriate. If there are frames representing **timeout** alternatives, then the process may need to be placed on the **event queue** (see Section B.10). Finally, information is planted in the process descriptor of the process executing the selec to identify the links on which it has become blocked (and whether it has joined the event queue): this information is required by any process which executes a rendezvous on one of the links in order to 'clear down' the calls on *all* links.

A process that becomes blocked during the selec code exits that code via a call to the scheduler.

B.9 Resources

Pascal-FC's resources have been modelled on the proposed protected record of Ada 9X. One of the motivations for the protected record is the desire of the real-time Ada community to have fast process synchronization for time-critical applications. Hence the feature has been designed in such a way that implementors should be able to achieve good run-time efficiency. The goals of Pascal-FC are different. The implementation described here was designed to be straightforward and, where possible, to make use of existing features of the interpreter.

B.9.1 Data structures

Each resource declared in a program causes the implicit declaration of a variable, which can be considered as a record with the following form:

```
type
  resframe =
    record
      boundary: procptr;
      occupier: procptr;
      SearchingForCandidate: boolean
    end;
```

This structure is similar to the monframe described in Section B.6.1. Though the language does not specify how mutual exclusion on resources must be implemented, the current implementation does in fact use blocking: a priority queue is maintained at the resource boundary, as was the case for monitors, and the boundary field points to a (possibly empty) linked list of process descriptors. The occupier field makes it easy to determine whether the resource is currently occupied. The SearchingForCandidate field has a role which is outlined later in this Appendix.

The other data structure associated with resources is the queue on each guarded procedure. For each such procedure, a variable is implicitly declared which is a pointer to a (possibly empty) linked list of process descriptors.

B.9.2   P-codes associated with resources

Five P-code instructions have been introduced into the intermediate code:

```
prslp     (sleep on a guard)
prjmp     (jump if not searching for candidate)
prsel     (try to select blocked process)
prcnd     (try to find a candidate)
prxit     (exit resource)
```

In addition to these codes, three of those already described in relation to monitors (mexec, mretn and enmon) are also used to implement resources.

Resource body code

The optional body of a resource has the same form as a monitor body; purpose and semantics are also the same. The existing mexec and mretn codes are, therefore, used.

Calling resource procedures

The calling sequence for a resource procedure is the same whether or not the procedure is guarded. As in the case of calls to monitor procedures, the normal procedure call is bracketed by additional instructions, which constitute entry and exit protocols. If the called procedure is guarded, the calling process will, on entry to the resource, begin execution at the first instruction generated by the guard expression (rather than the first instruction of the procedure body, as would be the case for an unguarded procedure). Conditional jump instructions ensure that a process finding a closed guard executes the prslp instruction and thereby becomes blocked on the relevant queue.

The entry protocol for a resource procedure is the enmon code used in the implementation of monitors. The exit protocol is, however, different. It consists of two instructions:

```
prcnd     addr    ; look for a candidate
prxit
```

The first of these causes the process to 'thread through' the code which evaluates all the procedure guards, having first marked the SearchingForCandidate field of the resframe variable true. The addr argument is the address of the first instruction of the first guard expression. The prxit instruction carries out simple 'housekeeping' operations.

Use of the guards

The code generated by the guard expressions is used in two different ways. A process wishing to execute a guarded procedure will evaluate one guard: it must block if the guard is false. By contrast, a process that leaves a resource needs to determine whether there is a process blocked on a guard that may now inherit mutual exclusion. In the current implementation, this is done as follows:

- all guards are evaluated and the addresses of queues with open guards are stacked;
- a search is then made among the stacked queues for a process to awaken.

A process searching for a candidate ignores queues with closed guards: it does not block on them as would a process attempting to execute a guarded procedure. Hence the new conditional jump prjmp has been introduced: it is used in conjunction with the SearchingForCandidate field of the resframe variable so that processes may behave differently, depending on whether they are attempting to execute a guarded procedure or looking for a candidate.

Consider now the behaviour of a process searching for a candidate. This operation is carried out whenever a process leaves a resource, either by encountering a closed guard or by completing an exported procedure.

Whenever a guard evaluates to true, the address of the associated queue is pushed onto the stack: such addresses are analogous to the select frames described previously in that they will later be used to attempt to find a process to awaken. When a guard evaluates to false, execution passes to the evaluation of the next (if there is one). This control of flow depends on the use of the prjmp instruction.

A prsel instruction is executed when the addresses of all queues for which the procedures have open guards have been stacked. This instruction is linked to the end of the 'chain' of guards in the resource. Its role is similar to the selec instruction. In the current implementation, a random choice is made to determine where the search should begin for a candidate (some or all of the queues may be empty). If a candidate is found, mutual exclusion is passed to it otherwise the resource boundary queue is investigated. If a process is blocked at the boundary, it now inherits mutual exclusion. The resource is marked as unoccupied if the boundary queue is empty.

B.9.3 Requeue

No new P-code instructions are required to implement the **requeue** statement: the compiler generates a normal procedure call (including entry and exit protocols if this is a call to another resource), followed immediately by a 'return from procedure' instruction. This implements the required semantics of abandonment of the procedure containing the **requeue** statement.

B.10   Timing facilities

Timing facilities are only required where real-time applications are envisaged, but all existing implementations of Pascal-FC do provide elementary timing features. The two principal features are:

- the sleep procedure
- the **timeout** alternative in the **select** statement.

The fundamental data structure underlying both of these is known as the **event queue**, which is a linked list of process descriptors. A process that is blocked by either of the above features has its process descriptor placed on the event queue. Processes on this queue are not ordered according to when they became blocked, but according to when they will become unblocked. As both sleep and **timeout** specify a period of blocking, it is easy to determine when unblocking will become due.

The 'wake time' of a process is represented by a field in its process descriptor. One such field is sufficient, for though a **select** statement may contain several **timeout** alternatives, the language defines that only one of them is effective: the others are ignored and the process only 'joins' the event queue once. A **timeout** or sleep with a negative or zero argument simply deschedules the process: it does not join the event queue at all.

The interpreter maintains a system clock: this is usually some integer type. The clock is updated periodically (for example, at the rate of one increment per second). Eventually this integer would overflow, but the rate of updating is always chosen that overflow does not occur in practice. Pascal-FC has been designed for teaching purposes rather than for serious real-time applications, so that program execution times are usually of the order of seconds or minutes. The rate of update is chosen so that overflow would occur, at the earliest, a matter of days after the program began to execute. For practical purposes, therefore, the system clock is monotonic.

Each time the system clock is updated, the process at the head of the event queue (if the queue is non-empty) is examined. If it is time to awaken it, then this is done: this is repeated for all other processes on the event queue whose wake time has now arrived. As the queue is ordered according to wake time, this procedure can safely cease when a process is found for which the wake time lies in the future.

References

Andrews G.R. (1981). Synchronising Resources. *ACM Transactions on Programming Languages and Systems*, **3**(4), 405–31

Andrews G.R. (1991). *Concurrent Programming: Principles and Practice*. Benjamin/Cummings

Barz H.W. (1983). Implementing Semaphores by Binary Semaphores. *SIGPLAN Notices*, **18**(2), 39–45

Ben Ari M. (1982). *Principles of Concurrent Programming*. Prentice-Hall

Ben Ari M. (1990). *Principles of Concurrent and Distributed Programming*. Prentice-Hall

Berry R.E. (1982). *Programming Language Translation*. Ellis Horwood

Booch G. (1987). *Software Engineering with Ada*. Addison-Wesley

Brinch Hansen P. (1972). Structured Microprogramming. *Communications of ACM*, **15**(7), 574–8

Brinch Hansen P. (1975). The Programming Language Concurrent Pascal. *IEEE Transactions on Software Engineering*, **SE–1**(2), 199–207

Brinch Hansen P. (1981). The Design of Edison. *Software Practice and Experience*, **11**(4), 363–96

Burns A., Lister A.M. and Wellings A.J. (1987). A Review of Ada Tasking. In *Lecture Notes in Computer Science*, volume 262. Springer-Verlag

Burns A. (1988). *Programming in occam2*. Addison-Wesley

Burns A. and Wellings A.J. (1990). *Real-time Systems and Their Programming Languages*. Addison-Wesley

Coffman E.G., Elphick M.J. and Shoshan A. (1971). System Deadlocks. *Computing Surveys*, **3**(2), 67–78

Courtois P.J., Heymans F. and Parnas D.L. (1971). Concurrent Control with Readers and Writers. *Communications of ACM*, **14**(10), 667–8

Davies G.L. and Burns A. (1990). The Teaching Language Pascal-FC. *The Computer Journal*, **33**(2), 147–54

Davies G.L. (1990). Teaching Concurrent Programming with Pascal-FC. *SIGCSE Bulletin*, **22**(2), 38–41

Dijkstra E.W. (1965). Solution of a problem in concurrent programming control. *Communications of ACM*, **8**(9), 459

Dijkstra E.W. (1968). Co-operating sequential processes. In *Programming Languages* (Genuys F., ed.), pp. 43–112. Academic Press

Eisenberg M.A. and McGuire M.R. (1972). Further comments on Dijkstra's concurrent programming control problem. *Communications of ACM*, **15**(11), 999

Gomaa H. (1984). A Software Design Method for Real-Time Systems. *Communications of ACM*, **27**(9), 938–49

Hoare C.A.R. (1969). An Axiomatic Basis for Computer Programming. *Communications of ACM*, **12**(10), 576–80

Hoare C.A.R. (1974). Monitors: an Operating System Structuring Concept. *Communications of ACM*, **17**(10), 549–57

Hoare C.A.R. (1985). *Communicating Sequential Processes*. Prentice-Hall

Holt R.C. and Cordy J.R. (1988). The Turing Programming Language. *Communications of ACM*, **31**(12), 1410–23

INMOS Ltd (1984). *Occam Programming Manual*. Prentice-Hall

Lamport L. (1974). A New Solution of Dijkstra's Concurrent Programming Problem. *Communications of ACM*, **17**(8), 453–5

Leach J. (1987). Experience Teaching Concurrency in Ada. *Ada Letters*, **7**(5)

Lister A.M. (1977). The Problem of Nested Monitor Calls. *ACM Operating Systems Review*, **11**(3), 5–7

Mitchell J.G., Maybury W. and Sweet R. (1979). *Mesa Language Manual, version 5.0*. Report CSL-79-3. Xerox Palo Alto Research Center

Owicki S. and Lamport L. (1982). Proving Liveness Properties of Concurrent Programs. *ACM Transactions on Programming Languages and Systems*, **4**(3), 455–95

Peterson G.L. (1981). Myths about the Mutual Exclusion Problem. *Information Processing Letters*, **12**(3), 115–6

Wellings A.J., Keeffe D. and Tomlinson G.M. (1984). A Problem with Ada and Resource Allocation. *Ada Letters*, **3**(4)

Welsh J. and Bustard D.W. (1979). Pascal-Plus – Another Language for Modular Multiprogramming. *Software Practice and Experience*, **9**, 947–57

Index